NEW STUDIES IN BIBLICAL THEOLOGY 23

Sealed with an oath

D0931755

Titles in this series:

NEW STUDIES IN BIBLICAL THEOLOGY 23

Series editor: D. A. Carson

Sealed with an oath

COVENANT IN GOD'S UNFOLDING PURPOSE

Paul R. Williamson

APOLLOS

INTERVARSITY PRESS
DOWNERS GROVE, ILLINOIS 60515

APOLLOS (an imprint of Inter-Varsity Press)
Norton Street, Nottingham NG7 3HR, England
Email: ivp@ivpbooks.com
Website: www.ivpbooks.com

INTERVARSITY PRESS
PO Box 1400, Downers Grove, Illinois 60515, USA
Website: www.ivpress.com
Email: mail@ivpress.com

First published 2007

British Library Cataloguing in Publication Data
A catalogue record for this book is available from the British Library.

UK ISBN-13: 978-1-84474-165-6
UK ISBN-10: 1-84474-165-6

Library of Congress Cataloging-in-Publication Data
These data have been requested.

US ISBN-10: 0-8308-2624-6
US ISBN-13: 978-0-8308-2624-7

Set in Monotype Times New Roman
Typeset in Great Britain by Servis Filmsetting Ltd, Manchester
Printed and bound in Great Britain by Creative Print & Design (Wales), Ebbw Vale

To Mum,
with love and gratitude

Contents

Series preface

New Studies in Biblical Theology is a series of monographs that
address key issues in the discipline of biblical theology. Contributions
to the series focus on one or more of three areas: 1. the nature and
status of biblical theology, including its relations with other dis-
ciplines (e.g. historical theology, exegesis, systematic theology, historical criticism, narrative theology); 2. the articulation and exposition
of the structure of thought of a particular biblical writer or corpus;
and 3. the delineation of a biblical theme across all or part of the biblical corpora.

Above all, these monographs are creative attempts to help thinking Christians understand their Bibles better. The series aims simul-
taneously to instruct and to edify, to interact with the current
literature, and to point the way ahead. In God's universe, mind and
heart should not be divorced: in this series we will try not to separate
what God has joined together. While the notes interact with the best
of scholarly literature, the text is uncluttered with untransliterated
Greek and Hebrew, and tries to avoid too much technical jargon. The
volumes are written within the framework of confessional evangel-
icalism, but there is always an attempt at thoughtful engagement with
the sweep of the relevant literature.

One of the major trajectories that ties the Bible together is the
theme of covenant. Indeed, only because of the misadventure of
doubtful translation do we say that the Bible has two 'Testaments'
rather than two 'Covenants'. Many Christian thinkers across the centuries have made 'covenant' the organizing principle by which they
understand the Old Testament, or even the entire Bible. Dr
Williamson has given us a fresh reading of the many passages that
contribute to this theme. The task is enormous, of course, since the
material is not only plentiful, but in many passages much disputed.
Inevitably, not every reader will be persuaded by every bit of exegesis
in this book. But few will be the readers who will not learn a great
deal from it, and who will not appreciate the firm but respectful way

Dr Williamson disagrees with his dialogue partners. And perhaps some of those who are much too indebted to atomistic exegesis, unable to see how the Bible hangs together, will glimpse something of the comprehensiveness and wholeness of God's self-disclosure in Scripture, and find their worship of the covenant-making God enhanced.

D. A. Carson
Trinity Evangelical Divinity School

Author's preface

The present study was first conceived as a dictionary article for IVP's *New Dictionary of Biblical Theology*. Part of the original article was subsequently expanded for a more focused contribution in IVP's *Dictionary of the Old Testament: Pentateuch*. Over a longer than anticipated gestation period, the material has continued to grow and develop, until it has reached its present shape. In many respects, however, it remains a work in progress, and is certainly not presented as a comprehensive analysis of the subject. For the latter a much larger volume and (for this author, at least) a much longer gestation period would be necessary. It is hoped, nevertheless, that this study will provide a stimulating overview of the various divine-human covenants in Scripture, as well as offering some insights into the role that covenant has in biblical theology. The most radical departure from the traditional covenantal schema is my dual-covenant approach to God's dealings with Abraham. This approach builds on the insights of my doctoral supervisor, Dr T. D. Alexander, and is defended in much greater detail in my earlier monograph, *Abraham, Israel and the Nations*. Interested readers will find there the detailed argument that the present volume must often take for granted.

The aim of the present study is to highlight the significance of covenant for biblical theology, and explore the role of this concept within God's unfolding purpose. The first chapter reviews some of the important issues that must be addressed in any biblical-theological investigation of covenant, not least, the meaning of this biblical idea. The conclusion reached is that covenant is essentially 'a solemn commitment, guaranteeing promises or obligations undertaken by one or both parties, sealed with an oath'. The primary function of this ancient theological motif, first introduced in the context of the flood, is understood as follows: to advance God's creative purpose of universal blessing.

The second chapter, therefore, sets the covenant idea into its biblical-theological context, namely, God's purpose to extend his rule and blessing throughout the world – a divine plan jeopardized but not eradicated by human rebellion. The suggestion that humanity's prelapsarian relationship with God should also be described as some form of covenant is explored but rejected.

The following five chapters examine each of the major divine-human covenants attested to in the Old Testament. The universal covenant with Noah is all-encompassing, serving mainly to guarantee the future survival of God's creation despite human rebellion. Rather than seeing this as a renewal of an earlier covenant established at creation, this Noahic covenant is understood as the covenant with creation subsequently alluded to in other OT texts (Jer. 33:19–26), which guarantees the ultimate fulfilment of God's creative purpose.

This purpose is further unpacked in the next major development in the history of the covenant idea: God's promises to Abraham. Two distinct, but related aspects of God's programmatic agenda, namely, nationhood and international blessing (Gen. 12:1–3), are solemnly confirmed by two distinct covenants established between God and Abraham. The national aspect of God's promises is the primary focus in the rest of the patriarchal narratives and we begin to see its fulfilment in the multiplication of the Israelites in Egypt, the exodus and the conquest.

The next major covenant, established with the nation of Israel at Sinai, sets out the covenantal obligations for those in whom God's national promise to Abraham is realized. In order to mediate blessing to others, Israel must model the kingdom of God on earth by living according to the Mosaic Law. Despite many renewals, this was a covenant that ultimately appeared to have failed. Israel failed to fulfil its obligations, hence jeopardizing the fulfilment of God's international agenda.

With the national dimension of the promise attaining fulfilment in the time of David (2 Sam. 7:1), the next covenantal development focuses in particular on the royal seed that had earlier been promised to Abraham (Gen 17:6, 16). As hinted at in the Abraham narrative itself, this royal seed would ultimately serve as the bridge between the national and international aspects of God's ancestral promises: thus the royal covenant established with David and his dynasty picks up the royal and international trajectories from the Abraham narrative, and identifies more explicitly the conquering seed through whom international blessing would eventually come.

Israel's failure and inherent inability to mediate blessing to the nations is addressed directly by the climactic covenantal development:

a new covenant through which all others would find their ultimate fulfilment. Chapter 7 explores how this new covenant is anticipated in the Old Testament's prophetic literature, and chapter 8 surveys how the New Testament portrays its fulfilment – along with all previous divine-human covenants – in the person of Jesus Christ and the kingdom he inaugurated.

Thus, by tracing the covenant trajectory from its conception in the primeval period to its consummation in the new heavens and the new earth, this study highlights that covenant is not only one of Scripture's more significant theological motifs, but that it is also a most important bonding agent in the cement that unites Scripture as a whole.

Like all such projects, this work could not have been completed without the help and assistance of others. I want to take this opportunity, therefore, to express sincere gratitude to those whose prayers have been a tremendous source of encouragement. The undergraduate and postgraduate students I have had the privilege of teaching at Moore College, as well as some of the folk from St Helen's, Bishopsgate, have acted as a sounding board for many of the ideas contained in this volume. The Principal and Moore College Council generously provided study leave, facilitating a period of writing that was uninterrupted with other teaching or administrative responsibilities. The support of my colleagues at Moore College has been a great help. In particular, Philip Kern and Peter O'Brien took time out of a busy schedule to read and comment on earlier drafts of this study. I am also greatly indebted to Professor D. A. Carson, Philip Duce and the editorial team at IVP, whose insights and observations have helped sharpen my own thinking and improve the clarity of expression in several places. While all these contributions have certainly enhanced the final product, naturally I alone am responsible for any shortcomings that remain.

Last but not least I want to express thanks to my family – Karen, Matthew and Andrew – whose love and support are a constant delight and whose various interests provide a healthy balance to my theological pursuits. Thanks also to my mum, whose Christian faith and perseverance were instrumental in my own salvation, and whose kindness, generosity and love have endured through many trials. I dedicate this book to her with love and gratitude.

Paul R. Williamson

Abbreviations

AB	Anchor Bible
ABD	*Anchor Bible Dictionary*, ed. D. N. Freedman, 6 vols., Garden City, NY: Doubleday
AnBib	Analecta Biblica
AOTC	Apollos Old Testament Commentary
ASV	American Standard Version
AV	Authorized Version
Bib	*Biblica*
BJRL	*Bulletin of the John Rylands University Library of Manchester*
BST	The Bible Speaks Today
BWANT	Beiträge zur Wissenschaft vom Alten und Neuen Testament
BZAW	Beihefte zur Zeitschrift für die alttestamentliche Wissenschaft
CBQ	*Catholic Biblical Quarterly*
CC	Continental Commentaries
CRBS	*Currents in Research: Biblical Studies*
CTJ	*Calvin Theological Journal*
ESV	English Standard Version
ET	English translation
GKC	*Gesenius' Hebrew Grammar*, ed. E. Kautzsch, trans. A. E. Cowley, 2nd ed. Oxford: OUP, 1910
HBT	*Horizons in Biblical Theology*
IBHS	*An Introduction to Biblical Hebrew Syntax*, B. K. Waltke and M. O'Connor, Winona Lake, Ind: Eisenbrauns, 1990
JAOS	*Journal of the American Oriental Society*
JB	Jerusalem Bible
JBL	*Journal of Biblical Literature*
JETS	*Journal of the Evangelical Theological Society*
J.-M.	Joüon, P., *A Grammar of Biblical Hebrew*, 2 vols.,

	trans. and rev. T. Muraoka, Rome: Pontifical Biblical Institute
JPS	Jewish Publication Society
JSJSup	Journal for the Study of Judaism Supplements
JSNT	*Journal for the Study of the New Testament*
JSNTSup	Journal for the Study of the New Testament Supplement
JSOT	*Journal for the Study of the Old Testament*
JSOTSup	Journal for the Study of the Old Testament Supplement
lit.	literally
MSJ	*The Master's Seminary Journal*
MT	Masoretic Text
NASB	New American Standard Bible
NCBC	New Century Bible Commentary
NEB	New English Bible
NIBC	New International Biblical Commentary
NICNT	New International Commentary on the New Testament
NICOT	New International Commentary on the Old Testament
NIDOTTE	*New International Dictionary of Old Testament Theology and Exegesis*, ed. W. A. VanGemeren, 5 vols., Grand Rapids: Zondervan,1997
NIGTC	New International Greek Testament Commentary
NIV	New International Version
NIVAC	New International Version Application Commentary
NJB	New Jerusalem Bible
NJPSV	New Jewish Publication Society Version
NKJV	New King James Version
NLT	New Living Translation
NovT	*Novum Testamentum*
NRSV	New Revised Standard Version
NSBT	New Studies in Biblical Theology
NT	New Testament
OT	Old Testament
OTL	Old Testament Library
PNTC	Pillar New Testament Commentaries
RB	*Review biblique*

REB	Revised English Bible
RevExp	*Review and Expositor*
RSV	Revised Standard Version
SBL	Society of Biblical Literature
SBLDS	Society of Biblical Literature Dissertation Series
SOTBT	Studies in Old Testament Biblical Theology
SOTS	Society for Old Testament Studies
TDOT	*Theological Dictionary of the Old Testament*, ed. G. J. Botterweck and H. Ringgren, trans. J. T. Willis, G. W. Bromiley and D. E. Green, 14 vols., Grand Rapids: Eerdmans, 1974–
TEV	Today's English Version
TNIV	Today's New International Version
TOTC	Tyndale Old Testament Commentaries
TynB	*Tyndale Bulletin*
UF	*Ugarit-Forschungen*
VT	*Vetus Testamentum*
WBC	Word Biblical Commentary
WMANT	Wissenschaftliche Monographien zum Alten und Neuen Testament
WTJ	*Westminster Theological Journal*

Chapter One

Biblical theology and the covenant concept

Biblical theology, covenant and the unity of Scripture

In terms of theological parlance, 'biblical theology' is possibly one of the most difficult concepts to tie down. While scholars of all persuasions happily use the terminology, they do not necessarily have the same thing in mind.[1] For some it simply refers to theological ideas expressed in the Bible, whether in part or the whole. Thus it may describe the theology of a particular book or corpus (e.g. the theology of Isaiah or the theology of the Pentateuch),[2] the theology of either part of the Christian canon (i.e. Old Testament Theology or New Testament Theology), or even a synthesis of biblical doctrine.[3] While all such theological reflection certainly falls within its broad compass, as a distinct theological discipline, biblical theology is arguably best thought of as a holistic enterprise tracing unfolding theological trajectories throughout Scripture and exploring no biblical concept, theme or book in isolation from the whole. Rather, each concept, theme or book is considered ultimately in terms of how it contributes to and advances the Bible's meta-narrative, typically understood in terms of a salvation history that progresses towards and culminates in Jesus Christ. As Rosner (2000: 3) has recently defined it,

> Biblical theology is principally concerned with the overall theological message of the whole Bible. It seeks to understand the parts in relation to the whole and, to achieve this, it must work with the mutual interaction of the literary, historical, and theological dimensions of the various corpora, and with the interrelationships of these within the whole canon of Scripture.

---

[1] See e.g. Barr 1999: 1–17.

[2] It is sometimes employed even with respect to putative underlying sources; e.g. the 'theology of the Yahwist', etc.

[3] In the latter case it may differ little, if at all, from dogmatic or systematic theology.

17

It is within the parameters of such a biblical-theological framework (what some have dubbed, 'pan-biblical theology') that the present study will explore the nature and relationship between the various divine–human covenants revealed in Scripture.

The validity of such an enterprise, however, has not gone unchallenged.[4] Perhaps the most serious of such challenges for constructing such a biblical theology in general, and one focusing on 'covenant' in particular, concerns the implications of theological diversity for the overarching 'unity of Scripture'. Indeed, given the presence of such theological diversity, for many scholars it is impossible to speak of the 'unity' of either part of the canon. Thus most mainstream scholarship rejects any idea of a unified theology of the Old Testament, preferring to think rather in terms of Old Testament *theologies*.[5] In a similar vein, most contemporary New Testament scholars reject the possibility of constructing a single New Testament theology, although not all would embrace the radical position advocated by Räisänen, who, following Baur's lead, identifies such sharp theological disagreement among New Testament authors as to undermine completely the task of constructing a single New Testament theology.[6]

Against such a negative premise concerning the extent of theological diversity within the scriptural canon, it is certainly difficult to see how biblical theology (as defined above) can be accepted as a legitimate scholarly enterprise: 'biblical theology cannot be maintained if there is no (at least underlying) unity in the Bible's theology'.[7] Without such fundamental unity, it is inconceivable how one might construct any coherent biblical theology of an overarching scriptural concept such as covenant. While one cannot deny that Scripture has indeed multifaceted voices, sometimes in dialectical relationship,[8] the core issue here is not whether Scripture speaks with one voice or many, but whether these many voices – regardless of their distinct emphases – are all essentially singing from the same theological hymn sheet. Evangelical scholarship has traditionally contended that such

---

[4] See Balla 2000: 20–27.

[5] Such a stance is sometimes masked by volumes whose titles imply a unified Old Testament theology; however, compare the title of Gerstenberger's (2002) recently published *Theologies of the Old Testament*.

[6] See Marshall (2004: 17–47) for a concise discussion and response. For a more comprehensive critique, see Balla 1997.

[7] Balla 2000: 24.

[8] 'Dialectic' is the interplay between opposing or paradoxical ideas, such as 'judgment and salvation' (i.e. opposites in tension).

is indeed the case, and that the key which unlocks this theological symphony is the Bible's meta-narrative as described above. Thus, while an investigation into the unity of Scripture clearly lies outside the scope of the current investigation, it is hoped that this study will demonstrate how the biblical-theological trajectory of covenant illustrates at least one way in which Scripture's numerous and diverse voices do blend together in perfect harmony.

The place of covenant in biblical scholarship

It is clear that from an early stage in the Christian era the significance of the covenant concept in biblical theology was recognized. Such is noticeably reflected in the canonical nomenclature applied to Christian Scripture: the Old and New *Testaments*.[9] Apparently, it was not until the Reformation period, however, that anyone constructed a biblical theology around this particular concept. This was done by Johannes Cocceius (1603–69), whose attempt to interpret the Bible holistically by giving central place to 'covenant' not only laid the basis for federal or covenant theology (e.g. as presented in the 1677 *magnum opus* of H. Witsius), but also anticipated more recent emphases by identifying covenant as the major biblical-theological trajectory that could be traced throughout salvation history.

While the centrality of the covenant idea was assumed by Reformed theology in the years that followed, some disagreement broke out over the precise nature and number of the covenants (e.g. in the famous Marrow Controversy [1718–23] of the Church of Scotland, debate raged over the postulated 'covenant of grace' and its relationship to the postulated 'covenant of redemption').[10] With the advent of modernity, however, new questions began to arise with respect to both the antiquity of the covenant concept in Israel's history, and its theological importance as a biblical idea. While such debate took place largely within the domain of Old Testament scholarship, more recently – through the impact of post-Holocaust ecumenical dialogue and E. P. Sanders's concept of 'covenantal nomism' – New Testament scholarship has become embroiled in its

---

[9] While the precise origin of this nomenclature is unknown, it was clearly quite early in the Early Church period.

[10] For a concise discussion of the Marrow Controversy and also the twentieth-century debate on the place of law and grace in federal theology, see McGowan 2005: 183–189.

own brand of covenant controversy as well. As discussion of the latter will be taken up in a subsequent chapter, here we will limit our focus to the discussion of covenant within Old Testament scholarship.[11]

Wellhausen and source criticism

In his highly influential *Prolegomena to the History of Israel*,[12] Wellhausen reconstructed the history of Israelite religion from (what he perceived to be) a primitive stage resting on the conviction of an indestructible natural bond between Yahweh and Israel, through the heightened ethical imperatives of the prophets (the highpoint for Wellhausen) to the slide into legalism in the post-exilic era. According to this reconstruction, the presentation of Israel's relationship with Yahweh in terms of a covenant was a relatively late development influenced primarily by the preaching of the prophets.[13] Through the latter, Wellhausen believed, the 'natural bond between the two [Yahweh and Israel] was severed, and the relation was henceforth viewed as conditional'.[14] From this the notion of covenant or treaty naturally developed.[15]

While some scholars by and large accepted Wellhausen's conclusions with respect to the antiquity and historicity of the Sinai traditions, others rejected the sharp dichotomy he had drawn between early Israelite religion and that which arose through the preaching of

[11] The following material is drawn largely from Nicholson's penetrating study (1986).

[12] First published as *Geshichte Israels*, vol. 1 (ET *History of Israel*; Berlin: Reimer, 1978), it was renamed *Prolegomena zur Geschichte Israels* in subsequent German additions. The second edition (1883) served as the basis for the first English edition, thus entitled *Prolegomena to the History of Israel*, Edinburgh: A. & C. Black, 1885.

[13] Prior to the prophets, 'The relation between the people and God was a natural one as that of son to father; it did not rest upon observance of the conditions of a pact' ('Israel' appendix to *Prolegomena*, 469). For Wellhausen, the traditions of Moses the leader of the exodus generation (historical episode) and Moses the Sinai lawgiver (literary fiction) were sharply distinguished. While Moses subsequently promulgated legislation for Israel (beginning at Kadesh), this was the beginning of an ongoing ad hoc process rather than a single act furnishing Israel with a national constitution (see Nicholson 1986: 4–5). The Sinai tradition arose later, from the need to stamp this growing legislative body of material with divine imprimatur by associating it with a single dramatic moment in the past.

[14] 'Israel' appendix to *Prolegomena*, 473.

[15] Wellhausen maintained that the key OT term for covenant is not used of a divine–human relationship in the eighth-century prophets, but was subsequently seen to fit very well their (as well as later prophetic) emphasis on the conditionality of Yahweh's relationship with Israel.

the eighth-century prophets, and maintained that there was a historical core to the Sinai traditions which reflected some sort of early covenant arrangement.[16]

Form and tradition criticism

The effect of form criticism, with its emphasis on the narratives as folk tales (German: *Sagen*), was to sharpen the historical questions even more: how much of the bondage–exodus–wilderness complex of stories was rooted in historical fact? While a kernel of such information was generally acknowledged, controversy continued over the antiquity and historicity of the covenant idea.[17] Indeed, of those who accepted the antiquity of the concept in Israel, several understood its early significance very differently; namely, as a pact of mutual protection made between various Hebrew tribes living in the vicinity of Sinai only later reinterpreted theologically in relation to the divine–human relationship of which Israel was party. This raises the question whether or not such a covenant (i.e. made between different social groups) could also have incorporated a covenant with Yahweh himself and, as such, constituted one of the distinctive, foundational aspects of Israelite faith – as was argued by Robertson Smith and several others.[18]

However, some explanation was thus required for the dearth of references to such a covenant in the literature of the eighth-century prophets. Solutions to this problem included the following: (a) memory of the formal act was unnecessary as long as the divine–human relationship remained intact; (b) the presence of numerous covenant images (e.g. Yahweh as king, father or vineyard owner) in the prophets and their frequent depiction of Yahweh in dispute with Israel indicate that the concept of covenant obligations is present even if the covenant term is not; (c) its absence in prophecy generally (not just pre-exilic) is due to prophetic emphasis on spiritual and

[16] Kittel (1895) perceived of this as an arrangement decreed by one of the parties (Yahweh), which later evolved into the idea of a reciprocal obligation inherent in the term. See Nicholson 1986: 8–9.

[17] According to Nicholson (1986: 9–13), while dismissed by some scholars (e.g. E. Meyer and [at least initially] H. Gunkel), its antiquity and core historicity was defended by others (e.g. C. Steuernagel; O. Procksch; H. Gressmann), although not at the expense of denying perceptible developments within the covenant tradition such as the transition from a unilateral to a more reciprocal arrangement or vice versa. As Nicholson observes, the latter highlights the underlying disagreement over the meaning of the term *běrît*. For more on this controversy in the early twentieth century, see Nicholson 1986: 13–27.

[18] See Nicholson 1986: 22–24.

ethical realities rather than formal covenant obligations; (d) the concept of covenant was not sufficiently developed at this stage, and would thus have led to an impoverished understanding of the divine–human relationship. While all such explanations found some support among Old Testament scholars, none proved persuasive enough to secure a consensus.

Eichrodt, Mowinckel and Noth

However, a new consensus on the antiquity and significance not only of the Sinai covenant, but also other covenantal traditions in the Old Testament (notably, the Abrahamic and the Davidic) did begin to emerge in the period following the First World War.[19] The three main factors leading to this new consensus are listed by Nicholson as follows:

1. As had been argued at an earlier time, covenant was seen to be a necessary feature of Israelite religion as a religion of 'election' and not a 'natural' religion. Scholars such as Hempel, Weiser and Galling maintained that covenant was key to the uniqueness of Israelite religion, a fact further stressed by Eichrodt in his monumental *Theology of the Old Testament*, a work that famously employed covenant and the related theology as the main organizing concept for Old Testament theology.[20]

2. A new area of research, the role of the cult in Israelite religion, came to prominence in the 1920s. Influenced by Gunkel, Greesmann, Pedersen and Grønbech, Mowinckel's seminal work on the study of the Psalms (1921–4) argued covenant (renewal) lay behind Israel's New Year festival (Tabernacles) in which Yahweh's kinship was annually re-enacted or 'actualized' in this cultic drama, and that it (covenant) was the link between individual and community 'blessing'.[21] Weiser (1925) went further, arguing that the New Year Festival was in fact a festival of covenant-renewal, and the theory of such a recurring covenantal festival is reflected also in Alt's seminal mono-

[19] According to Nicholson (1986: 28), this major swing of scholarly opinion is reflected in the second edition of Gunkel's *Religion in History and Presence* (1913, 1930).

[20] Eichrodt explained the sparsity of covenant in the pre-exilic prophets by their perceived need to counter the threat of dead externalism and mechanical routine, which they did by encouraging a spontaneous response coming from the heart (rather than mere obligatory duty).

[21] Mowinckel subsequently maintained that the narratives of Exod. 19 – 24 were simply a description (in the language of historical myth) of such a covenant renewal celebration from the monarchical period.

graph (1934) on the origins of Israelite law. This premise of such a recurring cultic festival incorporating a recital of the divine law led to the conclusion that the eighth-century prophets were covenant 'enforcers', whose ethical teaching clearly presupposed the covenant tradition inherent in Israel's cult.

3. Weber's earlier theory of an Israelite confederacy of tribes, akin to the later Greek amphictyonies, was firmly established by Noth (1930). According to Noth, the foundation of this twelve-tribe league or confederacy was reflected in Joshua 24, which presupposes a quite separate historical situation from that of the Sinai narratives. Thus understood, the covenant at Shechem was the means by which the Israelite tribes of the Sinai covenant incorporated into their community other Israelites who were already settled in the land.[22]

While not all of these ideas were new, they were given fresh impetus by the detailed and cogent manner in which they were presented. However, as Nicholson (1986: 34–44) suggests, other significant factors clearly contributed to the new consensus: (a) the rebirth of interest in Old Testament theology (as distinct from a purely 'history-of-religions' approach; (b) neo-orthodoxy's emphasis (e.g. Karl Barth) on supernatural revelation and assault on 'natural theology' created a climate more conducive to the idea of revelation in history and discerning the uniqueness of Israel's faith; (c) the renewed challenge to validate the relevance of the Old Testament as part of Christian Scripture (associated with the upsurge of anti-Semitism in Germany); (d) a shift of emphasis within the 'history-of-religions' school from uniformity and commonality to distinctiveness and individuality of national beliefs inevitably led to a focus on the covenant idea; (e) the growing influence of the study of the sociology of religion, especially that of Max Weber, who emphasized the *function* of religious beliefs in the structures and activities of society – hence the particular significance of covenant for Israelite society.[23]

[22] Noth thus rejected the idea that the Sinai covenant was a retrojection based on the Shechemite traditions of Joshua 24.

[23] Weber noted that in other ancient confederacies the deity guaranteed the oath sworn by the members to each other, whereas in Israel the covenant was not only between the tribes but also between the tribes and Yahweh, and it was this aspect that was the key to the stability of Israelite society vis-à-vis many of their neighbours (see Nicholson 1986: 39). As Nicholson illustrates (43–44), Weber's sociological analysis undoubtedly was the main factor that contributed to the new consensus on covenant in the era following the Great War.

In addition to the antiquity and significance of the Sinai covenant, general agreement was also reached on the origin and nature of the other two major Old Testament covenants; namely, the Abrahamic and the Davidic. Their antiquity was likewise defended on sociological grounds.[24] This general consensus over the antiquity of the major Old Testament covenants remained largely unchallenged until the underlying reconstruction of Israel's history, and in particular, Noth's amphictyony hypthothesis, came under increasing attack during the early sixties to mid-seventies.[25]

Alleged treaty parallels

A further factor that gave impetus to the study of covenant in the mid-twentieth century was the recovery of ancient Near Eastern treaties that, it was believed, shed considerable new light on the origin and significance of the covenant concept in ancient Israel.

The suggestion in the mid-twentieth century of clear parallels between ancient Near Eastern secular covenants, particularly the second-millennium Hittite treaties and certain portions of Deuteronomy, seemed to serve a critical blow to the earlier consensus (following Wellhausen) that covenant was a relatively late innovation in Israel's history. Basing their conclusions on Korošec's seminal study of Hittite treaty structures, several scholars identified analogous structures in the biblical material.[26]

These scholars insisted that the Hittite treaty documents reflected a remarkable consistency of form, outlined by Mendenhall as follows:

1. Title/preamble, giving names of suzerain and vassal
2. Historical prologue – brief history of relationships between the countries
3. Stipulations, both general and detailed
4. Deposit and public reading of the text

---

[24] Most notably, in L. Rost's influential study *The Succession to the Throne of David* (German original: 1926) and A. Alt's ground-breaking monograph, 'The God of the Fathers' (German original: 1929; ET in *Essays on Old Testament History and Religion*, 1–77).

[25] Note, the antiquity of the Davidic covenant, however, was challenged by some, including Noth – who believed it to be a late innovation.

[26] According to M. G. Kline (1975: 114 n. 2), D. J. Wiseman was apparently the first to make such comparisons (in a paper presented to SOTS in 1948). In any case, such comparisons were likewise suggested in important studies by other scholars (e.g. Mendenhall 1955; Baltzer 1964) in the following decades.

5. List of gods who are witnesses to the treaty
6. Curses/blessings for breaking/keeping the treaty

Mendenhall, whose work proved most influential in this area, concluded from these alleged parallels that the tribes of Israel were not bound together by blood-ties but by a covenant based on religion and modelled after the suzerain–vassal treaties established by the great Hittite king. Thus the covenant form reflected in the Old Testament traditions such as Exodus 20 – 24 and Joshua 24 could be dated accordingly.

In contrast to the second-millennium Hittite treaties, later Assyrian treaties were seen to have a simpler and more varied form, without historical prologue (with the possible exception of just one Assyrian treaty) and with the witnesses before the stipulations. Hence:

1. Title/preamble
2. Witnesses
3. Stipulations
4. Curses/blessings

Thus Mendenhall maintained that when empires arose again, notably Assyria in the seventh century BC, the structure of the suzerain–vassal treaty was notably different, and therefore the covenant idea in Israel must go back at least to the Mosaic era (i.e. the latter part of the second millennium BC).

However, while the above outline for the Hittite treaties was generally accepted (cf. Hillers 1969), others noted with McCarthy (1963) that the fourth element (deposit and public reading) is the least frequent, and thus omitted this in the outline (or else included it as part of the detailed stipulations), and presented the stipulations as two distinct parts:

• general stipulations
• detailed stipulations[27]

Moreover, although McCarthy agreed with Mendenhall that Israel used ancient Near Eastern treaty forms to describe its special relationship with Yahweh, he was much more cautious about using literary form to argue for an early date of the related Old Testament

---

[27] So e.g. Baltzer (1971); cf. also Craigie (1976).

passages. Thus, while recognizing treaty parallels with Deuteronomy (or more accurately, Ur-Deuteronomy), he nevertheless agreed with conventional critical dating of the latter to Josiah's reforms (i.e. seventh century BC).

Largely following McCarthy, Weinfeld (1965, 1972) highlighted further similarities which suggested that the writers of Deuteronomy were familiar with Assyrian treaties, even though the book they had produced was not a covenant or treaty document per se. In particular, he noted the extensive set of curses in Deuteronomy 28 paralleled the longer lists of curses in Assyrian treaties. In addition, he highlighted a significant amount of shared ideas such as that of undivided allegiance. While Weinfeld acknowledged some significant 'discrepancies' (such as the absence of historical prologue in the Assyrian treaties and a substantial difference in their objective vis-à-vis Deuteronomy's central law-code), he believed that these could be explained (a) by a gap in our knowledge of Assyrian vassal treaties (cf. neo-Assyrian 'royal grants', which do reflect the 'historical prologue') and (b) by the alleged coalescence in Deuteronomy of two originally distinct covenant types, a 'covenant of law' and a 'covenant of vassalship'.

Thus, while initially seen as supporting the antiquity of covenant in Israelite religion, further research into biblical parallels with suzerain–vassal treaties seemed to suggest otherwise, and scholarship was once again divided.

A 'return' to Wellhausen (Perlitt, Nicholson)

More trenchant criticism of the alleged treaty parallels came from Perlitt (1969) and Nicholson (1986), who essentially resurrected Wellhausen's view that the covenant concept was a relatively late development in the history of Israelite religion, no earlier than the Deuteronomic materials.[28]

Rejecting Mendenhall's form-critical approach altogether, as well as that of the comparative religions school, Perlitt dated the fully developed idea of covenant to the post-exilic era, and argued that all pre-Deuteronomic references to a *běrît* can be dismissed on source-critical grounds.[29]

---

[28] While not agreeing in every detail (e.g. contra Perlitt, Nicholson [1986: 191] concedes that 'the notion of a covenant between Yahweh and Israel was not so late a development as to have been completely unknown in the eighth century BC'), Perlitt and Nicholson agree on the basics of Wellhausen's analysis.

[29] For a detailed summary of Perlitt's monograph, see Nicholson 1986: 109–117.

Likewise dismissing alleged parallels between suzerain–vassal treaties as a 'blind alley', Nicholson made the following incisive observations to underline that the analogy is inexact and therefore fundamentally flawed:

1. Deuteronomy is not a legal document in the same sense as the ancient Near Eastern treaties.
2. Deuteronomy is not treaty-like in its manner of presentation, but a valedictory speech of Moses.
3. The Deuteronomic legislation deals with many matters not strictly pertinent to the suzerain–vassal relationship.
4. Deuteronomy contains two prologues unlike anything found in ancient Near Eastern treaties.
5. The designation of 'Yahweh as King' is conspicuous in Deuteronomy by its absence.

Nicholson also raised the matter of the appropriateness of such an analogy for the relationship between Yahweh and his people:

> Notwithstanding all the references in the treaties to the 'love' of suzerain for vassal and of vassal for suzerain, to the suzerain as 'father' and the vassal as 'son, such relationships were surely hardly ever like that. Vassals did not as a rule 'love' those who conquered, subdued and dominated them . . . To tell Israelites that Yahweh 'loves' them in the same way as a suzerain (e.g. Ashurbanipal or Nebuchadrezzar) 'loves' his vassals, and that they are to 'love' Yahweh as vassals 'love' their suzerains would surely have been a bizarre depiction of Yahweh's love of, and commitment to, his people, and of the love and commitment with which they were called to respond.[30]

However, while Nicholson may rightly question the appropriateness of the analogy if pressed too far, the fact that – as he clearly concedes – such 'love' and 'filial' language is used both in covenant texts like Deuteronomy and these extra-biblical ancient Near Eastern treaties, surely does suggest that the treaty parallels are not an entirely blind alley, and may perhaps serve to further our understanding of how such language needs to be interpreted in biblical covenant contexts.[31]

---

[30] Nicholson 1986: 78–79.
[31] Perhaps this should be qualified by the recognition that no human analogy or metaphor can ever be entirely exact.

Despite a number of protesting voices,[32] it appears that within contemporary mainstream scholarship, the reigning consensus is that the notion of a divine–human covenant was a relatively late development in Israel's history. This is reflected, for example, in McKenzie's recent and informative introduction to covenant (2000). While one could object to the circularity of his reasoning in a number of places, it is painstakingly clear that, whatever its socio-political origins, for him the concept (or image) of a divine–human covenant 'came to full expression relatively late in Israel's history' (2000: 25). Thus, as this brief survey of Old Testament scholarship on covenant has shown, the historical-critical study of covenant has come full circle, and the dominant approach within mainstream Old Testament scholarship owes much more to a critical reconstruction of Israel's history than to the narrative theology of the canonical biblical text.

Paying more attention to the latter, key contributions by evangelical scholars appeared in the latter part of the twentieth century. Defining covenant as 'a bond-in-blood sovereignly administered' (1980: 15), Robertson's study is primarily interested in the relationships between the various divine–human covenants in Scripture. As the title of his book suggests,[33] Robertson relates each of the covenants ultimately to Christ, depicting their relationship in terms of a single, overarching purpose that each covenant administration expands on until its ultimate fulfilment in Christ. Unfortunately, however, Robertson imposes on this biblical framework at least two additional covenants, a 'covenant of creation' (i.e. a covenant initiated with Adam), and a 'covenant of redemption' (i.e. what other Reformed theologians describe as 'the covenant of grace') through which 'the original purposes of creation are achieved – or even excelled' (1980: 63).

Dumbrell (1984) approaches the subject from a fairly similar perspective, maintaining that all of the major covenants in Scripture are developments of an original 'covenant with creation', implicit in the creation stories and attested to in a number of other biblical texts. Thus there is in essence one divine–human covenant with several different phases from its inception at creation through to its consummation in the new creation.[34]

---

[32] E.g. Zimmerli 1978: 50–55, and more recently Cross 1998: 3–21.

[33] *The Christ of the Covenants.*

[34] While not wishing in any way to detract from the fundamental unity of the various divine–human covenants suggested by both these scholars, it is unfortunate that they find it necessary to appeal to covenants whose exegetical basis appears (at least to the present author) to be somewhat tenuous (see pp. 52–58, 69–76 below).

Adopting a rather different approach, yet still operating within a Reformed framework, McComiskey's study (1985) differentiates between two types of covenant in the Old Testament: an unconditional, promissory type and an obligatory, administrative type. McComiskey places the Abrahamic (Gen. 15) and the Davidic in the former category, and understands the covenant of circumcision (Gen. 17), the Mosaic covenant and the new covenant in terms of the latter. The significance of such a distinction between the covenant depicted in Genesis 15 and the one described in Genesis 17 will be explored further in the present study (see chapter 4 especially).

In a bold attempt to steer a middle path between classical dispensationalism and Reformed theology, Walton (1994) provides a discussion of covenant from what he calls a 'revelatory' perspective.[35] His major thesis is that covenant is chiefly a vehicle for the (progressive) revelation of God to his people and the nations. While Walton has undoubtedly highlighted a neglected aspect of the function of divine–human covenants, to collapse covenant into revelation seems overly reductionistic. Thus, while utilizing his emphasis on the revelatory function of covenant, the present study will operate with quite a different definition of the covenant concept (see p. 43 below).

Unfortunately, even though these biblical-theological investigations by evangelical scholars have certainly made significant contributions to our understanding of the biblical theology of covenant, they have been largely ignored in the mainstream debate. Nevertheless, their insights are certainly of interest to those concerned with a holistic biblical theology of covenant. The present investigation, however different its conclusions may be in a number of places, intends to build on the important foundation that the latter scholars have laid.

The role of the covenant concept in Scripture

Covenant is without doubt one of the most important motifs in biblical theology, attested to not only by the traditional labels applied to the respective parts of the Christian Bible, but also by the fact that the concept looms large at important junctures throughout the Bible. It underpins God's relationship with Noah, Abraham, Israel, the

---

[35] For a helpful summary, in which he compares the theological ramifications of his understanding of covenant with covenant theology, classical dispensationalism and progressive dispensationalism, see Walton 1994: 182–183.

Levitical priesthood and the Davidic dynasty. It is also used with respect to God's relationship with the reconstituted 'Israel' of the future. Therefore, while 'biblical' and 'covenant theology' must certainly not be confused as synonymous, covenant is indisputably one of the Bible's core theological themes.

Covenant as a recurring theological motif

While the terminology applied to the major divine–human covenants in Scripture is fairly uniform (i.e. Noahic/Noachic; Abramic/Abrahamic; Mosaic/Sinaitic; Davidic/royal; new), there is less agreement over the precise number of such covenants and their relationship to one another. Indeed, while many acknowledge only those divine–human relationships to which covenantal terminology is expressly applied, others (mainly within Reformed circles) have identified several additional covenants, including an all-encompassing 'covenant of grace'.

This latter concept clearly lies at the very heart of what is known as 'Covenant Theology'. Ever since the heyday of federal theology in the seventeenth century,[36] covenant theologians have insisted that all post-lapsarian covenants between God and humans are underpinned and held together by a 'covenant of grace'. This meta-covenant, which is understood to have superseded a probationary 'covenant of works' between God and Adam that existed prior to the fall, is generally viewed as the outworking of a pre-temporal, inter-trinitarian 'covenant of redemption'. In any case, every post-lapsarian covenant explicitly mentioned in Scripture is viewed as an expression and development of this one supra-historical covenant that lies at the heart of redemptive history and keeps it advancing towards its ultimate goal: the new creation.

Admittedly, this concept of a single, overarching 'covenant of grace' helpfully serves to keep the continuity and theological relationship between the various divine–human covenants clearly in focus. Unfortunately, however, some of the terminology that has thus been introduced into the discussion has proved problematic and

[36] As noted above, two seventeenth-century Dutch theologians were particularly influential: Johannes Cocceius (often dubbed the 'father of federal theology' and certainly one of the first to attempt to write a biblical theology) and Herman Witsius (whose treatise on covenant theology remains in print today). However, while these two played a significant role in the propagation of federal theology, it had already taken root before their work was published – as is clear from its expression in the Westminster Confession of Faith (1643–8). For more on the history of federal theology, see Golding 2004: 13–66.

potentially misleading. Moreover, superimposing a covenantal framework on the entire canon is not without its difficulties, not least of which is the somewhat hypothetical nature of the major theological construct (i.e. the covenant of grace). Therefore, while fully acknowledging that all the divine–human covenants ultimately serve the same overarching divine purpose (see below), it seems preferable in a biblical-theological investigation to articulate that *purpose* as simply and unambiguously as possible. Thus, rather than speaking in terms of a single, overarching 'covenant of grace', the unity and continuity of the various divine–human covenants will be explored in terms of God's universal purpose – a purpose that is given clear expression in the Genesis creation narratives, and that finds its ultimate fulfilment in the new creation inaugurated through the death and resurrection of the Lord Jesus Christ.

Depending on how one views the Noahic, Abrahamic and Mosaic covenants, there are thus between five and ten explicit divine–human covenants in Scripture.[37] The following discussion will assume a total of seven (not including some covenant renewals by Israel such as Josh. 23 – 24; 1 Sam. 12; 2 Chr. 29 – 31; 2 Kgs 22 – 23), which will be examined under the following headings: the universal covenant (with Noah, his family and all creation); the patriarchal covenants (with Abraham and his seed); the national covenants (with Israel and its priestly representatives); the royal covenant (with David and his seed); and the new covenant (with a spiritually renewed and reconstituted Israel).

Covenant as the organizing theological 'centre'

While it has long been recognized that 'covenant is a major biblical metaphor for the distinctive relationship of the people of Israel with God',[38] some scholars – as already noted – have gone further, identifying covenant as the organizing theological centre (German: *Mitte*) around which the entire message of the Old Testament has been constructed, and providing the essential coherence between the Old Testament and the New.[39]

Certainly influential in this respect, Eichrodt's cross-sectional approach to Old Testament theology has been criticized on several fronts.

---

[37] The higher figure involves distinguishing between separate ancestral covenants (see below) and counting covenant 'renewals' such as Exodus 34 and Deuteronomy 29 – 30 as separate covenants.

[38] McKenzie 2000: 9.

[39] Notably, Eichrodt (1961, 1967).

1. It is too synchronic and not sufficiently diachronic.
2. It is too schematic and not sufficiently dynamic.[40]
3. It is basically misguided, since any attempt to systematize the Old Testament by means of one central concept or formula will be overly reductionistic and will inevitably suppress parts of the testimony that do not fit the overall scheme (e.g. it is difficult to incorporate the wisdom literature into Eichrodt's proposed theological centre).[41]

Despite such criticisms, other scholars have adopted Eichrodt's cross-sectional approach, while at the same time proposing alternative 'centres'. However, none of the alternative suggestions is without problems of its own. While any consensus on this issue seems more remote in the present postmodern climate than ever, it is perhaps worth noting that few of the proposed centres are altogether removed from Eichrodt's covenant idea.[42]

Nevertheless, given the fact that there are significant parts of Scripture in which the idea is certainly not prominent (e.g. the wisdom literature), it seems better to identify covenant simply as one of Scripture's major theological themes, rather than attempting to reduce all other trajectories so as to squeeze them into this mould.[43]

Covenant as a major unifying theological theme

As the above discussion has illustrated, the traditional nomenclature of the Christian Bible (i.e. Old Testament and New Testament) is not entirely misplaced. While covenant terminology may not be used as frequently in the New Testament (e.g. the Greek term for covenant, *diathēkē*, occurs only thirty-three times, mainly within the Pauline

[40] These first two criticisms are those of von Rad, for whom the whole idea of finding such an organizing theological centre in the OT was misguided, since, in his opinion, the OT was an amalgam of historical traditions, which by their very nature had no 'centre'; what eventually united them was the culmination of the 'story of faith' in Jesus Christ.

[41] For a helpful discussion of the problem of finding a theological centre in the OT, see Hasel 1991: 139–171. For a more concise analysis, see Scobie 2003: 85–87.

[42] I.e. it is difficult to unpack proposed 'centres' such as Yahweh, communion between God and Man, Yahweh the God of Israel and Israel the people of Yahweh, or the book of Deuteronomy without focusing primarily on covenant.

[43] Wright (2005: 56) similarly concludes that while 'it is futile to isolate any one theme or category as the sole organizing centre for the whole . . . the sequence of covenants in the canonical narrative does offer us one fruitful way of presenting the grand narrative that embodied Israel's coherent worldview'.

corpus and Hebrews),[44] the concept (i.e. the new covenant era inaugurated by the death and resurrection of Jesus Christ) lies at the very heart of New Testament theology.[45] Moreover, these new covenant realities experienced in Jesus Christ are repeatedly promised and foreshadowed in the Old Testament. All God's covenant promises anticipate this eschatological reality, and God's covenant commitment to Noah, Abraham, Israel, the Levitical priesthood and David typify or foreshadow it in one way or another. Indeed, even the wisdom literature, with its emphasis on 'the fear of the LORD' as the key to knowledge and wisdom, is closely related to the concept of living in covenant relationship with God. It is thus clear that the concept of covenant is much more pervasive in both Testaments than the mere frequency of explicit covenant terminology might lead one to conclude.[46]

Given its prominence and pervasiveness in the biblical text, no preaching programme or theological curriculum can ignore the biblical theology of covenant for very long. Indeed, even when not mentioned explicitly in the biblical text, covenant is seldom far from the surface. Some texts anticipate covenant realities, whereas others are built firmly on such a foundation. Hence one cannot faithfully expound or explain the Bible without paying particular attention to this important theological trajectory.

As well as its fundamental role in understanding the Bible as a whole, the covenant idea is essential for unlocking numerous biblical texts. Indeed, arguably, the meaning of many texts will be skewed unless covenant is brought into the hermeneutical enterprise (e.g. love/hate language is generally covenant related). Therefore, by reading texts against their implicit or explicit covenantal backcloth, their theological significance and practical import generally become so much clearer.

It is essential that, as those who through union with Christ participate in the 'new covenant', we understand not only what this is, but how it relates to the covenant history as disclosed in Scripture.

---

[44] McKenzie (2000: 84) lists the distribution as follows: (a) The four Gospels and Acts: Matt. 26:28; Mark 14:24; Luke 1:72; 22:20; Acts 3:25; 7:8 (b) letters of Paul: Rom. 9:4; 11:27; 1 Cor. 11:25; 2 Cor. 3:6, 14; Gal. 3:15, 17; 4:24; Eph. 2:12 (c) Hebrews: Heb. 7:22; 8:6, 8, 9 (2×), 10; 9:4 (2×), 15 (2×), 16, 17, 20; 10:16, 29; 12:24; 13:20.

[45] As highlighted most recently by Gräbe (2006: 68–150). Even John's Gospel, which never uses the word 'covenant', subtly echoes major covenantal motifs. See Pryor 1992 (esp. 148–150, 157–180); cf. also Chennattu 2006.

[46] Covenant terminology is much more frequent in the OT, the primary word (*bĕrît*) occurring some 285 times.

Pinpointing what is 'new' about the new covenant is therefore not merely a matter of academic interest; it is essential to understanding how our relationship to God through Jesus is both continuous and discontinuous with the relationship experienced by Israel under the 'old' covenant. Furthermore, to understand our covenant relationship with God and our place and role in salvation history, we must also understand the covenant promises made to Noah, Abraham, Israel and David – hence covenant serves as a crucial hermeneutical bridge that will help Christians move biblically and theologically from the period highlighted in the biblical text to the contemporary scene.

It is clear, therefore, that understanding the biblical theology of covenant serves more than to stimulate our intellect; rather, as we explore the covenant relationship enjoyed between God and people in the past, we further appreciate the covenant relationship with God that we enjoy in the present – both in terms of the privileges it encompasses and the responsibilities it enshrines.

The meaning of covenant terminology used in Scripture

While the term 'covenant' is one with which most people are at least vaguely familiar, a shared understanding of what is meant by this term can seldom be assumed. In some cases the intended nuance of this word is helped by the immediate context or associated terminology. For example, in a legal setting it refers to a formal agreement drawn up between two or more parties. In a socio-political setting it refers to the solemn undertaking agreed to by members of a particular party or group. In an ecclesiastical setting, it may describe the commitments made by members of a congregation, the marriage relationship established by the taking of mutual vows, or the topic of a forthcoming Bible study series. The focus of this particular investigation is obviously most in keeping with the latter, although even here we need to be careful, since, as has already been noted, examining the biblical theology of covenant and engaging in a study of covenant theology can mean two very different things. One is most likely to find the latter in a volume dealing with the practice of Christian baptism or systematic theology. 'Covenant Theology' is generally used to refer to a particular theological system of belief that serves as the basis for an associated set of ideas and/or ecclesiastical practice (e.g. most Presbyterians defend the rite of infant baptism on the basis of their covenant theology). The present investigation has little, if any, bearing on covenant theology in that sense.[47]

Rather, the concern here is with understanding a major theological trajectory in the Bible; namely, the series of covenants that God established between himself and various individuals or groups. Thus in the following chapters we will examine the biblical theology of covenant, not the pros and cons of covenant theology. Yet even with this important caveat, the definitional problem is not solved, as there is no universally agreed understanding of what is meant by 'covenant' in Scripture.[48] It is thus to this important issue that we now turn.

For some, covenant is almost synonymous with a relationship – or more precisely, a relationship involving promises; for others, a covenant necessitates that such promises are formalized in some way, mainly by means of a solemn oath and/or symbolic ritual. For still others, a covenant is essentially a unilateral obligation or mutual arrangement of some kind.[49] In the Old Testament it encompasses parity agreements between individuals and/or their families, oaths of allegiance by subjects to their king, international alliances between one nation and another, as well as several arrangements instituted between God and men.[50] The New Testament picks up the common Old Testament terminology (i.e. as used in the Septuagint), but as well as using it in its commonly accepted Old Testament sense (i.e. a formal agreement of one kind or another), it is often claimed that the New Testament also employs the Greek term in its more technically precise sense – a last will or testament (however, see p. 38 and the discussion in ch. 7 below).

Thus as McKenzie (2000: 3) correctly concedes, 'Defining "covenant" in the Bible . . . is not as easy as it might seem. Broadly, the word refers to an arrangement of some kind between two or more parties. But the exact nature of the arrangement is not always clear.' As he goes on to observe, some of the key questions that need to be addressed are as follows:

- To what extent is 'covenant' in the Bible promissory, and to what extent does it represent an obligation?
- Are both parties obligated or just one?

[47] For a recent discussion and defence of 'covenant theology' in the traditional Reformed understanding, see Horton (2006).

[48] For some scholars, this is due in part to the fact that even the biblical testimony is not in agreement (i.e. there is no uniform understanding of covenant in the Bible itself). This latter premise certainly warrants closer investigation.

[49] For more detailed discussion, see Nicholson 1986 (esp. 13–27, 83–117).

[50] For details, see below.

- Is the covenant imposed by one party on another, or are its terms negotiated and arrived at by mutual consent and agreement?
- Is a covenant in the Bible always between two parties, or can it involve more than two?

In one sense the obvious place to start is with the key terminology the Bible employs, although – as we will see – even this is problematic for a number of reasons.

The key terminology

Here we will limit our focus to the main biblical vocabulary for covenant, while acknowledging that (a) the covenant concept is not restricted to passages in which such terminology is explicitly used, and (b) there are several other terms closely associated with the covenant concept that shed light on what a covenant involved.

Hebrew

The primary Hebrew word for covenant is *běrît*. This word is used 286 times in the Hebrew Old Testament and, as noted above, is used of a wide variety of arrangements, some on a strictly human level, and others involving Yahweh also.

While *běrît* has arguably no real synonyms,[51] its associative field includes the following: *šěbû'â* (sworn oath); *'ālâ* (oath); *ḥesed* (steadfast love); *tôrâ* (instruction). Even when found in parallelism with *běrît*, words like *'ālâ* and *tôrâ* are not strictly synonymous (as the test of consistent reverse replaceability clearly demonstrates). Thus, as Nicholson (following Barr) puts it (1986: 103), while one may conclude that the making of a *běrît* involves the taking of an oath, one must not deduce from the mere taking of an oath that a *běrît* has been established.

Unfortunately, the lack of agreement over the etymology of this Hebrew word has added to the difficulty of tying down its essential meaning.[52] Proposed etymologies include the following:[53]

[51] So Barr 1974: 31–33; contra Weinfeld 1977: 256–260.

[52] This, of course, assumes that (a) there was some basic connotation that was implicit across its semantic range, and that (b) the usage of this term in the OT reflects that basic connotation in one way or another. While neither of these can simply be assumed, it seems to be the best way of explaining why this terminology is so consistently applied to similar concepts (i.e. relationships involving solemn obligations) across the OT literature.

[53] McKenzie 2000: 3 n. 2. For a more detailed discussion, see Weinfeld 1977: 253–255; Barr 1977: 23–38; Nicholson 1986: 94–103.

1. *brh* (I) – 'to eat' (reflecting the association between covenant initiation and a communal meal)
2. *brh* (II) – 'to see' (with the derived meaning, 'to choose, decide', hence the noun conveys a decision, obligation)
3. *birit* – an Akkadian preposition meaning 'between' (suggesting agreement between two parties)
4. *birtu* – an Akkadian noun meaning 'clasp, fetter' (hence a covenant is a 'bond')
5. *br* – a biconsonantal stem meaning, 'to set apart' (hence a covenant is a specially designated or set-apart favour or benefit)

The somewhat subjective nature of such etymological suggestions, not to mention the rather speculative nature of their results, has highlighted for others the unreliability of such an approach. As Barr has pertinently observed, the etymology of a word may be a completely blind alley, since (a) etymology concerns the prehistory of the word, and (b) it may have absolutely no bearing on the semantic function of the word as used by subsequent speakers and authors (in this case, those who authored and compiled the Old Testament). It is surely more profitable to examine carefully how the word is deployed across the breadth of the Old Testament, while not ignoring any extra-biblical literature that might possibly shed light on the meaning and nuances of the term.

Greek

In the Septuagint, *bĕrît* is generally translated by the term *diathēkē*.[54] Strictly speaking, this refers to a promissory obligation, and is commonly used in ancient Greek literature of a last will or testament, rather than of some kind of formal agreement or treaty – for which *synthēkē* might seem the more appropriate term. However, the latter implies an equality for those making such an agreement, whereas the former term serves to highlight that the 'covenant' is the result of one person's initiative, rather than merely being the result of a mutual agreement between two equal parties. This important distinction may thus help to explain why *diathēkē* rather than *synthēkē* is the preferred Greek term for the biblical authors.

As noted above, the New Testament follows the Septuagint in using the term *diathēkē*, rather than *synthēkē*, with respect to covenant.

---

[54] The only exceptions are the following texts: Isa. 28:15 (a covenant with death); Isa. 30:1; Dan. 11:6, 17 (all three texts describing equitable military alliances).

However, on at least two occasions (cf. Gal. 3:15; Heb. 9:16–17) it allegedly uses the term in its strict sense of a 'will or testament'. Nevertheless, even apart from the somewhat tenuous nature of the latter conclusion (see chapter 7 below), on both these occasions the concept is introduced primarily by way of illustration. Thus it would seem somewhat incongruous to use the allegedly distinct sense of the term in these verses to establish or qualify the meaning of covenant in its more general biblical usage. At most, these verses may highlight certain analogies between a *diathēkē* (in its literal sense) and the theological construct to which the term is most commonly applied.[55]

'Covenants' in the Old Testament between human beings

As noted above, in addition to its association with divine–human relationships, the term *běrît* is frequently used in the Old Testament with reference to interpersonal and socio-political agreements of various kinds; for example, see Genesis 14:13 (Abram's Amorite 'allies' are lit. 'owners of the *běrît* with Abram'); Genesis 21:17 (Abraham's pact with Abimelech); Genesis 26:26–31 (Isaac's pact with Abimelech); Genesis 31:44–50 (Jacob's pact with Laban); Joshua 9:3–21 (the Israelite treaty with the Gibeonites); Amos 1:9 ('covenant of brothers' implies a treaty made between Tyre and Edom); 1 Samuel 11:1 (the people of Jabesh-gilead attempted to negotiate a peace treaty with the Ammonites); 1 Samuel 18:3; cf. 1 Samuel 20:8; 23:18 (the personal loyalty agreement between David and Jonathan); 2 Samuel 3:12–13 (peace treaty between David and Abner); 2 Samuel 3:21; 5:3 (loyalty agreement between David and elders of Israel); 1 Kings 5:13 (Solomon's pact with Hiram); 1 Kings 15:19; 20:34 (loyalty pacts between Israel and Damascus); Hosea 12:1; cf. Hosea 10:4; (suzerainty agreement between Assyria and Israel);[56] Ezekiel 17:11–21 (treaty between Judah and Babylon); Jeremiah 34:8–20 (Zedekiah's agreement with the people of Jerusalem).

In addition to such socio-political commitments, the Old Testament occasionally describes marriage in terms of a *běrît*: Malachi 2:14; Proverbs 2:17 (cf. Hosea's use of the marriage metaphor in Hos. 1 – 3 for Yahweh's covenant relationship with Israel), and also mentions covenants of a more metaphorical nature: Job 5:23 (the expectation of a *běrît* of peace with the stones of the

---

[55] However, see the discussion in chapter 7, which argues for a consistent usage of *diathēkē* in the NT, including these two texts.

[56] Possibly Hos. 6:7 also refers to such a loyalty pact.

field and wild animals); Job 31:1 (Job's *běrît* with his eyes) and Isaiah 28:15, 18 (Jerusalem's political leaders' *běrît* with death).

While it would be misleading to describe these covenants as 'secular' – in that God was at least implicitly (and sometimes explicitly) involved in them as 'witness' and, as such, would certainly hold the covenant-breaker accountable – they clearly belong in a separate category from covenants that relate primarily to a divine–human relationship. Even so, the former obviously throw considerable light on the latter, as it was from the more secular idea of a *běrît* that the theological motif or metaphor most likely derives.[57]

It is clear from the texts surveyed above that a *běrît* covers a wide range of elective as opposed to natural human relationships:[58] a commitment between individuals or families; a suzerain–vassal treaty; a military alliance; and even a pact made with oneself. We must ask, therefore, what these arrangements have in common – other than their shared description as a *běrît*? At least two important observations are worth noting: (a) some form of divine sanction is generally implied for covenant-breakers; (b) the establishment of such a covenant was generally ratified by means of a solemn oath. Indeed, the latter could well be described as the *sine qua non* of a covenant.[59] While Lohfink (1967: 101–113) may have gone too far in actually defining a *běrît* in terms of an 'oath', it is now widely acknowledged that an oath was indeed an indispensable aspect in the ratification of a covenant.[60] Thus understood, it is this aspect that constitutes the most important common denominator between the various covenants attested to in Scripture. Each of them comprises an elective relationship formalized by means of a solemn obligation or oath. We may provisionally conclude, therefore, that one of the key concepts or basic ideas conveyed by the term *běrît* is the solemn nature of the agreement it enshrined; it had been sealed with an oath.

---

[57] The concept probably derives from formal kinship ties (so Cross 1998), which have subsequently been employed (along with vassal treaties) as a metaphor for a similar bond between God and human beings. For more on this – but reflecting the developmental views of mainstream OT scholarship – see McKenzie 2000: 11–39; Nicholson 1986: 83–117.

[58] For this important distinction between elective and natural relationship, see Hugenberger 1994: 171.

[59] Cf. the preponderance of oath-taking terminology in covenant-making contexts: cf. Gen. 21: 27, 31; 26:28, 31; 31:44, 53; Josh. 9:15–20; 1 Sam. 20:16–17, 42; 21:2, 7; 2 Kgs 11:4; Ezek. 17:13–19; 21:23. This is further attested by divine–human covenants; cf. 2 Chr. 15:10–15; Neh. 8:38; 10:29, and the numerous references to oath-taking in relation to the major divine–human covenants in the OT (see below).

[60] See Hugenberger 1994: 182–183.

However, this hypothesis must be further tested in the light of the other main category of *běrît* reflected in the Old Testament; namely, a *běrît* directly associated with a divine–human relationship.[61]

'Covenants' in the Old Testament between God and humans

As far as divine–human covenants are concerned, the first mention of any such *běrît* is in Genesis 6:18 (in association with Noah). Hosea 6:7, however, has traditionally been understood as referring to a covenant that was established between God and Adam, and thus for this (and other reasons) many interpreters identify the first divine–human *běrît* as the Adamic (often referred to as a probationary 'covenant of works' or, more recently, as 'the covenant of/with creation'; cf. Jer. 33:25). These latter ideas will be explored more fully below. At this stage it suffices to underline that, whether perceived as an entirely new development in salvation history or the renewal of an already existing covenant, the relationship between the Noahic or universal covenant and God's creative purpose is not in doubt. While first mentioned in Genesis 6:18, this covenant is apparently not ratified until after the flood (cf. Gen. 8:20 – 9:17), where God solemnly promises with an oath (cf. Isa. 54:9) to restrain the forces of chaos and maintain the created order.

The next example of a divine–human *běrît* is associated with Abram (Gen. 15:18), where the common idiom of cutting (Hebrew: *kārat*) a *běrît* is first employed. This particular idiom most probably derives from the ritual involved in the establishment of many such covenants (cf. Gen. 15:10; Jer. 34:18).[62] Different terminology is found in Genesis 17, a chapter whose focus is likewise on a *běrît* between God and Abraham. Here it is anticipated that the covenant will be 'set/given' (Hebrew: *nātan*; Gen. 17:2) or established (Hebrew: *hēqîm*), and there are some markedly different emphases.[63] Significantly, on at least three occasions the patriarchal narratives explicitly use the language of oath-taking in relation to God's covenant obligations to Abraham (cf. Gen. 22:16; 24:7; 26:3), an association of ideas that is further attested in numerous other biblical texts (cf. Exod. 6:8; 13:5;

---

[61] It is worth reiterating that Yahweh was party also to interpersonal and socio-political covenants, as attested to by the fact that Yahweh is explicitly involved in some cases (cf. 1 Sam. 20:8; 2 Sam. 5:3), and also by the fact that God held the covenant partners accountable (cf. Ezek. 17:16–21).

[62] Most understand this ritual in terms of a self-maledictory oath.

[63] The significance of these differences will be explored in detail below.

32:13; 33:1; Num. 11:12; 14:23, 30; 32:11; Deut. 1:8; 4:31 [and *passim*]; Josh. 1:6; 21:43–44; Judg. 2:1; 1 Chr. 16:16–17; Neh. 9:15; Ps. 105:9–10; Jer. 11:5; 32:22; Ezek. 20:28, 42; 47:14; Luke 1:72–73; Heb. 6:13, 16–17).[64] While Yahweh's covenant promises to Abraham are clearly alluded to in the subsequent patriarchal narratives, a divine–human *bĕrît* is not mentioned explicitly again until we reach the book of Exodus, where it also encompasses Isaac and Jacob, and serves as the basis for Yahweh's deliverance of Israel from Egypt (Exod. 2:24; 6:4–5; cf. Lev. 26:40–42; 2 Kgs 13:23; Neh. 9:8).

When the term is next found in Exodus (Exod. 19:5), it appears to anticipate the next major covenantal development; namely, the *bĕrît* established between Yahweh and Israel.[65] The ratification of this national covenant (generally described as Mosaic or Sinaitic) by means of a covenant-making ceremony involving blood ritual is described in Exodus 24.[66] Interestingly, there is no explicit mention of a divine oath in the context of the ratification of the covenant at Sinai, although a few texts appear to allude to such an oath (e.g. Num. 14:16; Deut. 28:9; 31:23; Ezek. 16:8, 59–60; 20:5–6; Mic. 7:20; cf. also Exod. 13:11),[67] and such is certainly mentioned explicitly in relation to the renewal or remaking of this covenant on the plains of Moab (cf. Deut. 29:12, 14, 19). The obligations imposed on the people were apparently 'inscripturated' in what is described as the 'Book of the Covenant' (Exod. 24:7). These obligations – at least in summary form – are subsequently engraved on 'the two tablets of the *testimony*' (Hebrew: *'ēdût*; Exod. 31:18 ESV; my italics), which, after

[64] In some biblical texts the precise referent intended by 'your forefathers' is ambiguous. However, in the texts listed, an allusion to Israel's ancestors (i.e. Abraham, Isaac, Jacob and his sons) seems to be the most straightforward interpretation.

[65] Although some (e.g. Dumbrell 1984: 81) insist rather that it refers back to the patriarchal covenant. Indeed, Baker (2005: 25) has recently argued that the traditional separation between the ancestral and national covenants is misleading in any case: 'the Mosaic covenant is a confirmation and elaboration of that made with Abraham, not something new or different'.

[66] It will be argued below that the blood-ritual involved in ratification of the Sinai covenant is an enacted oath rite (for the latter idea, see Hugenberger 1994: 194–214).

[67] Again, the precise referent point for some of these texts (esp. Mic. 7:20) is unclear. E.g. one might reasonably infer that the oath by which Yahweh assured the Israelites of their territorial inheritance was in fact made to their ancestors. In keeping with this, the reference to the oath Yahweh promised 'to you and your ancestors' in Exodus 13:11 (TNIV) could then be understood in terms of a vav explicative (i.e. 'to you, that is, to your ancestors'). Nevertheless, some of these texts are difficult to interpret in this way (e.g. Deut. 28:9; Ezek. 16:8; 20:5–6), and thus supply further evidence associating covenant ratification with the swearing of an oath.

their initial destruction and reintroduction, are referred to (Exod. 34:28 ESV) as 'the words of the *covenant*' (Hebrew: *bĕrît*). This national covenant is clearly the most prominent *bĕrît* in the Old Testament (lending some credence to its description as *the* Old Testament covenant), and is renewed at several important junctures in Israel's history (cf. Deut. 29:1; Josh. 24:25; 2 Kgs 23:1–3). Its precise relationship with the Levitical covenant(s) will receive more detailed analysis later (see chapter 3 below), but it seems that this national covenant also encompasses more specialized commitments between God and smaller sections of the covenant community; namely, the 'covenant of salt' with the Aaronic Priesthood (Num. 18:19) and the 'covenant of peace/perpetual priesthood' with Phinehas (Num. 25:12–13 ESV) and the covenant of faithful ministry with Levi (Jer. 33:22; Neh. 13:29; Mal. 2:4–5, 8).

Although the key Hebrew term is not used in the context of its initiation, the promises God made to David of a perpetual dynasty (2 Sam. 7; 1 Chr. 17) are explicitly referred to as a *bĕrît* elsewhere (cf. 2 Sam. 23:5; 2 Kgs 8:19 [cf. 2 Chr. 21:7]; 2 Chr. 13:5; Pss. 89:3, 19–27, 39; 132:11[?]; Isa. 55:3; Jer. 33:14–26). Moreover, the concept is probably implicit in other texts, which, though not using the actual term *bĕrît*, similarly underline the binding nature of the relationship between Yahweh and Davidic dynasty (e.g. 1 Kgs 9:5; 11:36; 1 Chr. 28:4; cf. Ezek. 37:24–25). The way in which oath-taking language is employed in biblical texts referring to the royal covenant (cf. Pss. 89:3, 35, 49; 132:11; Acts 2:20) again adds further weight to the conclusion that such was an indispensable part of the covenant concept.[68]

The only other divine–human covenant mentioned in the Old Testament is the future *bĕrît* anticipated by the prophets (cf. Hos. 2:18; Isa. 54:10; 55:3; 59:21; 61:8; Jer. 31:31–34; 32:40; 50:5; Ezek. 16:60–62; 20:37; 34:25; 37:26; Dan. 9:27[?]; Zech. 9:11; Mal. 3:1[?]).[69] The precise relationship between this 'new covenant' (Jer. 31:31) and its antecedents needs to be carefully explored, but whether it is perceived in terms of a covenant renewal (i.e. of the covenant initiated at Sinai) or as a radically new development, this covenant involves

---

[68] While God had earlier sworn an oath to David concerning his own kingship (cf. 2 Sam. 3:9), the divine oath enshrined in the royal covenant concerned David's dynasty more than David himself.

[69] While not using *bĕrît*, Ezek. 36:22–38 obviously alludes to this future covenant also, as is clear not only from the emphasis on spiritual cleansing that will facilitate the meeting of God's covenant demands (Ezek. 36:25–27), but also from the express use of the covenant formula (Ezek. 36:28).

facilitating the demands of love and loyalty that proved impossible under the written covenant code (i.e. the Mosaic law).[70]

The fact that these various arrangements, ostensibly dating from different periods, are described by the same Hebrew term certainly implies a common denominator of some kind, something that was best captured in the ancient Hebrew mind by the concept of a *bĕrît*. As we have seen, a cross-sectional examination reveals at least two significant points of commonality:

- A covenant ratifies an already forged or existing elective relationship.
- The ratification involves the making of solemn promises by means of a verbal and/or enacted oath.

This suggests, therefore, that a divine–human *bĕrît* may be defined as the solemn ratification of an existing elective relationship involving promises or obligations that are sealed with an oath.

Conclusion

The above analysis leads us to conclude that while a covenant involves an elective relationship, and incorporates obligations on one or both covenant partners, the key aspect without which it cannot be described as a *bĕrît* is the solemnizing of the promises and/or obligations by means of a formal oath. Even where this latter element is not expressly mentioned, a close reading of the biblical material leads one to the conclusion that such an oath was always implicit in so far as a *bĕrît* is concerned. Thus, in what follows, the following definition of a *bĕrît* will serve as the basis for our examination of divine–human covenants in Scripture: 'a solemn commitment, guaranteeing promises or obligations undertaken by one or both parties, sealed with an oath'.

---

[70] The ratification of this new covenant is obviously not recorded in the OT, but interestingly it is again premised on the basis of a divine oath (cf. Isa. 54:9; 62:8).

Chapter Two

Covenant and God's universal purpose

Covenant in its biblical-theological context

If covenant is one of the most important ideas in Scripture as a whole, it is certainly so in the case of the Pentateuch in particular. The term itself (i.e. *běrît*) is found some eighty-two times, and is used to describe both interpersonal (cf. Gen. 14:13; 21:27, 32; 26:28; 31:44; Exod. 23:32; 34:12; Deut. 7:2) and divine–human covenants. As noted previously, the former obviously throw considerable light on the meaning of the term; namely, that it is a solemnly sworn commitment, guaranteeing promises or obligations undertaken by one or both covenanting parties. However, the predominant usage – describing divinely established covenants or the stipulations incorporated within them – is more significant theologically. These divine–human covenants not only occupy a pivotal place within the Pentateuch itself, but are also clearly foundational for the revelation that unfolds in the rest of the Bible. The first of these divine–human covenants (certainly, the first mentioned explicitly) is the universal covenant established by God with Noah and all creation in the immediate aftermath of the flood.[1] However, before looking at this particular covenant more closely, we need to locate it within its biblical-theological context. This warrants a brief examination of creation and the divine purpose.[2]

Creation and the divine purpose

In the book of Genesis, creation does not stand as a prescientific attempt to explain the origin of the cosmos. Rather, creation func-

---

[1] Gen. 6:18 most likely anticipates the establishment of this covenant; see fuller discussion below.

[2] The following discussion is limited to the first three chapters of Genesis for the sake of manageability. Obviously, the major structural markers in Genesis would suggest that the second main text unit in Genesis extends from Gen. 2:4 to Gen. 4:26. Admittedly, Gen. 4:26 ends on a more positive note than Gen. 3:24, and points us better in the direction of the Bible's eschatological goal.

tions in Genesis as the prologue to history. As Anderson (1994: 25) observes:

> It sets the stage for the unfolding of the divine purpose and inaugurates a historical drama within which Israel and, in the fullness of time, the church were destined to play a key role. Thus creation stands in an inseparable historical relation to the ensuing narratives that span the generations from Adam to Noah, from Noah to Abr(ah)am, and from Abraham to Joseph.

Or as he has more recently (1999: 92) put it, 'In the book of Genesis, creation is not presented as an independent "doctrine" but belongs in the context of an extended story that moves from the beginning toward the fulfilment of God's purpose for all creatures and the whole creation.'

However we understand the relationship between the two distinct creation narratives in Genesis,[3] it is clear that both present humanity as the pinnacle of God's creative activity. In Genesis 1 this is reflected in the fact that humans are created last, and delegated responsibility for the rest of creation (Gen. 1:26–31);[4] in Genesis 2 it is clear from the anthropocentric focus of the chapter, and also from its formulaic introduction, which serves primarily to introduce the tragic story of Adam and Eve.[5]

---

[3] I.e. Gen. 1 – 2:3 and Gen. 2:4–25. In their canonical context, these must be seen as complementary rather than contradictory: each has a distinct focus and purpose in the narrative as a whole.

[4] As Lucas (2003: 136) observes, it is further reflected in the divine deliberation before the act in v. 26a, the threefold use of *bārā'* in v. 27, and their unique creation in the *imago dei* (cf. vegetation, fish, birds and animals 'according to their kinds'). Likewise Dempster (2003: 57), whose graph illustrates the extraordinary significance of the sixth day.

[5] While there have been several noted challenges to the view that the formulae are introductory, this has remained the consensus. As Hamilton (1990: 9–10) notes, there are several difficulties with the proposal that the *tôlĕdôt* phrases are concluding summaries, the most serious of which is the lack of correspondence between the alleged colophon and the preceding material (e.g. Gen. 25:12 does not sit easily as a colophon for all the material from 11:27b). It is unsurprising, therefore, that other interpreters have taken these statements (with the possible exception of 2:4a) as introducing a new section. With respect to Gen. 2:4, it should be noted that (a) here also the formula fits as a heading; (b) unless the verse is unnecessarily split, its use of 'Yahweh Elohim' connects it with Gen. 2 rather than Gen. 1. Thus the first *tôlĕdôt* section in Genesis (Gen. 2:4 – 4:26) traces what became of the universe God had so marvellously created (ending, nevertheless, on a note of hope).

The functional aspect of the creation of human beings is explicated in Genesis 1:26–28. Here it is disclosed that

- humans alone are created in/as God's image (Gen. 1:26a, 27);[6]
- as such, humans are to populate the earth and rule over the rest of creation (Gen. 1:26b, 28).

The ability to fulfil the first aspect of the creation mandate ('Be fruitful and multiply and fill . . .') is clearly an expression of the divine blessing shared by humankind, birds and fish (Gen. 1:28 ESV; cf. Gen. 1:22; 9:1), but not land animals (cf. Gen. 1:24–25) – presumably because such blessing in terms of numerical proliferation would have rivalled and indeed threatened such 'blessing' in terms of humanity (cf. Deut. 7:22). This first aspect of the divine instruction recorded here is clearly linked to the second; human procreation (i.e. multiplication of the divine image-bearers) and populating the earth are imperative for the second aspect to be carried out as divinely intended (i.e. God wants his rule – as represented by humanity – to spread throughout the whole earth).

Such a position of power and authority is clearly reflected in the second aspect of the divine mandate: 'subdue' and 'exercise dominion' (Gen 1:28 my trans.).[7] Thus it would appear that humankind is created as God's vicegerent: to reign in a manner that demonstrates his lordship over all creation.[8] As Wenham (1987: 33) correctly cautions:

This is of course no license for the unbridled exploitation and subjugation of nature. Ancient oriental kings were expected to

[6] For a concise discussion of various interpretations of this enigmatic concept, see Wenham 1987: 27–32. On the basis of its threefold use in Genesis (Gen. 1:26–27; 5:1–3; 9:6), Scobie (2003:158–159) plausibly argues that 'the image of God in humankind is to be understood primarily in terms of personhood: human beings are created for personal relations with God and with other humans'.

[7] The term *rādâ* is used of Israelite authority over their servants, Solomon's reign over Israel (1 Kgs 4:24 [MT 5:4]), and the dominion exercised by the ideal, messianic king (Num. 24:17–19; Pss. 72:8; 110:2), whereas the term *kābaš* is used of the Israelite subjugation of Canaan (Num. 32:22, 29; Josh. 18:1), David's subjugation of his enemies (2 Sam. 8:11), and Israel's eschatological subjugation of its foes (Zech. 9:15). So Dempster 2003: 59–60. Therefore, a close examination of the biblical usage of these terms debunks the notion that these texts provide a biblical mandate for environmental abuse and rape. Rather, as Scobie insists (2003: 157), this is 'a command to order, maintain, protect and care for – i.e., to exercise control in the best interests of – the subject', hence ' "dominion" means responsible stewardship' (2003: 158).

[8] Significantly, ancient Babylonian and Egyptian texts describe the king in such a manner (as the deity's vicegerent). Similarly, here in Genesis the focus is on humanity's *role* (as God's image) rather than on his *nature*.

be devoted to the welfare of their subjects . . . Similarly, mankind is here commissioned to rule nature as a benevolent king, acting as God's representative over them and therefore treating them in the same way as God who created them.

In a similar vein Anderson (1999: 91) insists that 'human dominion is to be exercised wisely and benevolently so that God's dominion over the earth may be manifest in care for the earth and in the exercise of justice'. Thus it is important to recognize that while 'humanity is crowned the royalty of creation' (Dempster 2003: 57), this kingship must conform to the heavenly archetype implied in the *divine* image.[9] Humanity is to exercise dominion not only on God's behalf, but also to do so just as he would.[10] As Dumbrell (2002b: 62–63) aptly puts it, 'Dominion is the service that takes its motivation from one's ultimate human relationship with the Lord God, on whose behalf dominion is exercised.'

What such lordship over creation entails is spelt out more fully in Genesis 2:4–25, in which there is a narrowing of focus to the place from which Yahweh-God's rule was to extend throughout the world.[11] Having formed Adam from the dust of the ground and breathed into his nostrils the breath of life (Gen. 2:7), God places him in the garden 'to work the ground [lit. 'it'] and take care of it' (Gen. 2:15 my trans.).[12] Merrill (1991: 15) has correctly noted that

This must be seen in the light of verse 5, which points out that before the creation of man no shrub or plant had sprung up because there was as yet no rain and, more significantly, no man to 'work the ground' . . . To work the ground is one definition of what it means to have dominion.

[9] See Dempster 2003: 59 n. 6.

[10] As Dempster further notes (2003: 60), 'The rest of the canon assumes the royal overtones of Genesis 1, indicating the unique authority assigned to the primal couple, and thus to all humanity.' In particular, he highlights two key passages: Ps. 8 and Dan. 7:13–14.

[11] Eden (Yahweh-God's throne-room) is clearly presented as the source of life, not only for the surrounding garden (Gen 2:10a), but also for the whole earth (Gen. 2:10b–14). The fact that God is consistently given this double-epithet by the narrator in Gen. 2 – 3 is almost certainly intended to highlight the fact that the Creator God is also the God who later entered into covenant with Israel.

[12] While 'garden' is the immediate antecedent, the feminine suffix seems to refer back to 'the ground' (cf. Gen. 2:5).

Human dominion is exercised even more clearly in the naming of the animals (Gen. 2:20) – in the ancient Near East, to name something was tantamount to exercising dominion, and the context suggests such a connotation here.[13] Thus understood, Yahweh is here delegating to Adam the sovereignty for which he has been created.[14] Therefore, as Merrill (1991: 18) concludes, 'God had created man for the express purpose of conveying to him the status and function of image, that is, man was to represent God in his dominion over all creation.'

Although the sixth day brought to completion God's creative activity, this is not where the narrative ends. Rather, attention focuses on the seventh day, on which 'God finished . . . and he rested . . . from all the work that he had done' (Gen. 2:3 ESV).[15] Significantly, the seventh day is distinguished from the preceding days in two important respects:

- The descriptive pattern so prominent in the previous six days (i.e. announcement, imperative, report, evaluation or temporal framework) is entirely absent.
- This day is uniquely blessed and set apart.

As Turner (2000: 25) observes, 'this final day, unique in its content and narrative form, forms the apex and goal of God's creativity'. While the point is not made explicitly in Scripture until much later,[16] it is reasonable to infer from the text that this sabbatical blessing was something in which God intended humanity (made in God's image) to share.[17] Thus, as Dumbrell (1984: 34)

[13] Cf. Goldingay (2003:109), who correctly insists that 'contexts need to determine whether naming is a sign of authority'. Interestingly, Adam does not analogously name his wife until after the fall (cf. Gen. 3:20). In Genesis 2:23 he is not naming but defining her category in relation to himself and the rest of the animal world.

[14] The same idea of delegated kingship over all creation is reflected in Ps. 8, a psalm in which there are clear allusions to the *imago dei* concept of Gen. 1:26–28.

[15] Some translations (e.g. NIV/TNIV) avoid the apparent contradiction between v. 2 and the preceding verse by rendering the former in the pluperfect (i.e. *By* the seventh day God *had* finished). Ancient versions (Samaritan Pentateuch, Septuagint and Syriac) emended the text to read 'sixth day'. All such efforts to make sense of the text are unnecessary, however, if the seventh day is concerned with a different order of 'work' – that which transcends the physical universe and is concerned, rather, with sacred time (so Turner 2000: 24–25; similarly, Dumbrell 2002b: 53–54).

[16] Cf. Heb. 3:7 – 4:11.

[17] The fact that God 'blesses' and 'sanctifies' the seventh day suggests that the author 'did not consider it as something for God alone but as a concern of the world' (von Rad 1972: 62).

asserts, 'By the divine rest on the seventh day the goal of creation is indicated.'[18]

A harmonious relationship between God, humanity and creation is already implicit in Genesis 1 (the description of creation as 'good' and finally as 'very good').[19] However, it is the second creation narrative (Gen. 2:4ff.) that especially highlights this idyllic situation. While in this narrative the order of events is noticeably different,[20] here again mankind is the focal point and is distinguished from the rest of creation by being delegated special responsibilities (cf. Gen. 2:15).[21]

The garden in which God places Adam is highly significant.

1. It is clearly portrayed as a microcosm of the blessing that God intended for the whole earth. Indeed, it could correctly be described as 'a centre of world blessing' (Dumbrell 1984: 35), reflected in its depiction as the source of the four rivers that water the earth. From the creation mandate to 'multiply and fill the earth' (Gen 1:28 ESV) one can reasonably infer that God's purpose was for humanity to extend the borders of the garden throughout the earth.

2. It is presented as a divine sanctuary – a place in which the immediacy of God's presence is experienced and enjoyed.[22] Such

[18] Dumbrell (1984: 35) further observes, 'This notion of divine rest which man is thereafter invited to share becomes a dominant one in the later Old and New Testaments and the institution of the Sabbath (Exod. 31:13–17) becomes the particular covenant sign of the concept. So the sabbath . . . becomes for Israel an invitation to enter into, and rejoice in, the blessings of creation . . . For in pointing back to creation, the sabbath points also to what is yet to be, to the final destiny to which all creation is moving.' See also Shead 2000b: 745–750; Dumbrell 2002b: 54–55.

[19] The connotation of 'good' is not perfect/in no need of development (cf. Gen. 2:18), but appropriate for God's intended purpose.

[20] The order in Genesis 2 is man (v. 7), trees (v. 9), animals (v. 19) and woman (v. 22), whereas in Genesis 1, vegetation (day 3) precedes both (a) animals and (b) mankind (day 6); cf. Gen. 1:11–12, 26–30. Such differences pose a problem only when these narratives are interpreted in terms of an eyewitness account of the chronology of creation. It is highly unlikely, given the stylized structure of Genesis 1 and the symbolic imagery in Genesis 2 – 3, that either narrative was so intended. See further, Futato 1998: 1–21.

[21] Contrary to what is sometimes suggested, it is not the manner of his animation or his description as a 'living being' (Gen. 2:7 TNIV) that distinguishes humankind from the animals; cf. Gen. 2:19; 7:22; 9:3.

[22] Strictly speaking, the whole creation is the divine temple complex, the garden (in Eden) was part of the inner sanctum (the Most Holy Place, as it were). Thus understood, Adam is portrayed as a priest in Genesis 2, just as he is portrayed as a king in Genesis 1. Hence Adam and Eve were made kings and priests to serve God, and Eden is the model or prototype for what the world was to become.

'gardens' (i.e. botanical gardens or parks rather than the domestic variety) were a common feature of ancient Near Eastern temples, and it is therefore not surprising that many of the features of Eden are echoed in the tabernacle and the temple.[23] The key aspect of Eden is its role as a divine sanctuary. 'Within Eden the first man and woman have the unique privilege of being able to relate to God face to face without fear or shame' (Alexander 2002: 132).

The continuation of this harmonious relationship between God, humanity and creation, however, was clearly contingent upon human obedience to God's command (Gen. 2:16–17). While the clear echoes of the Sinai covenant in this prohibition ('you shall not') and its associated punishment ('you will certainly die') certainly link Adam and Israel typologically (with an ominous warning implicit for Israel – divine expulsion from the land and their source of life), it is unnecessary to infer from these or other analogies such as their shared role as a royal priesthood (see Dumbrell: 2002b: 61–62) that Adam too had a covenantal relationship with God.[24]

As Genesis 3 discloses, the conditions pertaining to this idyllic situation in Eden were not met – with disastrous consequences not only for the human race, but also for creation as a whole.[25] The ideal world of the garden of Eden was completely disrupted by the disobedience of Adam and Eve.[26] This disobedience led to alienation from God, as Adam and Eve are exiled from the garden (and hence from God and their source of life); to alienation from each other, as the dynamic of their relationship changed; and to alienation from the created world with its thorns and thistles making agriculture difficult. As Alexander (2002: 117) observes, 'The story of the fall brings to a bitter end the harmony that was the hallmark of God's creative activity.'

[23] See Dumbrell 2002b: 57–61.

[24] Indeed, given the absence of a divine promise, still less an oath, the presence of a covenant here seems most unlikely.

[25] Some scholars have advocated a less negative reading of Gen. 3, and/or attached less theological significance to this text than has traditionally been the case. However, as Dempster (2003: 66) pertinently comments, 'such views suffer from exegetical myopia'. While the traditional vocabulary (the 'fall') may derive more from dogmatics than the biblical text, the actual concept of a tragic cosmic event is certainly scriptural, and Gen. 3 is the foundational text. Similarly, Goldingay (2003: 144–145), despite his objections to the traditional terminology and some of its unbiblical nuances (e.g. an alleged fall from immortality to mortality).

[26] The context shows that to eat fruit from the tree of the knowledge of good and evil is to be like God (Gen. 3:5, 22), and thus to decide for oneself what is good or bad; i.e. to grasp moral autonomy.

Once introduced, sin rapidly reaches avalanche proportions: Cain's murder of Abel, Lamech's vengeful boast,[27] and the utter corruption of humankind before the flood. Sin has thus radically disrupted God's universal purpose, so much so that he must undo his creation and begin again.[28]

However, while sin clearly disrupted God's universal purpose, it did not eradicate it. As Goldingay (2003: 146) observes, Adam and Eve's disobedience 'affected their relationship with God and it cut them off from the garden, but it did not cut them off from God'. Indeed, as he further observes (2003: 149): 'Expulsion from Eden is a terrible event, yet it does not undo the whole purpose of creation. That purpose now begins to find fulfilment as Adam and Eve have their first two children.' Moreover, as already hinted at in Genesis 3:15, God will ultimately reverse the disruption to his universal purpose caused by the serpent, and he will do so through the seed of the woman. While Genesis 3:15 can be interpreted simply in terms of perpetual, unresolved conflict between humanity and evil ('crush' and 'strike' [TNIV] translate the same Hebrew verb, suggesting a mortal blow in each case),[29] without resolution this does not appear to be much of a curse on the serpent. Rather, while certainly encompassing the ensuing conflict between humanity and evil, the emphasis in Genesis on a promised line of seed suggests that it is that particular seed (i.e. subsequently identified as the seed of Abraham) who would both receive a mortal wound and deliver such. Thus understood, the curse on the serpent indeed foreshadows the ultimate triumph of Christ and his church (cf. Heb. 2:14; Rom. 16:20).[30]

It is with the fulfilment of this divine 'promise' of the *protevangelium*, and in particular, tracing this promised line of seed, that the rest of Genesis to Kings is primarily concerned.[31] Prior to the flood, the promised line of seed is traced from Adam through Seth to

---

[27] It is not altogether clear whether this is a statement of fact or a threat of such.

[28] With others Alexander (2002: 134) notes that 'the flood narrative in 6:9 – 9:19 exhibits close parallels with Genesis 1. The description of the floodwaters gradually covering the entire earth, including the highest mountains, portrays a return to the earth's original state prior to the separation of the land and seas (cf. 1:9–10). With the retreat of the floodwaters and Noah's departure from the ark, we have the re-creation of the earth.'

[29] So e.g. Goldingay 2003: 141 n. 14.

[30] Dempster (2003: 68) sees further significance in Adam's naming his wife immediately after the divine speech of Gen. 3:14–19: this was an expression of faith in the promise of Gen. 3:15 and a reclaiming of dominion through naming his wife, 'the mother' (i.e. alluding to her role in providing the seed who would strike the serpent). While it is possible to see in Adam's act an expression of faith in God's promise, it is more difficult to see 'reclaiming dominion in faith' through naming his wife 'Eve'.

[31] For more on this, see Alexander 2002: 101–113.

Noah,[32] thus highlighting the theological significance of the latter's deliverance: Noah was saved from the disaster of the flood to ensure the survival and preservation of the promised line of seed, through which the consequences of the fall would ultimately be reversed. And it is this divine purpose – universal blessing through this promised seed – that the Noahic covenant and indeed all subsequent covenants serve to protect and guarantee.

The question of a covenant with Adam

As already noted, the covenant concept is generally acknowledged as one of the Bible's major theological themes – as reflected not only in the canonical nomenclature but also in the recurring appearance of such covenants at all the major points in salvation history. However, scholastic Reformed (or federal) theology in the seventeenth century developed a theological system in which the whole of God's engagement with the world was understood within a covenant framework. This covenant framework included a number of covenants whose biblical basis is not absolutely clear or explicit. Such covenants include an eternal, pre-creation 'covenant of redemption/peace' between Father and Son, a probationary 'covenant of works' with Adam prior to the fall, and a post-lapsarian, all-encompassing 'covenant of grace' (of which each of the explicit divine–human covenants from Noah to the climactic 'new covenant' is understood to be a concrete expression or an administration).[33] Accordingly, federalists maintain that there are two great covenantal epochs in history: the pre-fall covenant of works and the post-fall covenant of grace, bound together by the eternal, covenant of redemption established between the Father and the Son in eternity.

Federal theology's 'covenant of works'

While there has been some debate within the Reformed camp over how the first of these two covenantal epochs is best described,

---

[32] This seems to be the explanation of the two genealogies in Genesis 4 – 5: the first, as often in Genesis, traces the rejected line of seed, whereas the second traces the promised line. This does not imply that the entire line of Cain was reprobate or that the entire line of Seth was godly, although it is probably significant that key figures in each of the otherwise similar list of names reflect such characteristics. In any case, as the more detailed genealogy of Genesis 5 suggests, it is with Seth's line, culminating in the righteous Noah, that the narrator is primarily concerned.

[33] The covenant of grace is also seen to incorporate a post-lapsarian covenant between God and Adam, alluded to in the *protevangelium* of Gen. 3:15.

'covenant of works' is certainly the most commonly used nomenclat-ure.[34] Unfortunately, however, this way of describing the concept has also resulted in much misunderstanding over what Reformed theo-logy intends by this idea.[35] While some critics have understandably concluded otherwise, there is no suggestion of humans achieving a righteous status, or procuring it by their own efforts. However, even many advocates of such a 'covenant of works' recognize that the nomenclature is imprecise and potentially misleading.[36] For example, as Robertson (1980: 56) observes:

> To speak of a covenant of 'works' in contrast with a covenant of 'grace' appears to suggest that grace was not operative in the covenant of works. As a matter of fact, the totality of God's relationship with man is a matter of grace. Although 'grace' may not have been operative in the sense of a merciful relationship despite sin, the creational bond between God and man indeed was gracious.[37]

Different ways in which such grace was widely acknowledged are conveniently listed by Ward (2003: 117–123) under the following five headings:

1. God was not obligated to create humanity in the first place.
2. God was not bound to enter into covenant with humanity.
3. The covenant (of works) was necessary, a reality flowing from the nature of God.[38]
4. The reward is always of God's goodness, and the language of merit, in the sense of earning/deserving the reward, is held to be inappropriate.

---

[34] Other epithets include 'covenant of nature', 'covenant of life', 'Edenic covenant', and more popular in recent discussion, 'covenant of creation'. In a recent defence of federal theology, McGowan interestingly suggests replacing the trad-itional covenant nomenclature altogether, preferring rather to speak of 'the Adamic Administration' and 'the Messianic Administration'. Tellingly, he insists that 'it is . . . perfectly possible to maintain the relationship of headship [i.e. involving imputation of sin or righteousness] without positing covenants as the basis for the relationship' (2005: 190).

[35] For a number of potential misconceptions, see Robertson 1980: 56.

[36] E.g. Kline 1986; Robertson 1980.

[37] Here Robertson accurately represents traditional Reformed usage, which reserved 'grace' for the activity of God with respect to *fallen* humanity.

[38] Obviously, this and the previous observation are mutually exclusive; but in both, God's grace is emphasized.

5. God gave sufficient grace to Adam for him to keep the covenant if Adam willed so.

Despite some of its acknowledged limitations, this 'covenant of works' is understood by its advocates as having great theological significance, giving explanation to fundamental biblical doctrines such as the fallenness of humankind, the universality of sin and guilt, and the federal headship of Christ.

However, the concept of a 'covenant of works' has attracted strong critique even from those whose 'Reformed orthodoxy' is beyond question. Not surprisingly, this has largely been on the grounds of insufficient warrant for such an idea in Scripture. Thus Hoeksema trenchantly observes, 'Nowhere do we find any proof in the Scriptures for the contention that God gave Adam the promise of eternal life if he should obey that particular command of God.'[39] Such a covenant is likewise dismissed by John Murray because of the lack of exegetical support, although, with others, he is also uneasy about the imprecise terminology. Most tellingly, even advocates such as McComiskey are forced to concede that 'the application of the term *covenant* is not wrong, provided we understand it to be used in its broadest relational sense' (1985: 219). But this of course raises the question whether or not this 'broadest relational sense' conforms to the use of 'covenant' in the rest of Scripture.

Mainstream Old Testament scholarship

While the idea has been rejected by many within mainstream Old Testament scholarship, the historical-critical approach does not necessarily exclude the idea of a covenant with Adam. This is demonstrated, most famously, by the fact that Wellhausen embraced such a concept, as attested by the source-critical label ('Q') he applied to the putative 'P' material contained in the Pentateuch. Wellhausen's description of the priestly material, 'The Book of the Four Covenants',[40] highlights his conception that each of the four main blocks of this material was associated with a particular covenant (viz. the Adamic, Noahic, Abrahamic and Mosaic).

However, while the influence of Wellhausen's classical source-critical analysis persists to the present day (albeit with significant modification and qualification), the vast majority of contemporary

---

[39] Cited by Golding 2004: 109 (from Hoeksema 1970: 108).
[40] *Vierbundesbuch*; Latin: *Liber quatuor foederum* – hence 'Q' for short.

Old Testament scholars totally dismiss any idea of an Adamic covenant,[41] primarily on the grounds that 'there is no explicit reference to a covenant with Adam or Eve. The word *covenant* does not occur at all in Genesis until the Noah story' (McKenzie 2000: 46–47).[42] Attempts to discern an implicit covenant either with Wellhausen in Genesis 1:28 – 2:4 or with federal theologians in the wider context are thus forthrightly rejected as having 'no basis in scripture' (Day 2003: 102).[43]

An exegetical critique

The only explicit textual support for the existence of an 'Adamic covenant' is Hosea 6:7.[44] While this text may initially appear to settle all dispute, its interpretation is notoriously difficult. Even so, several Reformed theologians have pointed to this text as corroborating an 'Adamic covenant' of one sort or another.

The translation, and hence the interpretation, of the key phrase *wĕhēmmâ kĕʾādām ʿābĕrû bĕrît* (lit. 'and they like Adam have transgressed a covenant' my trans. of Hos. 6:7) is hotly disputed. Although several translations and commentators interpret *kĕʾādām* in a personal sense,[45] meaning 'like Adam', most interpreters emend the key word to read, *bĕʾādām* (in/at Adam),[46] taking the proper noun in its geographical sense – referring to the first town Israel reached after crossing into the Promised Land (Josh. 3:16). Indeed, arguably, a geographical interpretation may not necessitate a textual emendation at all (cf. the similar syntax *kammidbār* [Lit. 'as in the wilderness'] in Hos. 2:3; MT v. 5). Further support for this geographical understanding is found in the reference to Gilead (Hos. 6:8) and Shechem (Hos. 6:9) in the immediate context, and especially in the deployment of the locative *šām* (there) immediately after *bĕrît* in Hosea 6:7. While, as Robertson maintains (1980: 22 n. 2), 'the emphatic "there" could

---

[41] Exceptions usually belong to the Reformed camp; e.g. McComiskey (1985); Robertson (1980).

[42] Cf. also the dismissive comments by Barr (2003: 12–13) and Day (2003: 99, 102).

[43] Other suggested 'proof-texts' for such an Adamic covenant will be considered below.

[44] Some advocates (e.g. Robertson 1980: 19–21) point also to Jer. 33:20–21, 25–26. However, these texts (and others in Jeremiah) seem to point more generally to a covenant with creation. For this reason they will be discussed below in the material dealing with covenant and creation.

[45] E.g. AV; ASV; NASB; NIV; NLT; ESV; also Vogels 1979: 33; McComiskey 1985: 214–215.

[46] E.g. RSV; JB; TEV; NRSV; NJB; TNIV; also Wolff 1974: 121–122; Mays 1969: 100; Andersen and Freedman 1980: 435–436; Day 1986: 2–6; Hubbard 1989: 128.

represent a dramatic gesture toward the place of Israel's current idolatry rather than requiring a poetic parallel to the location at which Israel had sinned in the past', such usage of the term is without parallel in Hosea (cf. Hos. 6:10; 9:15; 10:9; 13:8) and the 'Book of the Twelve' as a whole.[47] Indeed, even with no adjustments to the Masoretic Text, the Hebrew may be translated in several ways that clearly militate against using it as a proof-text for a hypothetical Adamic covenant.[48] The significance of this must not be overlooked, for without Hosea 6:7 there is no explicit textual support for a covenant established between God and Adam. Thus a major difficulty for those who wish to identify a divine–human covenant in the context of the creation narrative is the fact that there is no unambiguous warrant for such a concept elsewhere.

Undaunted by this fact, several scholars have sought to find exegetical support for such a covenant in the Genesis creation texts themselves. Thus Niehaus resorts to form criticism in an attempt to validate the existence of such a covenant.[49] His case is undermined, however, by the rather forced and tenuous nature of some of his suggested analogies between Genesis 1:1 – 2:3 and a typical second-millennium suzerain–vassal treaty pattern.

A better case is offered by Bartholomew,[50] who clearly recognizes the deficiencies in the traditional defence of a covenant within the context of creation. Nevertheless, while the allusions to Genesis 1 – 2 that he detects in subsequent covenant texts validate the claim that these covenants are 'anchored in' and 'involve the fulfilling of God's creative purposes', this does not necessarily indicate 'a covenantal understanding of creation in Genesis 1 and 2' (1995: 29). Moreover, Bartholomew's attempt to explain the absence of key covenantal elements (i.e. an oath or covenant rite) in Genesis 1 and 2

---

[47] The 'Book of the Twelve' is the traditional Jewish title for the Minor Prophets. Increasingly, OT scholarship is attempting a holistic reading of this corpus (see e.g. Rendtorff 2005: 264–314).

[48] E.g. the consonantal text could also be rendered, 'like Edom they have transgressed a covenant', although the locative (*šām*) clearly militates against this interpretation also. The Septuagint understands *kĕʾādām* in a 'generic' sense: *hōs anthrōpos* (they are *like a man* transgressing . . .). Such an interpretation ('like mankind') was strongly supported by Calvin. A radically different interpretation, initially proposed by Dahood (1963: 123–124), is adopted by Stuart (1987: 98–99, 111), who renders the verse, 'But look – they have walked on my covenant like it was dirt, see they have betrayed me!', reading *ʾādām* as a variant of *ʾādāmâ*, *ʿābar* as 'to walk on', and *šām* as 'see'.

[49] Niehaus 1995: 143–159.

[50] Bartholomew 1995: 28–30.

is unconvincing; he maintains that 'the normal assurance and legalizing element of covenant' is unnecessary prior to the fall (1995: 30), but this surely raises the question whether *covenant* is a necessary constitutive element at this stage either (cf. Stek 1994). In a similar vein Goldingay (2001: 23) comments:[51]

> The fact that Genesis does not use the word 'covenant' until after the flood is unlikely to mean nothing. I suspect it suggests that there is no need for the formalising or legalising of the relationship between God and the world when the relationship is in its unspoiled state. It is when humanity is discovered to be wrong-minded from youth (8:21) and God has acted so destructively towards the world that God comes to make the kind of irrational promise that Noah receives, and to seal it with a covenant commitment.

More recently Goldingay (2003: 181) elaborates as follows:

> By not speaking of the relationship between God and the first human beings as a covenant, Genesis has perhaps implied that there was no need for formally binding commitments before the time of human disobedience and divine punishment. Those events have imperilled the relationship on both sides. God cannot trust human beings, and human beings cannot trust God. So now God makes a formal and solemn binding commitment to humanity.

Tellingly, McComiskey (1985: 217) can offer no better explanation to this issue (the non-usage of covenant vocabulary before Gen. 6:18) than the following:

> The intent may be that we are not to understand the relationship with Adam to be a *běrît* in the same sense that the word has in its other occurrences in the Book of Genesis. In the other instances where the word is used of a divine–human relationship, it connotes the assurance of a divine promise of blessing that the human participant did not previously possess.

[51] While certainly not in agreement with all the sentiment expressed here, I consider Goldingay's premise and conclusion essentially to be correct.

Surely this concedes too much, given that the latter understanding of a divine–human covenant applies not only in the rest of Genesis, but throughout the rest of Scripture.

Conclusion

It is difficult to get past the lack of unambiguous textual warrant for the existence of a covenant between God and Adam. While the absence of formal covenant terminology cannot be said to exclude the idea (cf. the absence of the key Old Testament term in 2 Sam. 7 and 1 Chr. 17, which record the establishment of the Davidic covenant),[52] the fact that such terminology is not introduced until Genesis 6:18, where it unarguably relates to God's covenant with Noah, must carry considerable significance.[53]

Moreover, it appears that advocates of such a pre-lapsarian Adamic covenant must define 'covenant' in a way broad enough to encompass the situation that prevailed in Eden (e.g. a divine–human bond or relationship sovereignly administered), hence ignoring or excluding aspects that appear to be absolutely intrinsic to the making of a covenant both elsewhere in the Old Testament and the ancient Near East generally (i.e. a commitment solemnly sealed with an oath).

While there is little evidence of such a solemn commitment prior to the fall, Robertson and others may initially seem to have a firmer basis for the alleged covenant established between God and Adam after the fall. Here, at least, is a substantive divine promise (Gen. 3:15) in some sense foundational for the covenants that follow. However, the fact that this promise was expressly made to the serpent rather than directly to the human pair does raise questions over calling it a 'covenant with Adam'.

It seems best to conclude, therefore, that while Adam and Eve were certainly involved in a divine–human relationship both before and after the fall, neither the pre-lapsarian relationship nor post-lapsarian relationship was understood in terms of a 'covenant'. This explains not only the lack of scriptural warrant for any such Adamic covenant, but also the insurmountable fact that the biblical narrator clearly chose not to employ the word 'covenant' prior to Genesis 6:18.

[52] As Eichrodt's oft-quoted statement underlines, 'The crucial point is not – as an all too naïve criticism sometimes seems to think – the occurrence or absence of the Hebrew word $b^e r\bar{\imath}t$' (1961: 17–18).

[53] This is acknowledged even by Robertson (1980: 18), who concedes that 'The biblical exegete should be concerned to determine the reason for this omission.' However, he himself does not appear to furnish his readers with any such explanation.

Chapter Three

God's universal covenant with Noah

Introduction of the covenant idea

Whereas historical-critical reconstructions generally dismiss the idea of a divine–human covenant as a relatively late innovation that has been retrojected unto Israel's earlier traditions,[1] the canonical text unambiguously suggests that the concept extended back into the primeval era. It is first explicitly introduced in Genesis 6:18, where it apparently anticipates the solemn oath God made to Noah (as the selected representative of all creation) in the immediate aftermath of the flood (Gen. 9:1–17; cf. Isa. 54:9).[2]

Although some have distinguished between the covenant mentioned in Genesis 6:18 and the post-diluvian covenant established between God and all living creatures (Gen. 9), a close reading confirms that the mention of 'covenant' at Genesis 6:18 is proleptical. God's initial speech to Noah (Gen. 6:13–21) lacks even the most basic covenantal element (i.e. a promissory oath). Moreover, while some have pointed to implicit covenantal associations in the fulcrum of the flood narrative, where God is said to have 'remembered Noah' (Gen. 8:1), the fact that 'covenant' is not explicitly mentioned there is probably significant; God remembered *Noah*, rather than his *covenant*. If the latter had already been established by this stage, analogous texts suggest that God would have remembered the covenant in question rather than the person(s) with whom it was associated (cf. Exod. 2:24; 6:5; Pss. 105:42; 106:45). Therefore, the mention of 'covenant' at this point simply anticipates the covenant ratified in Genesis 9 and discloses God's purpose in the divine selection and preservation of Noah and his family.

Of all the divine–human covenants explicitly mentioned in Scripture, this first such covenant has attracted much less scholarly

---

[1] For the covenant idea in general as a retrojection, see McKenzie 2000: 11–39; Nicholson 1986: 3–117. For the Noahic covenant in particular, see Barr 2003: 11 and Dell 2003: 111–112.

[2] For more on this, see below.

interest, sometimes being ignored entirely or receiving only passing mention due to its more tenuous links with a salvation history whose primary focus is God's dealings with Israel.[3] As Dell (2003: 111–112) observes, in mainstream scholarship this scholarly neglect is due also to the fact that the Noahic covenant has been viewed as a post-exilic attempt to bring covenant into closer harmony with creation ideas, which were likewise deemed late and understood as having been subordinated to the doctrine of redemption. However, as she goes on to highlight (2003: 112), in more recent scholarship 'creation ideas are being seen as a more shaping influence upon the thought and writings of the Old Testament'.[4] This is reflected in texts that not only bring covenant and creation into association, but also make such a covenant incorporating creation pivotal for eschatological hope.[5] Thus understood, the Noahic covenant is not marginal, but rather foundational for salvation history and a holistic biblical theology of covenant.

Covenant and (re-)creation

It is important to understand the Noahic covenant against its immediate literary and theological setting; namely, the catastrophic judgment of the flood. The latter, in turn, must be read against the backdrop of creation and the fall, for as Clines has underlined, 'the Flood is represented not just as a punishment for the sin of the generation of the Flood, but as a reversal of creation'.[6] Whereas Genesis 1 depicts creation in terms of separation and distinction, in Genesis 6 – 7 such distinctions are eradicated. In Genesis 1:6–8 God establishes a firmament to keep the heavenly waters at bay, but the opening of the 'windows of heaven' in Genesis 7:11 (esv) tears this protective canopy apart. Likewise, the distinction between subterranean waters and the earth established in Genesis 1:9 is obliterated by the 'fountains of the deep' bursting out in Genesis 7:11. In the flood, the creative process (bringing order out of a watery chaos) is thus reversed. Therefore, as Clines (1997: 81) aptly concludes, 'The flood [*sic*] is only the final stage in a process of cosmic disintegration that began in Eden.'

It logically follows from this that the climax of the flood narrative is best understood in terms of a 'recreation' – a restoration of the

---

[3] This is sometimes true even within conservative circles; e.g. McComiskey, Walton.

[4] This is due largely to the impact of literary and canonical criticism, as well as the renewed interest in Israelite wisdom (with its emphasis on creation theology).

[5] Such is the main thrust of Dell's essay, although she sees the trajectory taking shape over at least three developmental stages (2003: 130).

[6] Clines 1997: 80.

divine order and God's visible kingship that had been established at creation. As a comparison with the Genesis creation narratives again illustrates,[7] such is indeed the case: The earth is made inhabitable by the separation of the land from the water (Gen. 8:1–3; cf. Gen. 1:9–10). Living creatures are brought out to repopulate the earth (Gen. 8:17–19; cf. Gen. 1:20–22, 24–25). Days and seasons are re-established (Gen. 8:22; cf. Gen. 1:14–18). Humans are blessed by God (Gen. 9:1; cf. Gen. 1:28a), commanded to 'Be fruitful and multiply, and fill the earth' (Gen. 9:1b, 7; cf. Gen. 1:28b), and given dominion over the animal kingdom (Gen. 9:2; cf. Gen. 1:28c). God provides humanity – made in his image (Gen. 9:6; cf. Gen. 1:26–27) – with food (Gen. 9:3; cf. Gen. 1:29–30).

For all this parallelism, however, there is one very significant difference between the recreated world of the post-flood era and the original creation. As noted in Genesis 8:22, the world had not been restored to its pristine, pre-fall condition. Rather, it was still marred by human sinfulness, significantly described in similar terms that had previously (Gen. 6:5) provided the rationale for the deluge; what had earlier explained the necessity of the flood now highlights the necessity of the covenant that God was about to establish.[8] Thus understood, this post-diluvian covenant (Gen. 8:20 – 9:17) reaffirms God's original creational intent that the flood had placed in abeyance and that humanity's inherent sinfulness would otherwise continue to place in jeopardy.

Ratification of the universal covenant

While the formal declaration of the covenant oath (for the latter, cf. Isa. 54:9) is admittedly restricted to Genesis 9:8–17, the actual ratification of the Noahic covenant apparently begins with the offering of sacrifices in the previous chapter (Gen. 8:20).[9] Some

---

[7] The following observations are noted by several scholars; for a more detailed discussion, see Smith 1977: 310–311.

[8] As Wenham (1987: 206) comments, 'were it not for the changed logic of God, in that he now cites man's depravity as a ground for his mercy rather than for his judgment, the descendants of Noah would be heading for extinction in another deluge'.

[9] Barr (2003: 17–22) highlights a number of differences in the speeches here (Gen. 8:21–22; 9:1–7, 8–17), which admittedly call for explanation (e.g. the absence of 'covenant' in the first two speeches, and its preponderance in the third). However, such anomalies may be explained in terms of the different stages involved in the inauguration of this covenant, with sacrifice, promises and obligations preceding the formal annunciation of the solemn oath and its sign. This would explain the author's reluctance to insert a reference to 'covenant' in Gen. 9:1–7, regardless of how 'easy' such an interpolation would have been.

support for this may be found in the discernible chiastic pattern framing this section,[10] although the identification of such literary devices is admittedly a somewhat subjective enterprise that may sometimes reflect more the ingenuity of the modern commentator than that of the ancient author. In any case, the immediate context connects this sacrificial ritual with God's deliberation to preserve the created order without future disruption by flood (Gen. 8:20–22); hence these sacrifices serve to explain the basis of the covenant promises that follow.[11] Moreover, such a sacrificial ritual was apparently anticipated by God himself (cf. Gen. 7:2–3). Thus Noah's action here is more than a spontaneous expression of thanksgiving: it is apparently something that God himself had intended, if not in fact commanded.[12] Furthermore, the Noahic covenant is not alone in mentioning sacrificial ritual in the context of covenant ratification (cf. Gen. 15:9ff.; Exod. 24:5–6), which may indicate that such sacrificial ritual was a common precursor to a covenantal oath. The sacrifices of Genesis 8 are thus best understood as an intrinsic element in the establishment of the Noahic covenant. In any case, it is difficult to deny that it was these sacrifices that prompted the subsequent divine promise (Gen. 8:21–22) – a divine self-deliberation that forms the basis of the oath reflected in Genesis 9:9–11: never again will God's plans be interrupted by a suspension of the natural order. Hence humanity's creational mandate (cf. Gen. 1:26–30) is here renewed (Gen. 9:1–7) and a solemn guarantee of the preservation of life on earth, without further divine interruption, is given (Gen. 9:8–17).

---

[10] Waltke (2001:127) suggests the following:

   A God's resolve never again to destroy the earth or humanity 8:20–22
     B Command to be fruitful 9:1
       C Legislation with regard to blood 9:2–6
     B[1] Command to be fruitful 9:7
   A[1] God's covenant and sign never again to destroy all flesh 9:8–17

[11] As Wenham (2003: 29) insightfully observes, 'The text ascribes God's change of heart to Noah's sacrifice . . . Once again (cf. 4:3–6) Genesis makes a point about sacrifice through a narrative: here it illustrates how a righteous man's sacrifice can atone for the sins of others, in this case the sins of the whole human race.' Goldingay (2003: 177) objects to the 'odd logic' of the MT's verse division here, but his conjectural break in the syntax (taking Gen. 8:21a with Gen. 8:20 and beginning a new clause with 'The Lord said . . .') results in an even more striking anomaly, as Goldingay acknowledges. In any case, he seems to recognize that Noah's sacrifice played some role in God's forbearance.

[12] As Wenham (1987: 189) observes, 'The earlier insistence that seven pairs of clean animals be taken on the ark shows that the narrative presupposes the necessity of sacrifice.'

Human obligations of the universal covenant

The juxtaposition of the latter two passages (i.e. Gen. 9:1–7 and Gen. 9:8–17) highlights the fact that the Noahic covenant incorporates bilateral obligations. Admittedly, this covenant is unconditional in the sense that God's promises are not contingent upon human response or behaviour.[13] Even so, the introduction of divine commands indicates that the obligations enshrined in this covenant were not unilateral.

The opening pericope in Genesis 9 clearly focuses on the human obligations, as is underlined by the bracketing of these verses with divine imperatives (Gen. 9:1, 7), which echo the creation mandate in Genesis 1 – indicating that 'God's purpose for the population of the earth remained the same' (Hartley 2000: 104). Thus the primary obligation imposed on humanity was that of fulfilling the role appointed by God in the beginning (Gen. 1:28).

Once again, however, attention is drawn to the fact that the post-flood circumstances are subject to significant change in human relations (Gen. 9:2–3). While some see an allusion to the enmity between animals and humans that existed since the fall (cf. Gen. 3:15), the wording of Genesis 9:2 seems to indicate a new development here; a further breakdown in human relations with the animal kingdom. A degree of enmity will now exist between humans and the entire, non-domesticated animal world.[14] By implication, humanity's non-vegetarian diet – now divinely sanctioned (cf. Gen. 1:29) – would undoubtedly be a contributing factor.[15] The animals had now become 'fair game'.

---

[13] As Anderson (1994: 157) concludes, 'Although legal obligations are given in the Noachic covenant, the permanence of the covenant is based on the unconditional commitment of God to the human and nonhuman creation, for better or for worse . . . hope for the future does not rest on human performance or improvement . . . Rather, hope is based on God's absolute commitment to the creation.'

[14] Greek manuscripts add 'and over all domesticated animals', but, significantly, this class is not represented in the MT. Barr (2003: 16 n. 6) insists that the emphatic 'all' of Gen. 9:2 is enigmatic (such 'fear and dread' of humans is not shared by some creatures such as lions, tigers, crocodiles, cobras and sharks). However, he seems to overlook the fact that the text itself allows exceptions to this general situation (cf. Gen. 9:5). Moreover, even these more aggressive creatures usually prefer to keep their distance from humanity, generally attacking only when humans invade their domains. See also Goldingay 2003: 180.

[15] While together these two texts (Gen. 1:29; 9:3) imply that a vegetarian diet had been the divine ideal, the concept of animal sacrifice reflected in Abel's offering (cf. Gen. 4:4) may suggest that domesticated animals (as opposed to game) were implicitly part of the human diet from the beginning.

With these new circumstances in view, further responsibilities are imposed (Gen. 9:4–6). Animal life in general, and human life in particular, must be treated with the dignity it deserves. As a token of such respect, the consumption of blood (representative of the animal's life-force; cf. Lev. 17:11) is strictly prohibited. Moreover, while animal slaughter is permissible, the killing of humans (whether by other people or by animals) is a capital offence (Gen. 9:5).[16] Significantly, the reason given for such severe punishment is the fact that humans, even in the post-fall, post-flood world, retain their unique status as divine image-bearers (Gen. 9:6). Thus, in this new, postdiluvian era, Noah and his sons are commanded to carry out humanity's creation mandate, while at the same time treating animal life generally and human life especially with due respect.

Divine obligations and sign of the universal covenant

The formal declaration of the divine covenant in Genesis 9:8–17 is made up of two distinct parts: the first (Gen. 9:8–11) articulates the divine oath, whereas the second (Gen. 9:12–17) announces the covenant sign. As Turner (1993) plausibly suggests, the latter element, God's 'bow in the clouds' (Gen. 9:12–17), probably signified the domelike barrier (*rāqîaʿ*, 'firmament') restraining the 'waters above' (Gen. 1:6–8).[17] While this visible symbol in the sky would undoubtedly reassure humankind, its express intent was to remind God himself to keep his covenantal promise. Thus, unlike subsequent examples (i.e. 'circumcision' and 'sabbath'), this first covenant sign chiefly served to remind God of his covenant obligation.

In keeping with the divine deliberation of Genesis 8:21–22, the covenant is universal in scope – encompassing Noah, his sons, their descendants (Gen. 9:9) and 'every living creature' (Gen. 9:10, 12, 15–17) – and 'everlasting' in endurance (Gen. 9:16). In the present context the latter appears to signify 'as long as the earth endures' (Gen. 8:22 TNIV). In any case, the covenant emphatically guarantees

---

[16] Obviously, this legislation serves to curb the sort of violence that had precipitated the flood (cf. Gen. 6:11–13).

[17] Others have understood it as the hanging up of God's bow (same Hebrew word), indicating an end to divine hostility. Such an idea (that the 'bow in the clouds' somehow symbolizes a covenant of peace) receives some support from Isa. 54:9–10 and Hos. 2:18; see further, Batto 1987.

that a cataclysmic flood will 'never again' be repeated (Gen. 9:11–12, 15; cf. Gen. 8:21). As Westermann comments:

> Underlying the history of nature and the history of mankind is an unconditional divine Yes, a divine Yes to all life, that cannot be shattered by any catastrophe in the course of this history . . . [or] by the mistakes, corruption or rebellion of man. God's promise remains rock certain as long as the earth exists.[18]

God's universal covenant elsewhere in the Old Testament

As mentioned above, Dell (2003: 114–122) has recently highlighted the following prophetic texts that juxtapose covenant and creation ideas.

Hosea 2:18

Here Hosea anticipates a divine covenant with non-human creatures that will lead to peace, and is seemingly a reversal of the more chaotic picture portrayed in Hosea 4:3, thus echoing aspects of the covenant God established with Noah. Significantly, it implies that the covenant with Israel ('for them') would have wider ramifications than mere national concerns.

Isaiah 24:3–5; 33:8–9; 11:6–9

The first of these texts highlights the negative effects on the earth/world of breaking the everlasting covenant by ignoring laws and statutes. The covenant is not identified specifically, but the universal emphasis of the passage, the juxtaposition of chaos and lawlessness, and the description of the covenant as 'everlasting' may well suggest that it is the Noahic covenant that is primarily on view.

The connection between the Noahic covenant and the second of these Isaianic texts (Isa. 33:8–9) Dell (2003) mentions seems much

---

[18] This is Wenham's somewhat racy translation of the original German edition. The official ET (Westermann 1984: 473) by Scullion reads as follows: 'The unconditional approval that God gives to his creation is the basis of the history of nature and of humanity. It is the basis of all life which can be shaken neither by natural catastrophes of any sort nor . . . by the transgressions, corruption or revolt of human beings. God's assurance remains firm "as long as the earth lasts".'

more tenuous, and an allusion to the Mosaic covenant is just as likely.[19]

The third Isaianic text (Isa. 11:6–9) depicts the overturning of the natural enmity that exists between animals and that which exists between animals and men by the future Davidic king, suggesting a reversal of fallen creation to its pre-fallen state, and thus, a situation to which the Noahic covenant ultimately points.[20]

Jeremiah 5:22–25; 14:20–22; 33:20–26

While covenant is not explicitly mentioned in Jeremiah 5:22–25, there are clear echoes of God's seasonal guarantees and the boundaries he placed on the watery chaos in the context of the covenant with Noah (cf. Gen. 8:22; 9:11–15), which the present iniquity of the people is now placing in jeopardy.

A similar allusion to the Noahic covenant is probably reflected in Jeremiah 14:20–22, where it may be referred to even more explicitly (Jer. 14:21b).

In Jeremiah 33:20–26 God's 'covenant with day and night' is explicitly recalled.[21] This is most likely a reference to the Noahic covenant, as is the further elaboration in Jeremiah 33:25. Clearly, the covenant in question is considered permanent and unbreakable, and the assurance given here resonates with the strong affirmative language used in the context of the Noahic covenant (cf. Gen. 8:21–22).[22]

Ezekiel 34:25–30; 37:26; Isaiah 54:9–10

These three texts all mention a future 'covenant of peace' that echoes features of the Noahic covenant. In Ezekiel 34:25–30 this anticipated covenant (made by Yahweh with his rescued people) is depicted in terms of the rejuvenation of nature and the banishment of wild beasts.

Such a covenant of peace between Yahweh and the restored people of God is again heralded in Ezekiel 37:26; here it is described also as 'an everlasting covenant' and involves the people's multiplication, possibly echoing the creation mandate to 'Be fruitful and multiply' reiterated in the context of the Noahic covenant. While there is no

---

[19] Indeed, the negative effects of covenant disloyalty on the land are even more pronounced in the Mosaic covenant.

[20] See below.

[21] Dell inexplicably cites only Jer. 33:20–22. Presumably, this is an oversight on her part.

[22] For the suggestion that the covenant in view here refers to an antediluvian covenant with creation, see below.

explicit mention of nature here, the concept of God's sanctuary in their midst reminds the alert reader of the idyllic portrayal of harmony portrayed in Eden.

Isaiah 54:9–10 contains the most explicit reference to the Noahic covenant. Again, the context is Israel's hope of future restoration. This idyllic future is described in terms of a covenant of peace that is absolutely secure, like the solemn oath God made with respect to another flood. The simile drawn here between the Noahic covenant and God's future covenant of peace with Israel implicitly suggests that the turning point proclaimed here 'had a significance which far transcended Israel herself, and affected the whole world'.[23]

Rather than being an innovation of the prophets, this anticipated 'covenant of peace' may well be the projection of an older tradition into the future,[24] as the various echoes of the Noahic covenant might well suggest.

In addition to these prophetic texts, Dell discusses a number of psalmic/wisdom passages that may point to the antiquity of Israel's creation tradition.[25] Of the texts she mentions, however, few seem to be directly relevant to the Noahic covenant.[26] The link between the ideal king and the creative order in Psalm 72 echoes the similar concepts noted in some of the prophetic texts discussed above. The Noahic covenant is apparently alluded to in Psalm 104:9, where reference is made to God establishing boundaries to stop the waters from again covering the earth, and a similar allusion is perhaps intended in Psalm 148:6.

Theological significance of the universal covenant

The theological significance of the Noahic covenant is at least twofold. First of all, it is the basis for our present confidence in God as Sustainer. It is the Noahic covenant that gives us the assurance that God will sustain the creation order, despite the chaos that continually threatens to engulf it. As Rendtorff (1993: 108–109) has well observed

[23] Westermann (1969: 275) cited by Dell 2003: 121 n. 10.

[24] As suggested by Batto 1987, although he traces the peace motif back to a primeval myth in which the gods bound themselves under oath to maintain peace and harmony with creation and humankind in the aftermath of their abortive attempt to eradicate the latter after they had revolted against them.

[25] See Dell 2003: 122–124.

[26] While Job 5:23 mentions a covenant involving human and non-human creation, this covenant (as Dell concedes) is purely metaphorical for human harmony with the natural environment.

(in answer to the question 'How can we be sure that there will be no further "uncreation" of the earth?'):

> The answer of the primeval history is unequivocal: nothing at all suggests that this will not repeat itself. On the contrary, the declaration that "the imagination of man's heart is evil from his youth" is explicitly repeated (8:21; cf. 6:5) . . . The reason for the danger therefore still exists; the earth is no longer "very good" and can never again become so. And yet God lets it go on existing. He pledges himself to do so . . . So according to the idea behind the Bible's primeval history, the reason that human beings can trust the orders of creation is not to be discovered simply in creation itself. On the contrary, creation's existence is profoundly endangered by all the things that constantly happen in it, which are anything but good. The fact that it still goes on existing in spite of this is due to God's self-imposed obligation, his covenant with Noah. And that is the reason why human beings can have confidence in creation . . .

Secondly, given that the Noahic covenant provides the biblical-theological framework within which all subsequent divine–human covenants operate, its universal scope is undoubtedly significant. As suggested by the allusions to Genesis 1 noted above, the universal scope of this covenant implies that the blessing for which humanity had been created and the creation had now been preserved will ultimately encompass not just one people or nation, but rather the whole earth. Accordingly, while the patriarchal narratives reflect an obvious narrowing in focus, the universal emphasis of Genesis 1–11 is not lost entirely in the subsequent chapters of Genesis and beyond. Thus as Anderson (1999: 95–96) observes:

> An eschatology, or hope for future consummation, is incipient in the flood story. For the Creator moves human history from potential chaos toward a new age in which the relations between human beings, nonhuman creatures, and their environment will be reordered. The rainbow is a sign of the purpose of God that overarches history from creation to new creation . . . In Christian perspective, the Noahic covenant belongs to a history of God's covenants that leads up to the 'everlasting covenant' made through the blood (sacrifice) of Jesus Christ (Heb. 13:20). Christ's covenant of peace does not supersede the

Noachic covenant: it is built upon it, as the temple atop the graduated levels of a ziggurat rests on a broad foundation.

Dell (2003: 131) concludes in a similar vein:

God's final will is for peace and harmony in an ideal creation. The Noachic covenant is the pivot around which this promise of a bright future revolves . . . God has made a promise, an agreement, a covenant with all people and animals and with the earth, that he will never allow creative chaos to ensue and destroy the creation that is God-given. He will maintain order over chaos, and the sign he will forever maintain his covenant with the earth is the rainbow.

A creation covenant?

While the above analysis has acknowledged clear links between the Noahic covenant and creation, several scholars go further, suggesting that the Noahic covenant is in fact a renewal of an already-existing covenant – one that God had previously made in the context of creation itself. As already noted, traditionally federalist theologians have posited a pre-fall 'covenant of works' and a post-fall 'covenant of grace' (the latter commencing with Adam and attested to by the *protevangelium* of Gen. 3:15), but several recent advocates of an antediluvian 'covenant' prefer to speak in terms of an all-embracing covenant established between God and his creation. Such a covenant was not established between God and humanity at some point subsequent to creation; rather, this covenant of/with creation was established in the very act of creation itself.

Exegetical arguments for a creation covenant

An exegetical case for such a 'covenant with creation', allegedly implicit in Genesis 1 – 2, has been mounted, among others,[27] by Dumbrell (1984: 11–43), for whom this covenant was established with creation generally rather than with humanity in particular.[28]

---

[27] Cf. M. G. Kline's self-published *Kingdom Prologue* (1986), in which an exegetical case similar to Dumbrell's is mounted for a covenant with creation.

[28] Beckwith (1987: 99 n. 23) suggests that Dumbrell is following Robertson (1980) with respect to this alleged covenant with creation. While admittedly there are similarities, for Dumbrell (1984: 32) this hypothetical covenant was made with creation generally: 'There could . . . be no question of two parties involved in any basic

Dumbrell's argument leans heavily on his exegesis of Genesis 6:18, from which he infers that the covenant there announced is simply the confirmation of the covenant God had previously 'brought into existence by the act of creation itself' (1984: 43). This conclusion is based primarily on two observations: how the Noahic covenant is introduced and how its ratification is described.

Genesis 6:18 (cf. Gen. 9:8–17) introduces the Noahic covenant by using a possessive pronoun, '*my* covenant' (*bĕrîtî*). For Dumbrell, 'the most natural interpretation . . . is that an existing arrangement to be preserved is referred to, to which no more specific appeal is required than the denomination of it as "my covenant" ' (1984: 24).

The other major factor in Dumbrell's argument is the precise connotation of the other Hebrew verbs used in association with a 'covenant', especially the verb *hēqîm* (establish). As in Genesis 17 (in which the covenant concept reappears in the Abraham narrative after its initial introduction in Gen. 15:18), the verbs *nātan* (give) and *hēqîm* are used with reference to the Noahic covenant rather than the more idiomatic *kārat* (cut) – the verb most commonly associated with the initiation of a divine–human covenant in the Old Testament (cf. the Abramic covenant, Gen. 15:18; the Sinaitic covenant, Exod. 24:8; the Davidic covenant, Ps. 89:3; the new covenant, Jer. 31:31). Dumbrell maintains that the ratification of secular covenants reflected in the Old Testament is likewise described by this same verb and that none of the analogous verbs used in association with a *bĕrît* is strictly synonymous with *kārat*. Such verbs, he avers, are not deployed with reference to a covenant's actual initiation (i.e. the point of entry), but are consistently used in relation to covenants that have been established formerly.[29] From this Dumbrell concludes that it is 'more likely that in contexts where *hēqîm bĕrît* stands (Gen. 6:18; 9:9, 11, 17; 17:7, 19, 21; Ex 6:4; Lev 26:9; Deut 8:18; 2 Kings 23:3) the institution of a covenant is not being referred to but rather its perpetuation' (1984: 26). If, as Dumbrell insists, the verb *hēqîm* is used exclusively for perpetuating a pre-existing relationship, then one must inevitably concede that Genesis 6:18 refers to an already-existing covenant.

In addition to the above arguments, Dumbrell (1984: 33–39; 1989: 137–156) also finds implicit evidence for a creation covenant (i.e. a

---

arrangement which is entered into by God *by virtue of creation itself*' (emphasis mine), whereas for Robertson (1980: 67) it was established with humanity in particular: 'By the very act of creating *man* in his own image, God established a unique relationship between himself and creation' (emphasis mine).

[29] Cf. Dumbrell 1984: 25–26; see too McConville 1997: 748–749.

commitment to achieve the purpose of creation) in the opening creation narrative itself (i.e. Gen. 1:1 – 2:4a). Thus the covenantal relationship is implicit in humanity's unique function as divine image; sharing in divine rest is the covenant's goal, and it is conditioned on submitting to Yahweh's authority (i.e. living under Yahweh's kingship).

Other advocates of a creation covenant (e.g. Robertson 1980: 19–21) have looked for scriptural support to Jeremiah 33:20–26.[30] In these verses God expressly mentions his 'covenant with the day and with the night' (Jer. 33:20 my trans.) and seems to link this with 'the fixed patterns of heaven and earth' (Jer. 33:25 my trans.) that he has established. Thus Robertson asks (1980: 19), 'When did God establish a "covenant" with "day and night"?' and notes that there are really only two possibilities: 'These phrases apparently refer either to God's ordinances of creation or to the ordinances of the covenant with Noah. In both instances, the regularity of day and night play a prominent role.'

However, while conceding that Jeremiah could be alluding to Genesis 8:22, Robertson concludes in favour of an allusion to Genesis 1:14, mainly on the basis of a second Jeremianic text (Jer. 31:35–36), where a similar analogy is employed. Robertson acknowledges that this second text does not actually use the term 'covenant', but notes that the terminology it does employ – 'statute' or 'fixed order' (Heb. $h\bar{o}q$) – is used in parallel expressions elsewhere (e.g. 1 Kgs 11:11; 2 Kgs 17:15; Pss. 50:16; 105:10). Robertson further notes that the details given in Jeremiah 31:35 correspond with those of the creation narrative but not with the Noahic covenant:

> Quite interestingly, the reference to the sun and moon specifically as light-bearers for day and night is found in the creation narrative but not in the narrative describing God's covenant with Noah. Furthermore, the narrative of the creation activity of the third day refers to the stars as well as to the moon (Gen. 1:16), as does Jeremiah 31:35. The record of God's covenant with Noah makes no mention of the stars.

For these reasons Robertson concludes that both Jeremiah 31:34–35 and Jeremiah 33:20–26 allude to God's creation ordinances, and thus a covenant made in the context of creation, rather than to the covenant with Noah in the aftermath of the flood.

[30] Dumbrell also draws on this text for support in at least one of his publications (2002a: 26).

Exegetical arguments critiqued

Prior to Genesis 6:18 there is not even a hint of any covenant being established – at least between God and humans.[31] Explicit covenant terminology is conspicuously absent in the creation narrative. As noted previously, the absence of such covenant language does not preclude the possibility that God established a covenant in the context of creation (cf. the absence of explicit covenantal terminology in 2 Sam. 7). However, unlike the Davidic covenant – for which there is ample explicit support elsewhere (e.g. 2 Sam. 23:5; Pss. 89:3, 28, 34; 132:12) – the corroborative evidence for an antediluvian covenant between God and creation is somewhat tenuous. Moreover, while the situation for Adam and Eve prior to the fall may have been similar to the situation experienced under the terms of subsequent divine–human covenants, it was not identical. As Dell (2003: 129) suggests, Dumbrell 'understresses the part played by human sin in the inauguration of this [creation] covenant after the flood'. As noted previously, the fact that the biblical narrator chose not to employ explicit covenant terminology until after the fall and in the context of a major threat to the fulfilment of God's purpose must surely be significant.

As well as the glaring absence of corroborative evidence for his postulated creation covenant, Dumbrell's exegesis of Genesis 6:18 may itself be challenged. Exodus 19:5 analogously heralds the formal inauguration of the Sinaitic covenant (cf. Exod. 24:8), referring to the latter (as yet, unestablished) covenant as 'my covenant'. In keeping with his earlier suggestion, Dumbrell (1984: 80–81) again suggests that an element of continuity is reflected here by the pronominal suffix: 'The phrase "my covenant" contains the same unilateral implications as are suggested by references such as Gen. 6:18; 9:9ff, hinting thus that the Sinai revelation may in fact be further specification only of an already existing relationship.' This, however, is clearly a circular argument; Dumbrell is uncritically assuming that the Noahic covenant *must* be understood as an expansion of his postulated 'covenant with creation'. Without the latter premise, Dumbrell's conclusion with respect to the Sinaitic covenant is not immediately obvious. Indeed, it is seriously undermined by the fact that the Sinai covenant is presented as a new development in the Pentateuchal narrative. Furthermore, given the use of the verb *kārat* (cut) in Exodus

---

[31] However, Hugenberger (1994: 216–279) presents a compelling case for identifying a marriage covenant in Gen. 2:23–24.

24:8 (according to Dumbrell, a verb consistently deployed only in the context of the initiation of a new covenant), this is something that even Dumbrell himself must surely concede.

In any case, a careful reading of the relevant texts amply demonstrates the fallacy of Dumbrell's underlying premise. Weinfeld offers a more comprehensive list of such texts and therefore provides a better basis on which to evaluate Dumbrell's assertion.[32] In several of the texts cited by Weinfeld the key verbs do indeed refer back to established covenants rather than to the initiation of new covenants (e.g. 2 Sam. 23:5). Nevertheless, such is not uniformly so, and is clearly difficult to maintain for several texts (e.g. Num. 25:12; Deut. 29:12 [MT 11]; Ezek. 16:8; 17:13; 2 Chr. 15:12), arguably including the relevant covenantal texts in Genesis also (i.e. Gen. 6:18; 9:9, 11; 17:2, 7, 19). Moreover, while the causative verb *hēqîm* may be understood as 'to confirm' or 'to maintain' (e.g. Lev. 26:9; Deut. 8:18), it has a wide range of nuances in the Old Testament (see Williamson 2000a: 197–198). Thus a close examination of the relevant texts demonstrates that Dumbrell's conclusion is seriously flawed. For example, as Beckwith (1987: 99 n. 23) observes, the deployment of *hēqîm* in Exodus 6:4 illustrates that this verb does not necessarily suggest the confirmation or perpetuation of a previously existing covenant. Similarly, in Jeremiah 34:18 a strong case can be made in support of a covenant being instituted and not just renewed (cf. Jer. 34:10). Clearly, the context alone must determine the meaning attached to *hēqîm* in any given text, hence Dumbrell is mistaken simply to infer from the use of this verb that an already existing covenant is being maintained.[33] Rather, as Weinfeld (1977: 260) acknowledges, several verbs may be used to reflect the institution or ratification of a *bĕrît*, one of which is *hēqîm*. This being so, there is no compelling argument for interpreting Genesis 6:18 as alluding to the reiteration of a previously existing covenant. Rather, as a straightforward reading suggests, here the concept of a divine–human covenant is being introduced for the first time.

[32] Weinfeld 1977: 260.

[33] Dumbrell himself (1984: 25 n. 17) notes the exception of Ezek. 16:8 ('I spread the edge of my cloak over you, and covered your nakedness: I pledged myself to you and entered [*bô'*] into a covenant with you, says the Lord GOD, and you became mine' NRSV), suggesting that the legal formula might have been considered inappropriate in this context of a 'marriage' between Yahweh and Israel. However, it must be acknowledged that the prophets – including Ezekiel – reflect no such reluctance to use legal metaphor in relation to God's relationship with his people elsewhere. Moreover, the metaphor is surely no less 'inappropriate' in the absence of the exact legal formula.

But how then is its initial description as 'my covenant' to be explained? Well, rather than indicating that this is an already existing covenant, the initial description of the Noahic covenant (like the subsequent Mosaic covenant; Exod. 19:5) as 'my covenant' simply underlines its *unilateral* character. God describes the covenant as 'my covenant' because he initiated it and he alone determined its constituent elements. Even Dumbrell recognizes such a connotation for the pronominal suffix in both texts (i.e. Gen. 6:18; Exod. 19:5), and it is quite unnecessary to extrapolate further. Thus the use of *bĕrîtî* (my covenant) in Genesis 6 cannot be said to indicate, still less prove, that the covenant spoken of in this chapter is simply a reiteration or an expansion of a covenant already recounted (implicitly) in the opening chapters of Genesis. Rather, the possessive pronoun simply emphasizes the divine prerogative in every aspect of the covenant in view. Thus understood, Genesis 6:18 heralds the formal inauguration of the Noahic covenant that is subsequently set out in Genesis 8:20 – 9:17.

While some scholars have pointed to Jeremiah 33:20–26 for further support,[34] the references here to a covenant with inanimate created things seem to allude more to dimensions of the Noahic covenant reflected in Genesis 8:22 – 9:13 (esp. Gen. 8:22) than to an implicit 'covenant with creation' in Genesis 1 – 3. Admittedly, the somewhat similar analogy drawn in Jeremiah 31:35–37 may indeed allude to the fixed order established at creation, although this appears to build an argument from silence.[35] In any case, nothing is explicitly said in this particular context (Jer. 31:35–37) of a divine covenant with creation, and caution needs to be exercised before adjudging terminology to be 'synonymous' on the basis of Hebrew parallelism. Neither here nor elsewhere is it suggested that the cycle of day and night and the other cosmic ordinances established at creation were ratified by divine covenant *prior to that established with Noah.*

---

[34] Significantly, McComiskey (1985: 216) is reluctant to use Jer. 33 to support the extension of the covenant concept to the pre-Noahic period. It is unclear to me why Dumbrell has generally ignored (although cf. 2002a: 26) its possible significance for his postulated covenant with creation, as this would appear to be a rather obvious 'proof-text' for bolstering his case. Possibly the use of the verb (*śîm*, 'to set/place') on this occasion serves to explain Dumbrell's earlier caution (I am indebted to Michael Stead for this suggestion).

[35] This objection cuts both ways. However, given that the creation narrative is undoubtedly the more comprehensive account, the absence of some creation terminology in Gen. 8:22 – 9:17 is to be expected.

Nevertheless, while the conclusion that Genesis 1 – 3 must portray an antediluvian covenantal relationship is a non sequitur, Dumbrell and others are obviously correct to recognize several clear echoes of the creation narrative in the Noahic covenant. But these echoes suggest merely that God intended, through Noah, to fulfil his original creative intent; they do not necessarily presuppose the existence of a covenant between God and inanimate creation or indicate that the material in Genesis 1 – 3 must be understood covenantally. Rather, 'Creation can only be called a *běrît* from the point of view of its restoration after the flood' (Rendtorff 1993: 134).

The significance of the debate

While the preceding discussion may seem somewhat pedantic, it does have a direct bearing on our understanding of covenant. For Reformed theologians, apparently, any relationship involving God must be covenantal in nature – whether his relationship with creation in general or his relation with human beings in particular. Covenant is seen as framing or establishing any such relationship.

This, however, is not in fact what the biblical text suggests. Rather than establishing or framing such a divine–human relationship, a covenant seals or formalizes it. The biblical order is relationship, then covenant; rather than covenant, hence relationship.

Leaving aside creation for a moment, just consider the ensuing biblical examples of divine–human relationships that are subsequently sealed by means of a covenant: God was clearly in relationship with Abraham from Genesis 12, yet it is not until Genesis 15 that God formalizes that relationship by means of a covenant. Similarly, God was in relationship with Israel before the covenant he formally established with them on Mount Sinai. Likewise, God was in relationship with David long before he sealed that relationship by covenant in 2 Samuel 7. And a straightforward reading of Genesis 6 suggests that God was in relationship with Noah before sealing that relationship by covenant immediately after the flood. Thus the question is not whether or not a relationship existed between God and creation or between God and humanity prior to the fall. Undoubtedly, such a relationship existed. However, to insist on calling this relationship a 'covenant relationship' is another matter entirely. There is no indisputable evidence in the biblical text for doing so. This is hardly surprising if, as suggested above, a covenant was primarily a means of sealing or formalizing such a relationship; it did not establish it.

As Waltke (2001: 136) puts it, 'A covenant solemnizes and confirms a social relationship already in existence.'[36]

Hence our discussion throws important light on the precise relationship between creation and covenant. Rather than allowing creation to be subsumed under covenant,[37] covenant must be understood in the context of creation. The priority of creation over covenant has important ramifications for redemptive or salvation history. The latter is concerned not merely with the restoration of the divine–human relationship established at creation, but ultimately with the renewal of all things, including creation itself, which, as Paul reminds us, 'will be liberated from its bondage to decay and brought into the glorious freedom of the children of God' (Rom. 8:21 NIV). It is towards this eschatological objective that each of the divine–human covenants in Scripture advances. The glue that binds all the biblical covenants together is God's creative purpose of universal blessing. Each of the subsequent covenants simply takes us one step closer towards the realization of that divine goal.

---

[36] Waltke understands the verb (*qûm*) in Gen. 6:18 to signify the confirmation of a previously existing relationship (between God and Noah), rather than a new development in an existing covenant (cf. Dumbrell).

[37] In fairness to Dumbrell, it must be noted that he also is opposed to subordinating creation to covenant.

Chapter Four

God's programmatic covenants with the patriarchs

The patriarchal covenants in their biblical-theological framework

The Noahic covenant has never been abrogated, as is attested to by the ongoing validity of its sign – the rainbow. Therefore subsequent divine–human covenants must be viewed within the context of its all-encompassing framework. Rather than superseding the covenant established between God and Noah, the patriarchal covenants, despite their narrower primary focus, have the same ultimate objectives in view. This is clear from the programmatic agenda announced to Abraham in Genesis 12:1–3.

The programmatic agenda

Genesis 12:1–3 is clearly a pivotal text in so far as the book of Genesis is concerned. Heralding yet another new stage in God's dealings with humanity, it is set against the backdrop of the primeval prologue in general, and the Babel incident in particular. These three verses fix the agenda not only for the patriarchal narratives, but also for the rest of the Pentateuch and beyond. Therefore, this divine speech to Abram is one of the most important revelations in the whole of Scripture. Indeed, it has been well described as the Bible's Magna Carta. Here we find a synopsis of the divine agenda in which God's rescue plan for humanity is revealed. The necessity of such a rescue mission has been underlined repeatedly in the preceding chapters, in which the escalating spread of sin and judgment has been traced from the Garden of Eden to the Tower of Babel. But here in Genesis 12 God's redemptive plan is at last revealed. It has been hinted at in the previous chapters, but here it is disclosed most fully. As the apostle Paul puts it,[1] here God announces the gospel in advance to Abraham.

[1] See Gal. 3:8.

Bracketed by the narrator's comments (Gen. 12:1, 4a), this divine speech comprises a series of promises that are linked to Abraham's willingness to obey Yahweh's instructions. The first part of the divine speech is reasonably straightforward: God gives Abraham the command to 'Go!' and holds out the prospect of nationhood ('a great nation, blessing, and a great name'). However, while the initial part of this speech is relatively clear, the interpretation of the latter part is much more complicated. This is due to a couple of factors, both of which relate to Hebrew grammar. The verb 'to be' (*hyh*) found at the end of verse 2 is a volitional form; that is, a verb form that would usually be read as an imperative – although this is not how most English translations render it (cf. NIV; ESV; TNIV). So the first problem is whether God issues Abram with one command here, or with two?

The second problem relates to the form of the verb at the end of verse 3. Here the niphal form of the verb 'to bless' (*brk*) can indicate a passive idea (viz. these people will *be blessed through* Abram) or it can indicate a reflexive idea (viz. these people will *bless themselves by* Abram). Thus the interpreter faces an exegetical conundrum – which of these two possibilities is intended here? Does the niphal carry a passive or reflexive meaning with respect to this particular promise?[2] Deciding one way or the other is further complicated by the fact that where the promise is reiterated in the patriarchal stories, a different verb form is sometimes used, one which is generally reflexive in meaning.[3]

Therefore, while initially the interpretation of these verses may seem straightforward, the precise meaning is complicated by these two features of the Hebrew text. Given the tremendous theological freight of this passage, both issues must be examined carefully.

The imperative form of the verb hyh

As it stands, the traditional Hebrew text (MT) can be interpreted either as an emphatic consequence clause, 'so that you will indeed be blessed', or as a second command, 'Be a blessing'. While modern English translations clearly favour the former, most recent studies support the latter.[4] Unfortunately, therefore, this is an area over which scholarly opinion is sharply divided. Indeed, some have even

---

[2] For further possible translations, see below.

[3] Grüneberg (2003), however, has recently challenged this consensus as reflected in the standard Hebrew grammars, maintaining rather that 'The hithpael predominantly expresses a variety of middle nuances' (2003: 242).

[4] While the detailed investigation by Grüneberg (2003) is one important exception, some of his argument appears to be circular and perhaps overly dismissive in places.

suggested removing the problem altogether through textual surgery – by retaining the Hebrew consonants but supplying different vowel points,[5] the text may be emended to read, 'and it [i.e. "your name", v. 2c] shall be a blessing'. However, such an extreme measure is unnecessary, especially since it is possible to make sense of the text as it stands, and the latter is undoubtedly the harder reading.[6]

Support for reading the verb as a second divine command may be found in Genesis 17:1b, in which a similar construction (an imperative verb string involving *hyh* + X) is found, and here the verb undoubtedly retains its imperative force ('Walk before me and *be* blameless' Gen. 17:1 NIV; my italics). Further support for retaining the imperative reading can be adduced from the fact that both imperatives in Genesis 12:1–3 are directly followed by cohortatives – a construction that normally expresses purpose or result. Since the first of these imperative-cohortative clauses expresses a conditional promise, it seems reasonable to conclude that an identical construction in the same text-unit should be similarly interpreted (i.e. as a second conditional promise). Thus understood, Abraham's divine commission was twofold: he was to 'Go', and he was to 'Be a blessing!'[7] The significance of this twofold command–promise structure will be explicated below.

The significance of the niphal form of brk

Once again, there are two main lines of interpretation: the Hebrew verb here, *nibrĕkû*, has generally been understood either in a passive sense (i.e. 'all the families of the earth shall *be blessed* through you'), or in a reflexive sense (i.e. 'by you all the families of the earth shall *bless themselves*').[8] As mentioned above, this interpretative crux is

---

[5] The reader should understand that the original Hebrew text contained only consonants. The present system of vowel-points was introduced by Jewish scribes between AD 500 and 1000 to preserve the traditional pronunciation of the text they were transmitting.

[6] Generally, the harder reading is preferred unless there are good grounds for explaining its origin in terms of intentional change or unintentional corruption.

[7] How Abraham was to become a means of blessing is not spelt out explicitly, but the subsequent narrative would suggest that it related in some way to the 'seed' of which he would be the progenitor. Moreover, when Gen. 12:2 is read in conjunction with Gen. 22:16–18, Abraham's obedient faith and future posterity appear to play a crucial role.

[8] It should also be noted that the precise nuance given to the debated niphal form here has a direct influence upon the translation of the following prepositional phrase *bĕkā*. In agreement with a reflexive interpretation of *nibrĕkû* it is possible to translate *bĕkā* as 'by you' (so RSV; JB; NJPSV; NRSV [in footnote]; NJB). However, a local sense ('in you') or an instrumental sense ('through you') is equally possible, and as Dumbrell (1984: 71) suggests, 'a somewhat parallel use of the phrase in Gen. 21:12 ('for through Isaac shall your descendants be named' RSV) tips the scales in favour of an instrumental sense.'

compounded by the fact that two different verb forms are used in relation to this particular promise within the patriarchal narratives: the generally passive niphal is used in Genesis 12:3, 18:18, 28:14, whereas the primarily reflexive hitpael is used in Genesis 22:18 and Genesis 26:4. Since a reflexive meaning can be conveyed by both verb forms, should the traditional passive translation be abandoned?

The antiquity of the passive interpretation is reflected by both the Septuagint and the New Testament (cf. Acts 3:25; Gal. 3:8). Moreover, it can plausibly be argued that were a reflexive voice intended, this could have been communicated unambiguously through a consistent use of the primarily reflexive hitpael. Advocates of a reflexive translation, on the other hand, contend that a passive connotation could have been conveyed unambiguously by alternative verb forms (i.e. the qal passive participle or the pual), and that the meaning of the reflexive expression (to evoke blessing upon oneself using Abraham's name) is illustrated by several instances of this type of formula elsewhere (cf. Gen. 48:20; Ruth 4:11; Zech. 8:13).

However, the fact that the promises are explicitly related to the person of Abraham rather than to his name constitutes a serious problem for those who wish to interpret the verb reflexively. A further difficulty is that the context anticipates that the nations will participate in Israel's blessing (in v. 3a, what is expected to be the norm is expressed by the plural);[9] thus merely *wishing* for such blessing would be 'decidedly anti-climactic' (Dumbrell 1984: 70). Moreover, an exclusively reflexive interpretation of this text would appear to be ruled out also by the related texts in which the niphal is employed. This is most transparent in Genesis 18:18, where a statement concerning a mere wish expressed by other nations would hardly explain Abraham's international significance. It seems unlikely, therefore, that these occurrences of the niphal form of *brk* should be interpreted reflexively, despite the presence of the hitpael in Genesis 22:18 and Genesis 26:4. But how then are these occurrences of the hitpael to be explained?

One plausible way to account for the latter is by giving the niphal a 'middle' sense (i.e. 'win/find blessing'). This translation has the advantage of incorporating both a passive and reflexive meaning,

---

[9] The parallel plural reading ('those cursing you') attested in a number of witnesses most likely resulted from scribal harmonization.

which may help explain why the compiler of Genesis allowed both forms of the verb to stand unaltered in the final text.[10] Moreover, if a middle rather than a passive sense were intended, this would also explain why the more common passive verb forms (qal passive participle or pual) of *brk* were not employed. Furthermore, as Dumbrell (1984: 71) correctly points out, 'Such a sense would also be more congruent with the general Old Testament position on mission, whereby the nations are consistently presented as seekers, coming in to a reconstituted Israel.'

However, even if the niphal does carry this idea of 'to find blessing', this still leaves unexplained the distribution of the two forms of *brk* in the relevant texts. Why is the niphal used in Genesis 12:3, Genesis 18:18 and Genesis 28:14, but the hitpael in Genesis 22:18 and Genesis 26:4? Rather than assuming that the final editor used these different verb forms arbitrarily, or was somehow reluctant to impose uniformity on his text because of underlying source material, it is worth examining more closely how the niphal and hitpael are used in these particular texts. A close comparison suggests that, rather than being used synonymously, each verb form has a distinct nuance (Williamson 2000a: 227–228).[11] Where the niphal is deployed, a less direct situation is implied: the one through whom the nations will acquire blessing is Abraham (or, in the case of Gen. 28:14, primarily Jacob). In contrast, in contexts where the hitpael is found, the channel of blessing is the promised 'seed' through whom the anticipated blessing will be communicated directly (cf. Ps. 72:17; Jer. 4:2). Thus the hitpael form of the promise may be understood as action done on one's own behalf (i.e. a 'benefactive reflexive', *IBHS*, §26.2e) and translated as 'in your seed all the nations of the earth will acquire blessing for themselves', whereas the niphal may be understood as a middle, 'through you all the families of the earth will experience blessing'.

---

[10] However, as Walton (2001: 393) plausibly argues, it seems more likely that 'the Niphal and Hithpael were intentionally used with different nuances in mind'. Remarkably, however, this possibility seems to have been seldom entertained or examined, although compare Williamson (2000a: 227–228), Walton (2001: 393–394) and Grüneberg (2003: 191–241).

[11] Walton (2001: 393–394) arrives at a similar conclusion, albeit from a different direction. Cf. also Grüneberg's more comprehensive discussion, which concludes that the hitpael form of *brk* in Gen. 22:18 and 26:4 carries the force of a 'speech action middle' (i.e. 'utter blessing'), whereas the niphal form has a passive connotation.

The twofold agenda of Genesis 12:1-3

As noted above, the narrator's comments provide a structural frame-work for these verses.[12] Between his comments are two sets of conditional promises related by the theme of blessing.[13] The demarcation of these conditional promises is indicated, not only by the Hebrew syntax (the repeated imperative–cohortative structure), but also by their respective emphases. In the first segment (Gen. 12:1–2c) Abraham is to be the recipient of blessing, whereas in the second (Gen. 12:2d–3) he is to be the mediator of blessing. Whereas the first part of the divine speech focuses exclusively on the relationship between Yahweh and Abraham, the second half introduces the relationship between Abraham and others (i.e. those Yahweh will bless or curse accordingly). The promissory focus in these two sections of Genesis 12:1–3 is therefore not identical, and it is important that each is clearly defined and carefully distinguished. Unfortunately, however, this important distinction between the promises relating to nationhood and those relating to international blessing has often been overlooked. Clines, for example, misleadingly collapses both dimensions into his promissory category of 'divine–human relationship' (1997: 30). While divine–human relationship is certainly the glue that binds the national and international dimensions of the promise together, it is important not to blur the distinction between the promise of a 'great nation' and the promise of international blessing.

Related to the first imperative ('Go . . . !') is the prospect of national status, conveyed in the threefold promise of 'a great nation, blessing, and a great name' (Gen. 12:2). The 'great nation' and the 'great name' appear to define more precisely the nature of the anticipated 'blessing'. The use of the noun *gôy* (nation) signifies that a geopolitical

---

[12] The structure of the pericope may be set out as follows:

Yahweh told Abram,

'Leave your land, your clan and your father's house and go to the land that I will disclose to you,

so that I may make you into a great nation, bless you and make you famous.
Be a blessing,

so that I may bless those blessing you and curse anyone who despises you and so that through you all the families of the ground may experience blessing.'

Abram did as Yahweh said . . . (my trans.).

[13] There can be little doubt that the central theme of this pericope is that of blessing. This is reflected, not only by the frequent occurrence of the root *brk* (used five times in Gen. 12:2–3), but also by its climactic position at the end of the speech.

entity is in view. This is further supported by the fact that the existence of Abraham's descendants as a nation (*gôy*) is intrinsically related to the territorial aspect of the divine promise (Gen. 12:7; 17:8; 18:18). Abraham's landless descendants constitute a people (*'am*), but in order to be a nation (*gôy*) they must have territory of their own.[14]

The prospect of a 'great name' likewise relates to the overarching promise of nationhood. This is suggested by two things. First, by the implicit contrast with the failed aspirations of the tower-builders of Babel (cf. Gen. 11:4), whose attempts at civil organization (nationhood) had been thwarted by divine judgment. Secondly, by the fact that this same phenomenon – this idea of a 'great name' – is used in relation to David (2 Sam. 7:9) in the context of national security and international prestige.

Thus the first part of Genesis 12:1–3 relates primarily to Abraham, holding out to him the prospect of nationhood. There is, however, a subtle shift in promissory focus in the second part of this divine speech. No longer is the emphasis on a national entity that will stem from Abraham. Instead, the primary focus is transferred to an international community to whom Abraham will mediate blessing. Indeed, the fact that God no longer speaks in terms of a 'nation' (or even 'nations'), but rather of 'all the families of the ground' (Gen. 12:3 my trans.) is perhaps significant. While the Hebrew term *mišpĕḥâ* ('clan' or 'extended family') can parallel *gôy* (cf. Jer. 10:25; Ezek. 20:32; Nah. 3:4), its deployment in the present context may hint at the non-political nature of the blessing enshrined in this international promise. This may also be alluded to by the use of the term *'ădāmâ* (ground) – that which Yahweh had earlier cursed (Gen. 3:17–19). These dispersed clans of the ground that Yahweh had cursed will be reunited by the blessing that will be mediated through Abraham.

It is clear from Genesis 12:3a that such blessing will not come automatically to 'all the families of the ground'. Rather, it is contingent on their attitude to Abraham. As Mitchell (1987: 30) underlines, 'The promise of blessing is conditional. Only those on good terms with Abraham will acquire blessing, while those hostile to him will be the object of God's devastating curse.' Potential recipients of such blessing must 'bless' Abraham. Blessing Abraham, like its antonym in Genesis 12:3 (i.e. 'disdain'), denotes deeds rather than mere words.[15]

---

[14] The three major constitutional aspects of a *gôy* are identified by Clements (1977: 426–433) as race, government and territory; cf. Speiser 1960: 157–163.

[15] See Mitchell 1987: 126–131.

How such 'blessing' or 'disdain' translates into action is not spelt out, but both are clearly indicative of a particular mindset. Either one is favourably disposed towards Abraham and identifies with him in some way, or one adopts a contemptuous attitude and treats him lightly – as someone of no importance. In either case, one's relationship with Abraham is what determines whether blessing or curse is experienced.

It may thus be concluded that Yahweh's speech in Genesis 12:1–3 anticipates two quite distinct prospects linked by a logical progression: the first section (Gen. 12:1–2c) focuses on national blessing promised to Abraham; the second section focuses on international blessing promised through Abraham. While clearly distinct, these two promissory goals are nevertheless related by the fact that the blessing promised in the second part of the divine speech is in some way dependent upon the promise related in the first; that is, Abraham's role as a mediator of blessing is contingent upon his being a recipient of blessing. Moreover, its climactic position at the end of the speech indicates that 'The primary motive behind the call of Abraham is God's desire to bring blessing, rather than cursing, upon the nations of the earth. The promise that Abraham will become a great nation . . . must be understood as being subservient to God's principal desire to bless all the families of the earth.'[16] Thus, while Yahweh's purposes primarily interest Abraham and the nation that will derive from him, ultimately they have a much wider concern: 'all the families of the earth' (Gen. 12:3 ESV) who, through Abraham, will also experience blessing. In other words, God's plans for Israel were always subservient to his universal purpose, his plans for all the families of the earth.

As indicated above, this twofold agenda of Genesis 12:1–3 is clearly significant. As well as providing an overview of salvation history, it prepares the reader for what would otherwise be a most anomalous feature of the ensuing narrative: the inclusion of two starkly different reports of covenants being made between God and Abraham.

The patriarchal covenants

Most interpreters take it as axiomatic that God's covenant with Abraham is a single entity instituted in several stages (between two

---

[16] Alexander 2002: 146.

and four). How these 'stages' are understood is determined by the perspective from which the interpreter is operating (i.e. whether a 'diachronic' or a 'synchronic' approach to the text of Genesis is adopted).[17]

Scholars operating from a diachronic perspective generally consider the 'stages' of the Abrahamic covenant to be a literary construct as opposed to chronologically distinct events. This literary construct, it is suggested, has developed from the amalgamation of different sources or traditions that allegedly lie behind the final form of the Abraham narrative. Thus understood, Genesis 15 and Genesis 17 are simply variant accounts, from different periods, of what is essentially a single event or episode in the Abraham saga. The idea of distinct or chronologically separate stages in the establishment of the Abrahamic covenant has been introduced artificially by the editorial process that took place during the compilation of the Abraham cycle. Thus what originally were two separate accounts of a single Abrahamic covenant now appear as two chronologically distinct stages in the covenant relationship.

However, as well as involving several unwarranted presuppositions with respect to the literary and theological differences between Genesis 15 and 17 (see Williamson 2000a: 81–95), such diachronic analyses fail to explain the inclusion of these two covenant pericopes in the final form of the Abraham narrative. The latter must be addressed, for – unless one uncritically assumes a somewhat piecemeal and incoherent process of final redaction – each of these chapters makes its own distinct theological contribution to the narrative as a whole.

From a synchronic perspective, those who hold to a single Abrahamic covenant typically understand its staged revelation in terms of Abraham's developing relationship with Yahweh. Opinion is divided over when the covenant is initially established (i.e. whether in Gen. 12 or Gen. 15), but it is agreed that subsequent chapters focusing on God's promises to Abraham simply confirm and amplify the same covenant. Thus understood, Genesis 17 is not an alternative account of the establishment of the Abrahamic covenant, but is either a renewal of the previously established covenant, or the next phase of its development, in which its promissory aspects are

---

[17] A diachronic approach looks at how the shape of the text may have developed through time, whereas a synchronic analysis looks at the shape of the text at a single point in time; namely, the final or canonical form of the text.

supplemented with important, but previously undisclosed, obligatory dimensions.

However, the problem with these suggestions is that they fail to explain the long time lapse between these two 'stages' of covenant-making, or to account adequately for the significant differences between Genesis 15 and 17 – both in terms of their covenantal framework and their promissory emphases.

The covenant of Genesis 15

Like the Noahic covenant (cf. Gen. 8:20), the establishment of the covenant in Genesis 15 is introduced by a sacrificial ritual (Gen. 15:9). This strange ritual has generally been interpreted as a self-maledictory oath akin to Jeremiah 34:18. Those obligating themselves to the covenant pass between the cleaved animals, essentially declaring the same fate for themselves should they fail to carry out their responsibilities. Although this interpretation has not gone unchallenged,[18] mainly because it involves a serious theological conundrum (viz. can God really put himself under such a curse?), it remains the current consensus and is thus reflected in most of the commentaries. The fact that Abram chases away the birds of prey is undoubtedly significant. Usually the carcasses of such cleaved animals would have become food for the carrion birds, but here Abram prevents this – possibly signifying that God would not ultimately suffer such a fate, because he would keep his solemn promise and would, in any case, triumph over the covenant curse. But, whatever the precise symbolism, the important point to note is that God alone (represented by the theophanic imagery of fire and smoke) passed between the dissected animals, indicating the unilateral nature of this particular covenant. Indeed, the fact that there is no 'sign' associated with this particular covenant is probably explained by the complete absence of human obligations. Thus the covenant established in Genesis 15 is unilateral, more akin to a 'Royal Grant'[19] than to a 'suzerain–vassal treaty', with obligations being undertaken by God alone.

These obligations – the promises solemnly guaranteed in Genesis 15 – relate to Abraham's posterity and territory (i.e. 'nationhood'). Significantly, there is no mention in Genesis 15 of any international

[18] E.g. G. J. Wenham (1982: 134–137). Gooder (2000: 58) misleadingly suggests that Wenham defends the view that the imagery in Gen. 15 speaks of a self-maledictory oath, whereas in fact he argues quite the reverse.

[19] So Weinfeld 1977: 270; however, cf. Haran 1997: 207 n. 8.

dimensions, or indeed of royal descendants or a perpetual divine–human relationship (cf. Gen. 17). Rather, the promises here relate solely to the establishment of a 'great nation' (Gen. 12:2) in a carefully defined geographical region (Gen. 15:18–21). Moreover, the chronology for the fulfilment of this covenant is stated quite explicitly (Gen. 15:13–16). Nothing is revealed (at least in Gen. 15) in relation to events subsequent to the establishment of nationhood. The covenant in Genesis 15 is not described as 'everlasting' (cf. Gen. 17:7, 13, 19), nor is the land said here to be an 'everlasting possession' (Gen. 17:8). Thus the focus of the covenant ratified in Genesis 15 seems to be somewhat narrower than that of chapter 17. Genesis 15 is purely national, whereas Genesis 17 incorporates both national and international dimensions. Moreover, the framework of each is clearly distinct, as a closer examination of the covenant of Genesis 17 will demonstrate.

The covenant of Genesis 17

In contrast to the unilateral framework of Genesis 15, the 'eternal' covenant of Genesis 17 is plainly bilateral. Such is clear not only from how it is introduced ('Walk before me and be blameless *so that* I may establish my covenant with both you and your descendants' Gen. 17:1 my trans.), but also from the way it is set out more fully in the following verses ('As for me . . . As for you . . .' [Gen. 17:4, 9 my trans.]). The human obligations are twofold, one ethical and the other ritual.

Irreproachable behaviour (Gen. 17:1) is a prerequisite for the establishment of this covenant, the verbal inflections in Genesis 17:2, 7 implying that this covenant had not yet been established with Abraham. The idiom of 'walking before someone' primarily suggests the idea of loyalty and devotion, such as a subject to his king.[20] The second part of this imperative ('and be blameless') enlarges on how such loyal devotion should be expressed. The idea is not one of sinless perfection or moral faultlessness – such would be an impossible goal, and as readers we already know from Noah's description back in Genesis 6 that what God was demanding of Abraham here is possible. Rather, the idea here seems to be being whole or complete; being totally dedicated to God. Hence the irreproachable behaviour in view here has as much to do with Abraham's attitude as with his actions. He was to be fully committed to God.

---

[20] See Hamilton (1990: 461) for a range of OT texts illustrating this particular nuance. Cf. also Sarna 1989: 123; Sheriffs 1996: 43–45.

In addition to this prerequisite of irreproachable behaviour, the rite of male circumcision is necessary in order to 'keep' the covenant and enjoy its benefits (Gen. 17:9–14). Circumcision also functions as the 'sign of the covenant' (Gen. 17:11), a feature that seems to be in keeping with a covenant that is not just promissory in nature. Thus, unlike the earlier 'covenant between the pieces' (Gen. 15), the covenant of Genesis 17 incorporates human obligations as well as those undertaken by Yahweh. The latter is bilateral, whereas the former is unilateral.

As well as this clear difference in framework, there are also important differences in the promises contained in each chapter. The promissory emphasis in Genesis 17 is markedly different from Genesis 15. Although the promises of Genesis 15 are not altogether absent (cf. Gen. 17:8), the stress in Genesis 17 is on Abraham's international significance. His numerical proliferation (Gen. 17:2) is elaborated chiefly in terms of his becoming 'the father of multitudinous nations' (Gen. 17:4–6 my trans.; cf. Gen. 17:16), a prospect further encapsulated in the new name he receives at this point in the narrative. While most interpreters have understood this promise of multinational fatherhood in a physical sense (i.e. Abraham would be the progenitor of several nations, not just Israel), the fact that only the Israelites and Edomites could actually trace their lineage to Abraham and Sarah suggests that the focus is wider than mere biological ancestry. This is further suggested by the fact that the covenant community is extended in Genesis 17 to include non-biological members of Abraham's household. Moreover, in every other place where the precise grammatical construction found here is employed (i.e. the inseparable preposition *lĕ* [to/for] joined to the noun *'āb* [father] in a 'resultative sense'),[21] a non-physical concept of fatherhood is undeniably in view (Williamson 2000a: 158–159). Hence this promise of multinational fatherhood is best interpreted in a metaphorical sense (i.e. Abraham will be their benefactor, akin to Joseph's 'fatherhood' in Gen. 45:8). Thus understood, Abraham will be 'the father of multitudinous nations' not in terms of biological ancestry but in terms of mediating divine blessing to them.

How the latter will materialize is elucidated in Genesis 17:6b–8. This covenant will be established (i.e. perpetuated) through a particular line of Abraham's descendants, who alone will inherit the blessings promised to Abraham (the promise of becoming 'a great

[21] See GKC, 119*t*.

nation' through which blessing will be mediated to the nations). This special line of Abrahamic descent will begin with Isaac (cf. Gen. 17:19–21), and from it will come a royal line of 'seed' (the 'kings' of Gen. 17:6 and Gen. 17:16; cf. Gen. 35:11). Admittedly, it is not explicitly stated in Genesis that God will perpetuate this covenant through these royal descendants of Abraham. Nevertheless, such an inference may be drawn from the fact that the context of each of the three texts in Genesis that mention these 'kings' is the transfer of covenant promises from one generation to the next (cf. Gen. 17:7–8, 17–21; Gen. 35:12). Moreover, the association of international blessing with the ideal Davidic king in Psalm 72:17 further suggests that the patriarchal promise will ultimately be fulfilled through a royal descendant of Abraham, arguably the subject in Genesis 22:17b–18 also.[22] It would appear, therefore, that Abraham will become the 'father [i.e. the spiritual benefactor] of multitudinous nations' through this royal 'seed'.

One covenant or two?

It is clear from the above analysis that the covenants mentioned in Genesis 15 and Genesis 17 are manifestly different in both nature (temporal/eternal; unilateral/bilateral) and primary emphases (national/international). The suggestion that they are simply two stages of the one covenant is seriously undermined by the inexplicable gap of some thirteen years between them, and by the consistent projection of the covenant in Genesis 17 into the future (lit. 'I will give my covenant' [Gen. 17:2]; 'I will establish my covenant' [Gen. 17:7 my trans.]). Both these anomalies, as well as the significant differences between the two covenant chapters, suggest a more plausible synchronic explanation: these chapters focus on two distinct, but related covenants (Williamson 2000a: 212–214).

Such a conclusion is further suggested by the fact that the different emphases in Genesis 15 and Genesis 17 mirror the two separate strands set out in the programmatic agenda of Genesis 12:1–3. Genesis 15 concentrates on the divine promise to make Abraham a 'great nation' (Gen. 12:2), whereas Genesis 17 focuses more on the divine promise that through Abraham 'all the families of the ground will experience blessing' (Gen. 12:3 my trans.). Thus understood, two distinct covenants were established between God and Abraham. The first (established in Gen. 15) solemnly guaranteed God's promise to

[22] See Alexander 1997: 255–270 and 1998: 191–212.

make Abraham into a 'great nation'. The second covenant (anticipated in Gen. 17, but not yet established) similarly guaranteed God's promise to bless the nations through Abraham and his 'seed'.

The fact that Genesis 17 anticipates a further covenant ratification in the Abraham narrative also explains several anomalous aspects of its climactic chapter (Gen. 22), not least the rationale behind this extraordinary test of Abraham's faith.[23] If, as suggested above, Abraham's compliance with the divine command in Genesis 17:1 was a prerequisite for the establishment of the second covenant, his submissive obedience in Genesis 22 clearly fulfils such a requirement. The covenantal significance of this incident would also account for the necessity of a sacrifice (even after Isaac's life had been spared), the timing of the second divine speech (Gen. 22:15–18), and the marked emphasis on Abraham's obedience (Gen. 22:16b, 18b; cf. Gen. 26:5). Most importantly, it would explain why the international aspect of the divine promise – the aspect of the programmatic agenda that had not yet been ratified by divine covenant – was reiterated at this particular point (Gen. 22:18). Admittedly, typical covenant terminology such as *běrît* or *kārat běrît* is not expressly used in the immediate context.[24] Nevertheless, against the backdrop of the preceding chapter (cf. Gen. 21:22–31), the sacrificing of the ram and God's swearing of an oath may well suggest that this is indeed a covenant-making occasion.[25]

Therefore, through his obedience to God's most difficult command (Gen. 22:2), Abraham supremely demonstrated his irreproachable behaviour, and so fulfilled the stated prerequisite for the establishment of this particular covenant (Gen. 17:1). In so doing, Abraham typified the kind of righteous behaviour expected of his covenant

---

[23] Although, cf. Vaughn 2004.

[24] Day (2003: 101) thus objects to the suggestion that Genesis 22 recounts the ratification of the covenant of circumcision (Gen. 17). However, he apparently ignores the biblical and extra-biblical evidence he himself has earlier presented (2003: 96–97), which demonstrates that swearing an oath and cutting a covenant may be virtually synonymous in covenant-making contexts.

[25] As Davies (2003: 76) observes, while the verb is a perfective (i.e. qatal), the context suggests that it is used in its performative sense ('I hereby swear' cf. GKC §106i and J.-M. §112f–g) as opposed to being a truly past use of the perfect, and hence recalling an earlier oath. While Davies (2003: 77) concedes that 'the concept of a divine oath is certainly related to that of a covenant, just as the oath sworn with invocation of the gods was an essential element of ancient Near Eastern treaties', he is not prepared to concede that all covenants involved oaths, and quite correctly notes that 'not all oaths were parts of a covenant'. However, while the latter point must be accepted, the biblical material does seem to suggest that oaths were indeed an intrinsic aspect of what is meant by a *běrît*.

heirs (Gen. 18:18–19) and later demanded of his national descendants (Gen. 26:5; cf. Neh. 9:13).

The covenant heirs

Within the rest of the book of Genesis, as in the Abraham narrative itself, attention focuses primarily on the promise relating to Abraham's 'seed'. This does not lessen the significance of the other promissory aspects, but simply highlights that the promise of 'seed' was in some sense foundational. Such an inference is clearly a logical one to draw, given that without descendants, there would be no-one to inherit the land, nor would there be anyone through whom blessing could be mediated to other people(s).

As noted above, Genesis 17 suggests that the covenant of circumcision will be perpetuated, not with Abraham's descendants generally, but with a particular line of descendants that will commence with Isaac (Gen. 17:16–21). Confirmation of this is found in Genesis 21:12 ('it is through Isaac that offspring shall be named for you' my trans.). This verse is especially interesting because of the contrast implied in the context (cf. Gen. 21:13) between Abraham's biological descendants generally and a special line of descendants traced exclusively through Isaac. While both, because of their Abrahamic ancestry, will expand to national proportions, only Isaac's descendants will perpetuate the line of descent in and through which all God's covenant promises will eventually be realized.

Given Isaac's special promissory status, the introduction of Nahor's family tree in Genesis 22:20–24 is not nearly so abrupt or unexpected as it might appear otherwise. The only obvious literary function of this short genealogy is to introduce the reader to Rebecca, through whom the special line of 'seed' would be continued.[26] It is unsurprising, therefore, that the remainder of the Abraham narrative should focus primarily on the coming together of Isaac and Rebecca,[27] and Isaac's unique position as Abraham's covenant heir (Gen. 25:1–11).

[26] As Wenham (1994: 119–120) observes, the mention of one female grandchild within this male-dominated genealogical snippet raises the reader's expectations. Less plausibly Hamilton (1995: 118) suggests that 'the emphasis in this genealogy is on one of the nations of the earth (Nahor's descendants) who find blessing in Abraham's descendants'.

[27] As is clear from Gen. 24:67, the death of Sarah (Gen. 23) and the marriage of Isaac and Rebecca (Gen. 24) should be read together as a literary unit.

In the patriarchal stories that follow, the special line of Abrahamic descent is further refined. The fulfilment of the promises concerning Ishmael is dealt with first (Gen. 25:12–18), after which attention shifts to Isaac, to whom the covenant promises are confirmed (Gen. 26:2–5). The nation descended from Esau is gradually ruled out of the reckoning, and the reader's attention is skilfully directed to the family line of Jacob, most significantly by the words of the blessing conferred on Jacob in Genesis 27:28–29, and subsequently, in Genesis 28:3–4. In both texts, especially the latter, there are very strong allusions to the promises made to Abraham. By contrast, the blessing conferred on Esau is analogous to the promises made to Ishmael (compare Gen. 27:39–40 with Gen. 16:12). Jacob's role as covenant heir is confirmed in Genesis 28:13–16, in which divine promises (i.e. land, seed and international blessing) are reiterated. In the subsequent revelation at Bethel (Gen. 35:9–15) the promise of royal progeny is added, further verifying that the special line of Abrahamic descent will be traced exclusively through Jacob. While the promise of international blessing is not stated explicitly in Genesis 35, a distinction is drawn between a 'nation' and a 'company of nations' that will come from Jacob (Gen. 35:11 ESV). Admittedly, several commentators interpret the second clause as qualifying the first (i.e. 'a nation, that is, a company of tribes'). Even so, it is still acknowledged that there is some allusion here to the multitudinous nations of Genesis 17. This may suggest, therefore, that like the multitudinous nations of Abraham, this company of nations will not necessarily be related to Jacob in a biological sense (see Williamson 2000a: 156–162). Thus understood, two different prospects are again anticipated: a national entity and an international community.

Before presenting his family history of Jacob (Gen. 37:2ff.), the narrator first traces that of the elder son to whom the covenant promises did not apply (Gen. 36).[28] The purpose of this genealogy seems to be similar to that relating to Ishmael in Genesis 25:12–18. Just as the latter alludes to the fulfilment of God's promises made in relation to (non-elect) Ishmael, so Genesis 36 alludes to the fulfilment of God's promises made in relation to (non-elect) Esau (cf. Gen. 27:39–40). Moreover, as Wenham (1994: 341) astutely observes, both this genealogy and the earlier one relating to Ishmael (Gen. 25:12–18)

---

[28] Cf. the short family history of Ishmael introduced at a similar point in the narrative in Gen. 25. Cf. also the placement of Cain's line (Gen. 4) before that of Seth (Gen. 5).

draw attention to the fact that the non-elect descendants settled outside the Promised Land, and are thus excluded from the line of promise.[29]

Not unexpectedly, therefore, the remainder of the patriarchal narrative focuses exclusively on the family history of Jacob's sons, four of whom are singled out for special attention (i.e. Joseph, Reuben, Judah and Benjamin). Of these four, Judah is possibly the most significant, in that the Joseph story is abruptly interrupted by an episode in which Judah's 'seed' occupies centre stage. While the full significance of the brief liaison between Judah and his daughter-in-law Tamar is only later disclosed (cf. Ruth 4:18; Matt. 1:3), the striking similarities with the birth story of Jacob and Esau (Gen. 25:24–26), together with the emphasis on Judah's 'seed', strongly suggests a special role in the promissory agenda for Judah. Genesis 38 thus provides yet another illustration of God's providence operating in the establishment of the special line of Abrahamic descent.

While the subsequent Joseph narrative is concerned primarily with how Jacob's extended family came to settle in Egypt, at least some attention is focused on their numerical growth (Gen. 47:27; cf. Gen. 48:4, 16), thus continuing the major focus of the patriarchal narratives on Abraham's 'seed' through whom the covenant promises – and hence God's universal purpose – would eventually be realized.

[29] Hamilton's suggestion (1995: 401) that the Edomite king list may allude to the promise of Gen. 17:6, 16 is not convincing. As Hamilton himself notes, this promissory aspect was reiterated in the previous chapter to Jacob (Gen. 35:11), whereas no such promise was made in the case of Esau. Rather, this seems to have been part and parcel of the very birthright he despised and the blessing from which he was excluded.

Chapter Five

God's national covenant with Israel

The national covenant in biblical-theological context

Of all the divine–human covenants in the Old Testament, the one formally established between Yahweh and Israel at Sinai is certainly the most prominent, not only in terms of the space devoted to it within the Pentateuch, but also in terms of its numerous echoes, renewals and theological significance within the Old Testament as a whole. Indeed, as McKenzie (2000: 4) observes, 'This is the one considered *the* Old Testament covenant.'

However, while a disproportionate amount of space may be devoted to the covenant(s) established between Yahweh and Abraham's national progeny,[1] the Israelites, it is important to realize that these national covenants do not in any sense supersede the patriarchal covenants. Rather, the latter are the theological backbone supporting the national covenants and against which they must be understood (cf. Lev. 26:42–45).[2] It is important to emphasize this, as it guards against any misreading of the Sinai covenant in terms of a temporary suspension, still less an annulment, of the programmatic agenda announced to Abraham. The giving of the law was not intended to set aside the promise (cf. Gal. 3:17); rather, it was the means by which the goal of the promise would be advanced in and through Abraham's national descendants (Gen. 12:2; cf. 18:18–19).

The hermeneutical key to the exodus event and its sequel (the Sinai covenant) is found in Exodus 2:23–25. From this text it is clear that God's intervention on behalf of the Israelites in Egypt was prompted by the covenant promises he had made to Israel's ancestors. Thus the deliv-

[1] There is some debate over whether the covenant ratified on the plains of Moab constitutes a distinct entity or is simply a 'renewal' of the covenant established with the Sinai generation.
[2] However, while the national covenant is clearly a fulfilment and development of the ancestral covenants, it nevertheless constitutes a separate covenant (*pace* Baker 2005: 25), as reflected in its ceremonial inauguration and distinct covenant sign.

erance from Egypt and God's revelation at Sinai must be interpreted in the light of the programmatic agenda set out in Genesis (cf. the allusions to the patriarchal promises in Exod. 3:7–8, 16–22; 6:4–6; 13:5, 11).

The book of Exodus begins by outlining the initial fulfilment of the promise relating to phenomenal expansion of Abraham's biological descendants (cf. Gen. 15:5). The extended family that had gone down to Egypt (Gen. 46:27) had grown into a multitude in the interim period (Exod. 1:6–10). Moreover, it continued to do so despite the genocidal policy of ethnic cleansing instituted by a new regime in Egypt (cf. Exod. 1:11–12, 20; 5:5). Evidently, the divine promise concerning the proliferation of Abraham's physical descendants had begun to materialize.[3]

Furthermore, by the end of Genesis the first prerequisite for the inheritance of the Promised Land had been met: Abraham's descendants had become 'migrants in someone else's land' (Gen. 15:13a my trans.). The opening chapters of Exodus recount how the second requirement (viz. the slavery and oppression of Abraham's descendants; cf. Gen. 15:13b) unfolded when a new king (presumably also meaning a new dynasty) established himself over Egypt (cf. Exod. 1:11–14; 2:23–25; 3:7–10). Moreover, as the story progresses

---

[3] Note the allusion in Exodus 1:7 to the creation mandate (Gen. 1:28) inherited by Noah (Gen. 9:1) and subsequently Abraham (Gen. 17:6). As Carpenter (1997: 608) observes, 'The multiplication of the enslaved Israelites in Egypt is not a biological or an environmental issue first of all; it is essentially a theological issue, in which the Lord has involved himself. It is a matter of God's remembering his promises and covenant with the descendants of Abraham, Isaac, and Jacob (Exod 2:24). The multiplication that occurs is a result of his original blessing at creation that he had placed on his "creation community" now being placed on these people (see Exod 1:7, which employs key words given in Gen 1:28) . . . God's command for humankind to be fruitful (*prh*), multiply (*rbh*) and fill (*ml'*) the earth has been placed on the enslaved Israelites and has become a reality for the descendants of Abraham, Isaac, and Jacob in Egypt, for they were fruitful (*prh*), multiplied (*rbh*) and filled (*ml'*) the earth. Furthermore, we are told they became "exceedingly powerful." This last expression links the development of "the Israelites" . . . into a nation – a promise fulfilled to Abraham given in Gen 18:18, along with the original blessings placed upon humanity. Israel has inherited these blessings as recorded in Gen 18:18, and they are the means by which God has developed Abraham into a great and powerful nation . . . As a result, . . . [a]lthough the original persons who enjoyed God's blessings, including Jacob and Joseph, have died, the blessing continues, for the God of the patriarchs continues his faithfulness, and the creator God remembers his plans for humankind. And death is not triumphant over the promises and covenants of God.' It is important to note that the use of creation language is not confined to these opening verses of Exodus, but – as Enns (2000a: 147–148) underlines – pervades the subsequent narrative: the opposition of Pharaoh to the Israelites' fulfilment of the creation mandate (Exod. 1:9; cf. 1:6–7); the story of Moses' birth (Exod. 2:1–10; cf. Gen. 1 and Gen. 6 – 9); the parting of the Red Sea (Exod. 14; cf. Gen. 1:9); the giving of the law (an act of re-creation); and the tabernacle – itself a microcosm of creation (see below).

the stage is further set for the promised deliverance of Genesis 15:14 (Exod. 3:16–22; 6:2–8; 7:1–5; 11:1–3). Thus the exodus event constitutes the fulfilment of the preliminary stage of the prospect held out in the covenant of Genesis 15: the prospect of nationhood. The 'great nation' promised by God to Abraham (Gen. 12:2) is about to emerge on to the world stage. Indeed, this is the very purpose of the exodus event: to bring to birth the nation with whom God will establish a special relationship (Exod. 6:7; cf. Gen. 17:7–8).

Therefore, as Anderson (1999: 137) correctly concludes, 'In the final form of the Pentateuch (Torah), the Mosaic covenant is subordinate to the Abrahamic. In this canonical context the Abrahamic covenant, which guarantees the promise of land and posterity, is the overarching theme within which the Mosaic covenant of law is embraced.'

The revelatory purpose of the national covenant

In essence, the Sinaitic covenant spells out the type of nation that Yahweh intended Israel to be. It is clear from the obligations imposed upon Israel that being in special relationship with Yahweh involved more than privilege; it entailed responsibility. Israel, Abraham's promised descendants, could continue to enjoy the divine–human relationship anticipated in Genesis 17:7–8 only by maintaining the socio-ethical distinctiveness enshrined in God's instructions to Abraham ('walk before me, and be blameless' Gen. 17:1). Like their ancestor, Israel must 'keep the way of Yahweh by doing what is right and just' (Gen. 18:19 my trans.). Like Abraham, Israel must 'obey Yahweh's voice and keep his requirements, commandments, statutes and laws' (Gen. 26:5; own trans., which changes the original pronouns to suit usage in text; cf. Exod. 19:8; 24:3, 7).[4] Having Yahweh as their God entailed conformity to his holy character (cf. Lev. 19:2). Thus the primary concern of the Sinaitic covenant was on how the promised divine–human relationship between Yahweh and the 'great nation' descended from Abraham (Gen. 17:7–8) should be expressed and maintained.

The bilateral nature of the covenant is reflected in the conditional framework (i.e. 'If you obey . . . then . . .' TNIV; similarly, ESV) of Exodus 19:5–6. For his part, God would make Israel unique among the nations: they would be his 'special treasure' (*sĕgullâ* implies a special

---

[4] As Kaiser (1992: 126) underlines, 'the very terms used for Abraham's obedience were the ones that would later come to denote the whole Mosaic law'.

value as well as a special relationship),[5] a 'priestly kingdom' and a 'holy nation'. As Dumbrell (1984: 87) suggests, the use of the term 'nation' (*gôy*) rather than the more customary 'people' (*'am*) may well indicate an allusion here to the promise of nationhood in Genesis 12:2. In any case, this text clearly indicates what kind of nation God intends Israel to be: a holy nation, set apart to God from all others. As such, Israel was clearly to function as 'a light to the nations'.[6] While ultimately Abraham's individual and eschatological 'seed' inherited this mission (cf. Isa. 42:6; 49:6; 60:3), such a role is at least implicit in Israel's description here as a 'priestly kingdom'. The latter phrase (found only here in the OT; although cf. Isa. 61:6 for a similar idea) has given rise to various interpretations, but its most straightforward sense (i.e. 'kingdom of priests') suggests that it is a statement of Israel's distinct status as 'a servant nation'. The whole nation has thus inherited the responsibility formerly conferred on Abraham – that of mediating God's blessing to the nations of the earth. Such a mission is also suggested by the explanatory statement that follows: 'because [*kî*] all the earth is mine' (Exod. 19:5). As Dumbrell maintains, 'the *kî* clause functions not as the assertion of the right to choose but as the *reasons* or *goal* for choice' (1988: 146, emphasis his). Israel's election as Yahweh's 'special treasure' was not an end in itself, but a means to a much greater end. Thus understood, the goal of the Sinaitic covenant was the establishment of a special nation through which Yahweh could make himself known to all the families of the earth.

To be such a nation, however, Israel must 'keep my [God's] covenant' (Exod. 19:5). In order to do so, Israel must fulfil the obligations inherent in this particular covenant, as the following chapters clearly indicate.[7] The principal obligations ('words') are set out in the

[5] The noun is used elsewhere of a king's private treasure (cf. 1 Chr. 29:3; Eccl. 2:8). It is related to the Akkadian word *sikiltu*, meaning 'personal property'. Hence Israel was Yahweh's personal and precious possession.

[6] For more on this, see Kaiser 2000 (esp. chs. 1 and 4).

[7] Like most interpreters, I take the covenant spoken of here to be the one subsequently ratified on Mount Sinai (Exod. 24:1–11). Following Dumbrell, Enns (2000b) suggests that the covenant spoken of here in Exod. 19:5 refers back to the ancestral covenant. However, while not wishing to deny the element of continuity between these covenants, the covenant obligations imposed on Israel (i.e. '*keep* my covenant') seem to anticipate the covenant code disclosed in the following chapters, that which the people somewhat naively commit themselves to obey (cf. Exod. 24:3, 7; cf. Exod. 19:8). More radically, Goldingay (2003: 370) flatly denies any idea of God establishing a covenant with Israel until Exodus 34, on the grounds that there is no explicit divine intention to do so or indeed a statement concerning covenant-making on God's part even in Exodus 24. However, the words and actions of Moses (Exod. 24:8) clearly point more in the direction of covenant initiation than 'sealing or reconfirming or

Decalogue (Exod. 20:1–17); the more detailed obligations ('judgments') are contained in the 'Book of the Covenant' (Exod. 20:22 – 23:33).[8] While various attempts have been made to discern structural parallels with ancient treaty patterns,[9] there is little consensus as to the extent and significance of the suggested parallels. It would seem, however, that these laws – like the rest of the Sinaitic obligations (i.e. as disclosed in Leviticus) – had a revelatory purpose; just as ancient law-codes generally made a statement about the king who had promulgated them, so the covenant obligations revealed at Sinai disclosed something of the nature and character of Yahweh. Therefore the law made a statement not only about Israel (as a 'great nation'; cf. Deut. 4:6–8), but also – indeed, more importantly – about Israel's God. Unfortunately, Walton (1994: 24–46) rather overstates the case by actually defining 'covenant' as 'God's program of revelation'. Nevertheless, this revelatory function is certainly a crucial element in the Sinaitic covenant and constitutes the thematic link between the two main parts of the book of Exodus – the deliverance of Israel from Egypt and the revelation of Yahweh at Sinai. Just as Yahweh had made himself known to Pharaoh (cf. Exod. 5:2) and the

---

renegotiating of a covenant' (Goldingay 2003: 370), and as covenant mediator (cf. Exod. 19), Moses is clearly representing God in what he says and does at this point.

[8] The relationship between the stipulations contained in the Decalogue and the more detailed (and varied) stipulations contained in what is commonly referred to as 'the Book of the Covenant' (i.e. Exod. 20:22 – 23:33) is variously interpreted. For some, the latter's stipulations are an extended (and non-contemporaneous) commentary on the former; i.e. the basis of the Sinaitic covenant was the 'Ten Words' (indeed, for many, a hypothetical form of these in a shorter and more uniform format), which was later supplemented by the material contained in 'the Book of the Covenant', and added non-historically to the Exodus account by a later editor(s). Following Albrecht Alt, many have drawn the distinction between apodictic (simple prohibitions) and casuistic (case: if/when . . ., then . . .) laws contained in this section of Exodus, without necessarily following him in the conclusions he attempted to draw from this regarding origins and application of the same (for more on this, see Whybray 1995: 110–115). The similarities between some of the biblical stipulations and other ancient Near Eastern law-codes have not gone unobserved (cf. Pritchard 1978: 159–223; Boecker 1980: 135–175). One striking parallel is between the *lex talionis* in Exod. 21:23–25 and the laws of retaliation found in the Code of Hammurabi; cf. Hyatt 1971: 234 for details. Nevertheless, as Hyatt himself acknowledges, 'there can be no question of *direct* borrowing from that or any other known ancient code, for there are numerous differences in detail' (1971: 220). In any case, as Durham (1987: 318) concludes, 'Wherever these laws originated, and whenever they stand now as an exposition and an application of life lived in relationship with Yahweh.'

[9] See e.g. Kitchen 1989 and 2003: 283–294. For more on this enterprise in general, see pp. 24–26 above. For the idea that the arrangement of Exod. 19 – 24 is logically coherent, and consistent with typical ancient Near Eastern covenant ratifications, see Polak 2004.

Egyptians (as well as to Israel and the surrounding nations) through the deliverance of the exodus, so he would further make himself known to Israel and the nations through the covenant relationship established at Sinai. Therefore, by fulfilling these covenant obligations, Israel would reveal Yahweh to the surrounding nations.

Given Israel's particular role – as a model of God's kingdom on earth – it was vital that the nation remained distinct from other nations, especially those Israel was about to dispossess. While the point is not made explicitly until later (Lev. 18:24–29; although cf. Exod. 23:20–33), Israel's distinctiveness was also necessary for retaining possession of the territorial inheritance. Expulsion from the Promised Land would in turn jeopardize the fulfilment of God's ultimate objective – the blessing of all nations through Abraham's royal 'seed'. Therefore, just as the Noahic covenant had guaranteed the preservation of life, in particular human life, on earth, so the Mosaic covenant guaranteed the preservation of Israel, Abraham's national posterity, in the land.

The ratification of the covenant at Sinai

The formal ratification of the Sinaitic covenant takes place in Exodus 24. Like earlier divine covenants (cf. Gen. 8:20–21; 15:9–10; 22:13–14), a sacrificial ritual is involved (Exod. 24:3–8).[10] No explanation is offered with regard to the ritual described here. While there is some correspondence with later sacrificial rites (cf. those of Exod. 29:16, 20 and Lev. 1:5, 11) in which blood is sprinkled upon the altar, the rite described here in Exodus 24:6 is nowhere repeated in the Old Testament, making its precise meaning difficult to ascertain. One plausible suggestion is that the symbolism is analogous with the more primitive covenant-making ritual reflected in Genesis 15 (and apparently revived in the early sixth century; cf. Jer. 34:18–20).[11] Thus

---

[10] For many scholars, this 'covenant-making' section interrupts the unit (Exod. 24:1–2, 9–11) describing the 'summit meeting' on top of Sinai. However, a covenant ratification at this stage (between Moses receiving instructions concerning the summit meeting and actually implementing them) is not incongruous with the overall flow of the narrative.

[11] On the basis of this analogy Bush (1992: 103) concludes, 'the bloodshed chillingly symbolizes Israel's acceptance of the covenant and its requirements'. However, for objections to the interpretation of the rite in Genesis 15 as a self-maledictory oath, see Wenham 1987: 332–333. Wenham interprets the symbolism of Genesis 15 as the promise of Yahweh's presence among his people, Israel (represented by the clean animals).

understood, the splattered blood (Exod. 24:6, 8) chillingly symbolizes the fate of the covenant breaker(s). Alternatively, the blood ritual may simply serve to consecrate the human agent as in the case of priesthood (so Nicholson 1986: 172–174), whose consecration (cf. Exod. 29; Lev. 8) may also be understood as part of a covenantal arrangement (so Dumbrell 1984: 94). In any case, while the precise significance of the symbolism remains unclear, the twofold application of the blood (i.e. to the altar and the people) would appear to underline the bilateral nature of the covenant so ratified.

Following the sacrificial ritual, the inauguration of the Sinaitic covenant apparently continues (*contra* Nicholson 1986: 121–133) with another ceremony associated with the ratification of covenants elsewhere: a covenant meal (Exod. 24:9–11; cf. Gen. 26:26–31; 31:43–54).[12] Admittedly, the consumption of food in the presence of God 'cannot be understood as *ipso facto* the making of a covenant with God' (Nicholson 1986: 126; cf. Exod. 18:1–12). However, as Nicholson himself acknowledges (1986: 127), here in Exodus 24 the context is clearly covenantal, and his *prima facie* case for rejecting the covenantal significance of this rite is not quite as obvious as he suggests. Nicholson clearly views the meal as an alternative to the ritual described in Exodus 24:5–8, whereas it may just as easily be understood as supplementary (cf. Gen. 31:54). Therefore, while Nicholson (1986: 131–133) is undoubtedly correct to highlight the significance of the fact that this group survived its *visio dei*, his exegesis of Exodus 24:11 seems overly reductionistic.

The sign of the Mosaic covenant: sabbath

Not surprisingly, the Sinaitic covenant conforms to the pattern for covenants involving bilateral obligations; namely, it had a 'sign': sabbatical rests (Exod. 31:13–17; cf. Isa. 56:4; Ezek. 20:12, 20). More surprising, however, is the fact that the stipulated covenant sign is only identified as such after Moses has received Yahweh's instructions concerning the establishment of Israel's cult (Exod. 25:1 – 31:10). These instructions were delivered to Moses during his extended

[12] Admittedly, nowhere else in the OT is such a covenant meal associated with a divine–human covenant. However, it seems unlikely that this was simply an ordinary meal or a graphic manner of emphasizing that they survived their experience of seeing God. Perhaps, as Enns (2000b: 492) tentatively suggests, such a meal may already have been on view in Exod. 24:4 (unlike the burnt offering, which was 'consumed' by God, the fellowship offering is one in which people normally participated) – although (as Enns concedes) no such connection is explicitly made in the text itself.

period on Mount Sinai (cf. Exod. 24:12–18), immediately after the covenant ratification ceremony had taken place (Exod. 24:1–11). The fact that the covenant sign is mentioned at this point in the narrative, just after the cultic instructions and just prior to Moses receiving from God the 'tablets of the testimony' (Exod. 31:18 ESV), suggests three things.[13]

First, that the detailed instructions Moses received with respect to the organization of the cult (i.e. the tabernacle, the ordination of the Aaronic priesthood and their priestly duties; Exod. 25:1 – 31:12) are also an intrinsic part of this particular covenant. By placing the covenant sign here, readers are reminded that the preceding cultic instructions are also part of the nation's response to Yahweh, its covenant partner. This inference is further suggested by the fact that the primary concern of the Mosaic covenant was to maintain the unique divine–human relationship between Yahweh and Israel, and thus some means of sustaining communion between a holy God and a sinful people was absolutely essential.

Secondly, the present juxtaposition of instructions regarding the tabernacle and the sabbath implies that there is an important connection between the sabbath and the tabernacle. This is further suggested by the fact that, after the breach and remaking of the covenant in Exodus 32 – 34, Moses prefaces the instructions to erect the tabernacle with instructions concerning the sabbath (Exod. 35:1–3).[14] As Childs (1974: 541) observes:[15]

---

[13] The suggestion (cf. Noth 1962: 240–241; Cassuto 1967: 403–405) that this pericope is placed here primarily to emphasize that scrupulous sabbath observance applies even to work on the tabernacle and its paraphernalia is unlikely for a number of reasons:

- Such an application is not explicitly stated in the text.
- The instructions here reflect a much wider application ('everyone who does [any] work') than a prohibition concerning tabernacle construction per se.
- The description of the sabbath as 'a sign in perpetuity' suggests a much broader application than the construction of the tabernacle.
- When Moses passes on this instruction to Israel (Exod. 35:2–3), it is again applied generally ('everyone who does [any] work') and the only specific application ('kindling a fire') has no obvious connection with the building of the tabernacle, etc.

Nevertheless, while this may not have been the primary reason for locating the covenant sign at this climactic point, clearly sabbath-keeping applied equally to construction work related to the tabernacle.

[14] This is not to deny a further significance in the bracketing of the rebellion narrative with the sabbath law; namely, the covenant is now proceeding as planned.

[15] Likewise, Dumbrell 1984: 104.

The tabernacle represents the fulfillment of the covenant promise: 'I will make my dwelling with you . . . I will be your God and you shall be my people.' But the actual sign of the covenant is the sabbath. Therefore, the observance of the sabbath and the building of the tabernacle are two sides of the same reality. Just as the sabbath is a surety of Israel's sanctity (31.13), so the meeting of God with his people in the tabernacle serves the selfsame end (29.43).

Thirdly, its climactic location suggests that observance of the sabbath was not just another one of Israel's covenant obligations (cf. Exod. 20:8–11; 23:12), but had particular significance – a point further underlined by its description as a perpetual covenant 'sign' (Exod. 31:13, 16–17), by the priority Moses gives it after the covenant has been broken and remade (cf. Exod. 35:1–3), and by the severe penalty imposed for breaking the sabbath.[16]

While the obligation to 'keep sabbath(s)' has a certain priority (although ESV's 'above all' may be a bit too strong here), the rationale for this is its cognitive function as a perpetual reminder of Israel's special status:[17] desecrating the sabbath is, in effect, renouncing one's special relationship with Yahweh. That the sabbath prohibition was not intended to be an absolute requirement (or indeed the most important covenant obligation), even under the Mosaic law, is clear from the teaching of Jesus (cf. Mark 2).

[16] As both Exod. 31:14a and Exod. 31:15b make clear, the *kārat* (cutting off) penalty (Exod. 31:14b) refers to exclusion from the covenant community through death, not merely physical expulsion. Compare also Num. 15:32–36. The suggestion that the example from Numbers is specifically a breach of the offence listed in Exod. 35:3 (viz. kindling a fire on the sabbath), hence carrying the death penalty, reflects a misconception that in Exodus 31 two conflicting penalties for sabbath-breaking, expulsion (Exod. 31:14b) and execution (Exod. 31:14a, 15b), are implied. When the full implication of the *kārat* penalty is understood, there is no discrepancy whatsoever. Thus the severe penalty attached to sabbath-breaking further highlights the theological importance of this covenant sign; cf. Gen. 17:14.

[17] Fox's (1974: 562) threefold categorization of the term *'ōt* in the Hebrew Bible seems to provide a generally acceptable framework from which to establish the connotation of the term here and elsewhere. The context seems to rule out the thought of a convincing proof; keeping sabbaths is not designed to prove anything in Exod. 31. The idea of a symbol sign is also excluded, for the explanation(s) offered here in Exod. 31 do not throw light on the sign's meaning, but rather explicate its theological significance. Thus the third of Fox's categories, cognition signs, seems best to fit the context of Exod. 31, for 'keeping sabbath' seems to function here primarily as a mnemonic device, intended to remind the Israelites of their special status as Yahweh's people and their obligation to keep his law.

As in Exodus 20:11, emphasis is placed here (Exod. 31:17) on the sabbath's significance as a perpetual reminder of God's rest after the work of creation. Thus by copying Yahweh's example,[18] the Israelites are in some sense participating in and pointing forward to the goal of creation: entering into the enjoyment of God's rest. Like other covenant signs, therefore, the sabbath expresses the essence of the blessing anticipated by the covenant itself; in this case, entering into the blessedness of divine rest.

The covenantal significance of the tabernacle

As suggested by its canonical location (see above), the instructions to erect the tabernacle must clearly be understood in terms of the covenant itself. As Dumbrell observes, this is further indicated by the fact that both here (cf. Exod. 31) and subsequently (cf. Exod. 35) the erection of the tabernacle and the covenant sign (sabbath) are juxtaposed, lending support to his conclusion that 'in some sense the building of the tabernacle and the observance of the sabbath are simply two sides of the same reality' (1984: 104). Thus interpreted, the tabernacle (signifying Yahweh's kingly presence in the midst of his people; see below) vouchsafed Israel's enjoyment of 'rest' in the Promised Land – itself a foretaste of the ultimate restoration of God's creation intention for humankind.[19] Therefore the tabernacle not only gave expression to (and facilitated the maintenance of) the divine–human relationship which was at the centre of the Mosaic covenant, but also anticipated its ultimate goal.

As Dillard and Longman (1995: 69) observe, 'the location, archi-tectural design, building materials, and accessibility of the tabernacle all highlight the fact that a holy God dwelt in the midst of the Israelite people'.[20]

---

[18] Note the particularly bold anthropomorphism ('and was refreshed', Exod. 31:17; cf. Exod. 23:12) found only here. As Durham (1987: 414) puts it, 'If even Yahweh stopped to catch his breath after six days of customary labor, so also should Israel.'

[19] As Enns (2000a: 149) avers, such an allusion is suggested, not only by the con-struction materials (which speak of heavenly order amid earthly chaos), but probably also by the sevenfold repetition of the phrase, 'The LORD said unto Moses' in chapters 25 – 31, the final of which introduces the sabbath command: 'In the midst of a fallen world, in exile from the Garden, the original "heaven on earth", God undertakes another act of creation, a building project signifying a return to pre-fall splendour' (Enns 2000a: 149).

[20] The following observations are drawn largely from Dillard and Longman's insightful and concise discussion (1995: 68–70). For a more comprehensive analysis, see Suh (2003).

1. The tabernacle was set up in the middle of the Israelite encampment – traditionally in the ancient Near East the place of the king's tent. Moreover, when on the move, the ark (located in the Holy of Holies of the tabernacle) led the way, analogous to a Near Eastern king leading his army into battle.

2. The tabernacle area was compartmentalized as follows: a courtyard, a Holy Place and a Most Holy Place, reflecting different gradations of holiness: outside the camp was the realm of the Gentiles and the unclean – to which the ritually polluted were exiled temporarily. Closer to God's presence, the Israelites in covenant with Yahweh resided in the camp encompassing the tabernacle; however, only Levites could reside in the immediate vicinity of the tabernacle. Moreover, only consecrated Aaronic priests could enter the tabernacle itself, and only the High Priest could enter (and only on the Day of Atonement) the Most Holy Place.

3. As one drew closer to the Most Holy Place the ground became progressively more holy. This is reflected in the correlation between proximity to the Most Holy Place and the preciousness of the construction materials used (e.g. the curtains; the metals). Thus the very building materials symbolically represent the fact that a holy God lived in the midst of his people. While recourse to more fanciful and allegorical approaches often tends to miss the wood for the trees, the extensive use of gold and blue fabrics seems to be another indication that the tabernacle was a royal residence, and the arrangement of the furniture 'stands as a vivid reminder that only those who have made atonement for their sin and uncleanness may approach God'.[21] Whatever the precise significance of the various fixtures (i.e. the chest/seat, the table, the lampstand), they certainly indicated that the tent was God's abode (these three items comprised the main items of furniture in an ancient home).

Thus the tabernacle represented God's dwelling in the midst of his people. Such is clearly the significance of the fact that following its erection, a cloud covered it and the glory of God filled it (Exod. 40:34).

However, the tabernacle also served another function – underlined by its description as a 'Tent of Meeting'. As such it eventually replaced the earlier 'Tent of Meeting' spoken of in Exodus 33:7–11, where Moses enjoyed his 'face to face' audiences with Yahweh. Like that earlier tent, the tabernacle was to be a place of divine–human

[21] Alexander 2002: 192.

communion – although for such communion between Israel and God, sanctification was necessary (hence the significance of the altar situated near the entrance to the tabernacle).[22]

As a symbol of God's relationship with his people, the tabernacle thus served an important function in the life and religion of the people of God. However, it was a temporary institution until the people of God were established in the Promised Land – after which, like their more permanent personal dwellings, God's dwelling took on the form of a house. Nevertheless, even this was but the foreshadowing of the New Testament reality, when God's Son would make his tabernacle among his people (John 1:14) and, ultimately, bring heaven down to earth in the New Jerusalem (cf. Rev. 21 – 22).

The covenantal status of the Levitical priesthood

Although the consecration of Aaron and his sons as priests (Exod. 28 – 29; Lev. 8) is not expressly related in covenantal terminology, a number of passages elsewhere apply covenantal language to the Levitical priesthood (Jer. 33:21–22; Neh. 13:29; Mal. 2:1–9). Admittedly, it is difficult to determine whether the latter passages allude to the 'covenant of peace' (Num. 25:12 ESV) – further defined as a 'covenant of perpetual priesthood' (Num. 25:13 ESV) – awarded to Phinehas for his loyalty to Yahweh, or to a covenant made with the Levitical priests more generally. Certainly, some kind of covenantal relationship had been established with the latter prior to the incident recorded in Numbers 25, as illustrated by the description of the priestly gratuities as 'a covenant of salt forever' (Num. 18:19 ESV) – apparently suggesting the permanence of this arrangement (cf. 2 Chr. 13:5). It is thus possible that a covenant between Yahweh and the priests had been in operation from the inception of the Levitical priesthood.

In any case, these priestly covenants seem to have served the same general purpose as the Mosaic covenant with which they are so closely related; namely, the priests facilitated the maintenance of the divine–human relationship between Yahweh and Abraham's descendants. Significantly, it was when they failed to do their part in this latter respect that they were accused by Malachi of having 'corrupted the covenant of Levi' (Mal. 2:8 ESV). Thus the Priestly and Mosaic

---

[22] For the covenantal significance of Israel's cult, see Beckwith 2000: 754–762.

covenants, while remaining distinct, run in parallel with one another, and are closely related in purpose; namely, maintaining the relationship between God and Israel.

The breaking of the covenant and its re-establishment

The fragility of the divine–human relationship between Yahweh and Israel (at least, on Israel's part) is illustrated by the crisis that arose from the episode involving the golden calf (Exod. 32 – 34). Even as Moses was receiving the covenant stipulations, the Israelites were breaking them – graphically depicted by the shattering of the inscribed tablets by Moses when confronted firsthand with the people's apostasy (Exod. 32:19).

Whatever the precise significance of the golden calf for Aaron and the Israelites,[23] the narrator leaves us in no doubt about its sinful offensiveness to Yahweh.[24] The seriousness of this breach of the covenant is highlighted in a number of ways: (a) Yahweh's implied repudiation of the Israelites as his people;[25] (b) the suggestion that Moses could supersede Israel as covenant heir (Exod. 32:9–10); (c) Moses' reaction – in both action and speech – when he saw firsthand how the people had sinned; (d) the repeated description of the offence as a 'great sin' (Exod. 32:21, 30, 31); (e) the inadequacy of the executions carried out immediately by the Levites to make atonement for the people's great sin (Exod. 32:27–32);[26] (f) the prospect of further

---

[23] Its intended function ('to go before us'; Exod. 32:1; cf. Exod. 23:20, 23) and its designation ('your *'ĕlōhîm* who brought you up out of the land of Egypt'; Exod. 32:4; cf. Exod. 20:2) seem to imply that they saw it as representative of Yahweh himself, rather than some new deity to replace him. Nevertheless, the plural forms used in association with *'ĕlōhîm* make it equally clear that it is a 'grotesque parody' (Moberly 1983: 47). As Moberly later points out (1983: 163), the same is true of 1 Kgs 12 (where again only one *deity* is represented), therefore McKenzie's assertion (2000: 21) that the plurality of 'gods' in Exod. 32 betrays literary dependence on 1 Kgs 12:28 strangely misses the point; viz. the pejorative nature of the comment in *both* Exodus and Kings.

[24] As Gowan (1994: 221) observes, 'The golden calf is seen by Moses and by the author of the passage as a direct violation of the first two commandments.'

[25] Clearly, Israel's special status as the people of God is called into question: Yahweh describes them to Moses as 'Your people whom you brought up' and 'this people' (Exod. 32:7, 9). Their description by the narrator as 'his people' (Exod. 32:14) suggests that Yahweh accepted the force of Moses' appeal to their election by Yahweh.

[26] While these executions carried out by the Levites certainly underline the serious consequences of covenant breaking for the nation generally, no rationale is offered here, whether with respect to their function (cf. Num. 25:11) or their apparently

divine judgment ahead (Exod. 32:33–34);[27] (g) the plague – a sign of covenant curse – with which Yahweh struck the people because they had made the calf (Exod. 32:25); (h) the way that Israel's fate is left semi-suspended, as Yahweh contemplates his next move.[28]

It is thus clear that Israel deserved to forfeit their privileged status as the people of God, the covenant having been broken even before the final stage of its formal establishment – the depositing of the covenant code in the ark of the covenant (Exod. 25:16; 40:20). Significantly, however, God desists from annihilating the Israelites when Moses appeals to the promise of nationhood – that which had been unconditionally guaranteed in Genesis 15 (Exod. 32:7–14). Moreover, an allusion to the wider purposes of God elicits Yahweh's promise to accompany his people after all (Exod. 33:12–17).[29] It is clear, however, that this change of heart is due solely to Yahweh's own gracious character (Exod. 33:19; cf. Exod. 33:3, 5; 34:9),[30] and it is on this basis that the covenant is 're-established'.[31] God's grace, nevertheless, still

---

random basis; perhaps the Levites targeted the ringleaders and those within the camp who were clearly 'out of control', although this is admittedly speculative.

[27] While this singularly menacing threat may have materialized (in part) when the people were subsequently struck with plague (Exod. 32:35), it is most unlikely that Israel took this plague to be the end of the matter (Gowan 1994: 228).

[28] While Yahweh's initial refusal to accompany the Israelites any longer (Exod. 33:3) further underscores the seriousness of their offence, Yahweh presents it more as an expression of grace than of judgment.

[29] Admittedly, there is some ambiguity in Exod. 33 over whether or not Yahweh is going to accompany his people – not helped by the unfortunate addition of 'with you' in Exod. 33:14 (ESV; NIV/TNIV). However, as Moberly plausibly suggests (1983: 61–65), two quite different things are probably on view: (a) Yahweh's general guidance through his angel (Exod. 33:2; cf. Exod. 32:34; 23:20–23); (b) Yahweh's personal presence in their midst as represented by the tabernacle shrine (i.e. at this stage the plans for the tabernacle are suspended, as is reflected in the temporary makeshift 'Tent of Meeting' and its location mentioned in Exod. 33:7–11). Alternatively, this is simply the writer's way of showing us God struggling with his options (Gowan 1994: 229).

[30] It is important to see that the issue with which Yahweh (and Moses) wrestles in these verses is 'the moral problem of how a holy God can abide with a sinful people' (Moberly 1983: 67). The resolution for which Moses intercedes successfully here is the maintenance of Yahweh's relationship with Israel purely on the basis of his grace. While the request to see Yahweh's glory may initially appear somewhat abrupt, it is much less so when it is noted with Gowan (1994: 232–233) that elsewhere in Exodus God's glory is associated with his presence and guidance; hence this is less a request for a *visio dei* in general, but a request that God would visibly demonstrate his answer to Moses' intercession.

[31] Such grace does not exclude any idea of further judgment, as is clear from the theophany Moses does experience (Exod. 34:5–7), and the freedom Yahweh is said to have in exercising mercy and compassion (Exod. 33:19). Even so, the emphasis in Exod. 34:6–7 is clearly on Yahweh's grace, rather than on his wrath or the obedient response of his people (cf. Exod. 20:5).

demands covenant obedience on the part of Israel. Thus the remaking of the covenant is followed by underscoring Israel's covenant obligations – first those that were particularly relevant in view of the people's recent behaviour (Exod. 34:11–27),[32] and then the covenant code or Decalogue (Exod. 34:28–32).[33] Moses' special role in this renewed (or remade) covenant is highlighted not only by the secondary position of Israel (Exod. 34:27b),[34] but also by the attention drawn to his ongoing work of covenant mediation (Exod. 34:29–35).[35]

As Enns helpfully points out, the golden calf episode is significantly bracketed by the command to keep the sabbath (cf. Exod. 31:12–17; 35:1–3; that is, an instruction to observe the sabbath – itself the covenant sign – is found immediately after the instructions to build the tabernacle and immediately before those instructions are carried out – their implementation having been disrupted by the breach of the covenant involving the golden calf). 'The framing of the rebellion narrative by the Sabbath law indicates that although God's plan has almost been destroyed, it is now proceeding undiminished. God will be with his people, no matter what happens' (2000a: 149).

However, as the subsequent story reveals (cf. the book of Numbers), such an assurance was not intended to offer grounds for complacency for any particular generation who might nevertheless fail to enter the Promised Land – whether through faithlessness, disobedience, or both.

The covenant and Israel's cult

As well as being an expression of worship, the cultic ritual was pedagogical: the Passover taught the later generations about Yahweh's

[32] As Moberly (1983: 95–96; emphasis his) avers, 'The point of these laws is not to renew the covenant on conditions different from those previously obtaining (Ex. 20–24) – their continuing validity is taken for granted – *but to select and emphasize those particular aspects which are relevant to the sinful tendencies which Israel has displayed.*'

[33] Exod. 34:27 seems to identify 'these words' with the immediately preceding stipulations (i.e. Exod. 34:11–26), whereas Exod. 34:28 seems to refer to the ten words inscribed on the original tablets (cf. Exod. 34:1). For a defence of this reading, see Moberly 1983: 101–106.

[34] As Moberly suggests (1983: 105), this renewed covenant is in some sense dependent upon Moses, who has successfully interceded on behalf of his people.

[35] Through the unusual expression 'Moses' face was radiant' (lit. 'horned'; Exod 34:30 my trans.), the writer appears to suggest that God made Moses what the people had wished of the calf – a mediator of the divine presence.

saving power; the sacrifices focused on Yahweh's mercy, justice and the necessity of substitutionary redemption. Thus, like the sacrifices associated with the ratification of the Noahic, Abrahamic and Mosaic covenants, the cultic ritual helped visualize theological truths and was both symbolic and typical – symbolic in that it was a physical representation of a spiritual reality (i.e. the necessity of death to sustain communion between sinful human beings and a holy God); typical in that it foreshadowed an even greater reality (the ultimate means through which human beings and God would be eternally reconciled).

Regular offerings

Leviticus gives details of five regular offerings.[36] All except the cereal offering involved animal sacrifice, so they are often referred to as sacrifices. The ritual is the same in most cases. Indeed, Leviticus says more of the ritual than of the spiritual reality behind it.[37] The verb 'to make atonement/to cover' (*kipper*; cf. *kappōret*, 'mercy seat') occurs frequently in Leviticus 1–7 (e.g. Lev. 1:4.). It is probably related to the noun meaning 'ransom price' (*kōper*), and would therefore mean 'to pay a ransom (for one's life)'. While its precise connotation is a much debated issue, as well as the idea of ransoming or restoring to favour by means of suitable payment there is also the idea of propitiation; that is, the averting of God's wrath that human sin has aroused (cf. Gen. 8:21; Job 1:5; Ps. 85:2–3; Mic. 7:18–20).

The fact that the performance of such priestly ritual is anticipated from the inception of the national covenant (cf. the instructions regarding the tabernacle's furniture and personnel in Exod. 25 – 30) indicates that the people's inability to keep their covenant obligations (i.e. as set out in Exod. 20 – 23) is clearly assumed. This elaborate system of making amends not only demonstrates the seriousness of such failure, but also implicitly casts such failure on the part of the congregation as inevitable. That this is indeed the case is demonstrated clearly by the legislation concerning the Day of Atonement ritual, when even the most consecrated Israelite, the Aaronic high priest, must make atonement for his own sins as well as the people's.

The Day of Atonement

While structurally Leviticus 16 is the conclusion of the first major section of the book, it also functions as the book's theological centre,

---

[36] Burnt, cereal, fellowship, sin and reparation.
[37] The psalms and the prophets give more emphasis to inner spiritual attitudes.

binding the two halves together. On the annual Day of Atonement the holiness and purity of both the tabernacle and the nation are in view. As an essential aspect of maintaining harmonious divine–human relationships, the Day of Atonement (Yom Kippur) involved three distinct rituals: (a) the purification of the sanctuary; (b) the sending away of the scapegoat; (c) the presentation of two burnt offerings.

The first closely parallels the ritual involved in the purification offering. The high priest entered the Most Holy Place and sprinkled blood on the ark of the covenant to cleanse both it and the Most Holy Place from pollution caused by sin. This procedure was repeated twice, first with the blood of a bull (atoning for the sins of the high priest and his family), then with the blood of one of two goats (atoning for the sins of the people).

The high priest then placed his hands on the other goat presented by the people (its selection was determined by lots), confessed the totality of Israelite sin over it, and expelled it into the wilderness. Like the person responsible for the incineration of the remains of the first goat, the person responsible for taking the second goat into the wilderness had subsequently to wash his clothes prior to returning to the camp.

In a similar fashion, prior to commencing the third ritual (the burnt offerings) the high priest had to bathe himself (although, in his case, it seems, he put on the same unwashed vestments). Similar to the earlier purification offerings, the two rams atoned for the sins of the high priest and the people respectively.

The role of the scapegoat is unique to the Day of Atonement, sym-bolizing the removal (into the most non-sacred space) of Israel's sin. Thus the blood of one goat is brought into the Most Holy Place, while the scapegoat is driven to the furthest point from God (the wilderness). The question of the precise relationship between both aspects of the ritual is difficult to answer categorically: does the purification offering deal with impurities and the scapegoat with sins? Does the scapegoat complete what the purification offerings could not do (i.e. atone for the sins of the priests)? Or do the two aspects simply fulfil the same function from different points of view? However the details are to be understood, the main point is clear: in some way this movement (of the two goats) restores harmony between God and Israel.

As these two examples illustrate, the central thread running through the Levitical legislation is Yahweh's holiness, as explicitly stated in several places in the book: 'Therefore be holy, because I am holy' (Lev. 11:45; 19:2; 20:26 my trans.). Sacrifice was the means of making the unholy pure again and restoring fellowship in the presence of a holy God who cannot tolerate the presence of sin and uncleanness. In other words, sacrifice was the means by which the central blessing of the covenant – communion between Yahweh and his people – was ensured and maintained.

Covenant renewal at Moab

If covenant is the key theological concept in the Pentateuch as a whole, it is especially so in the book of Deuteronomy. To some extent this is reflected in the book's formal structure, as suggested by the structural parallels (however inexact) drawn by various scholars between Deuteronomy and ancient Near Eastern suzerain–vassal treaties.[38] However, it is equally clear from the book's content and vocabulary. The key Hebrew term (*běrît*) occurs some twenty-six times in Deuteronomy – more than any other book in the Old Testament except Genesis (twenty-seven times) and Chronicles (thirty times). Moreover, the book is essentially an invitation to the next generation to renew the covenant that Yahweh had formerly established at Sinai: the new generation had to obligate themselves to the Mosaic covenant before taking possession of the Promised Land.

The relationship between the covenants at Sinai and Moab

Although in one sense Deuteronomy records a remaking or renewal of the Mosaic covenant with a new generation, there are some significant differences in emphasis, which may suggest that this covenant further qualifies the conditional nature of Israel's unique relationship with Yahweh – especially in relation to her future tenure in the

---

[38] The following similarities are often suggested:

Hittite Treaty Pattern	Deuteronomy
1. Preamble	1:1–5
2. Historical prologue	1:6 – 4:49
3. (3) General stipulations	5 – 11
(4) Detailed stipulations	12 – 26
4. Deposit and public reading	31:9–13, 24–26
5. Witnesses	30:19, 31:26, 32:1
6. Blessings and curses	27 – 28

Promised Land. Yahweh had earlier guaranteed the staged removal of the Canaanites (Exod. 23:30; 34:11). He had also indicated that Israel would likewise be expelled if they failed to meet their covenant obligations (Lev. 18:24–30). This is reiterated even more emphatically in Deuteronomy (cf. Deut. 4:25–26; 8:18–20; 28:21–24, 63; 29:21–28; 30:17–18).

Given the book's negative prognosis, it is clear that such exile from the land is anticipated in Deuteronomy as inevitable. As McConville (1993a: 133–135) observes, Israel's inability to be a faithful covenant partner is highlighted in various ways:

1. The prominent position of Israel's failure in the past (Deut. 1:26–46) at least hints at such recurring phenomena.
2. Calling attention to Israel's unimpressive track record (Deut. 9 – 10) before the long series of laws that they are required to keep, further hints at the likelihood of future failure.
3. Finally, the inevitability of such future failure is reflected in the way that both Moses' third address (Deut. 29:22–28) and song (Deut. 32:15–25; cf. Deut. 31:16–22) assume that the people will indeed fail to fulfil the covenant requirements and so will experience the covenant curses. Indeed, rather than alternative possibilities, in Deuteronomy 30:1 the blessings and curses are presented as successive realities in Israel's life.

Thus as McConville (1993a: 134) concludes, 'The alternatives placed before the people both at 11:26–32 and in ch. 28 seem to be mocked by a theology that claims Israel is constitutionally incapable of choosing the way of life.'

Happily, however, the book does not end on such a negative note. While Israel's incorrigibility makes exile inevitable, even exile to the most remote parts of the earth (Deut. 30:4) will not thwart God's ultimate purpose; rather, the promises made to Abraham will find further fulfilment (Deut. 30:5); the divine–human relationship will be sustained by an inner change (Deut. 30:6).

Therefore, the covenant in Deuteronomy is not simply a remaking of the Sinaitic covenant with a new generation. It is a reaffirmation of obligations laid out in the 'covenant of circumcision' (Gen. 17; cf. Deut. 30:6–10) for all future generations (Deut. 29:14–15), and an anticipation of the 'new covenant' that will guarantee that a divine–human relationship between Yahweh and Abraham's 'seed' will be maintained forever (cf. Jer. 31:31–34) by facilitating the important ethical obligations through Yahweh's circumcision of his people's hearts (Deut. 30:6; cf. Deut. 10:16).

The terms of the covenant in Deuteronomy

The terms of the national covenant ratified at Moab are stated most succinctly in Deuteronomy 26:16–19. While this passage does not use the term 'covenant', the concept is clearly implicit. Indeed, the unusual form of the verb 'to say' (these are the sole Old Testament occurrences [twice] of the hiphil of '*āmar*) possibly reflects covenant or treaty vocabulary.

There is some uncertainty over the best way to translate the opening clause in both verse 17 and verse 18 (cf. NRSV and ESV/TNIV). While the hiphil (causative) form of the verb would suggest 'you have made the Lord say that . . .', it may be better to understand it here in the sense of accepting or consenting to what someone says; thus, 'you have agreed to Yahweh's declaration that . . .' Whatever translation is adopted, it is clear that each declaration incorporates obligations undertaken by both parties to the covenant. There may even be some symmetry in the twin declarations (so Mayes 1979: 339). Thus understood, Deuteronomy 26:17 refers to one obligation undertaken by Yahweh (viz. that he will be Israel's God) and three obligations undertaken by Israel (viz. that they will walk in Yahweh's ways, keep his statutes, commandments and ordinances, and obey his voice). Deuteronomy 26:18–19, on the other hand, refers to one obligation undertaken by Israel (viz. that they will keep Yahweh's commandments) and three obligations undertaken by Yahweh (viz. that Israel will be his special possession, that he will set them above the nations, and that they will be his holy people).

Deuteronomy does not spell out when, precisely, this reciprocal commitment was formally ratified between Yahweh and the Israelites addressed at Moab. There are several allusions to the fact (cf. Deut. 27:9; 29:1, 10–15), but the ratification ceremony is nowhere actually described. Thus the reference to 'this day' in Deuteronomy 26:16 (also 'today' in Deut. 26:17, 18) is somewhat enigmatic. The most straightforward explanation is that, by the very act of assembling and listening to the covenant stipulations through Moses – the mediator of the covenant – the present generation of Israelites were identifying themselves with the commitment that had formerly been made at Sinai, and thus were tacitly giving their consent to the terms of the covenant. It is possible, however, that the record in Deuteronomy is quite selective; that is, an actual ceremony took place at the conclusion of Moses' speech, something that the compiler or the final editor has simply taken as read. In any case, however we understand the allusion to covenant ratification here, it is clear that by means of the reciprocal agreement drawn up between Yahweh and the Israelites on the plains of Moab the special status of Israel in the purpose of God was confirmed (cf. Deut. 29:13).

Again, it is important to remember that Israel's special status (as the people of God) was not an end in itself, but rather a means to an end – namely, the fulfilment of God's universal purpose. By shaping her national life by the laws and institutions of the Mosaic covenant, Israel would bear eloquent testimony to the nations surrounding her (cf. Deut. 4:6–8; 28:9–10). Thus the 'fame, praise and glory' (Deut. 26:19 my trans.), whether heaped upon Israel in the first instance or not (Cf. the NEB/REB translation: 'to bring him praise and fame and glory'), ultimately belong to Yahweh himself (cf. Jer. 13:11; 33:9).

The essential obligation to which Yahweh committed himself was to be Israel's God. Such an obligation was not new. Rather, this was something that was promised as far back as the patriarchal era (cf. Gen. 17:8). Indeed, it is this prospect, and all it entailed (Deut. 26:18–19; cf. Exod. 19:5–6), that serves to tie the Abrahamic and Mosaic covenants together (Deut. 29:12–13).

Thus understood, Yahweh's commitment to be Israel's God evidently assumes the fulfilment of the promise of nationhood (i.e. the fulfilment of the promises concerning both descendants and land). While the former has at least seen a preliminary fulfilment (Deut. 1:10–11; 10:22; 26:5; cf. Deut. 6:3; 13:17), the promise of land remains unfulfilled. Accordingly, Yahweh's fulfilment of the territorial promise is one of the major emphases in Deuteronomy. In fact, with some justification Millar claims that 'in Deuteronomy, to speak of the fulfilment of promise is, in essence, to speak of the land' (1998: 55). While this is a little overstated, it is only just – as is clear from the number of references linking the occupation of the land to the fulfilment of the patriarchal promise (cf. Deut. 1:20–21, 25, 35; 3:18, 20; 4:1, 40; 6:1, 10, 18; 7:1, 8, 12; 8:1, 18; 9:5; 10:11; 11:9, 21; 12:1; 19:8; 26:3, 15; 27:3; 30:20; 31:7, 21, 23; 34:4). Significantly, the boundaries delimited in Deuteronomy 1:7–8 are substantially those of Genesis 15:18–21. Thus Deuteronomy anticipates the imminent fulfilment of the covenant God established with Abraham in Genesis 15, a covenant guaranteeing the first aspect of God's programmatic agenda: nationhood (Gen. 12:2).

Israel, on her part, has committed herself to do everything that Yahweh desires: essentially, by keeping Yahweh's commandments (i.e. the statutes and the ordinances as delineated in Deut. 5 – 26). As Alexander underlines, the obligations to which Israel committed herself were essentially an expression of love and loyalty (2002: 253–264). Love is never mere sentiment or feeling in Deuteronomy; rather, love expresses itself in obedience (cf. Deut. 5:10; 7:9; 10:12–13; 11:1, 13, 22; 19:9; 30:16.). By contrast, disobedience is indicative of the lack of love (cf. Deut. 13:3). Not surprisingly, therefore, 'the central core of Deuteronomy consists of a long list of obligations which the Israelites were expected to keep' (Alexander 2002: 258).

As Yahweh demanded exclusive allegiance, this love must be expressed also in absolute loyalty. The Israelites must love only Yahweh; thus the strong emphasis in Deuteronomy against any idolatrous behaviour (cf. Deut. 4:15–16; 5:7; 6:14; 7:4, 16; 8:19; 11:16, 28; 13:2, 6, 13; 17:3; 28:14, 36, 64; 29:18; 30:17–18). Complete loyalty was essential for the covenant relationship between Yahweh and Israel to be maintained. Israel's continued tenure in the Promised Land depended on it, for – as noted above – this was her *raison d'être* as the people of God.

Subsequent renewals of the national covenant

While the national covenant was periodically renewed in the nation's subsequent history, there is insufficient evidence for the idea of the annual covenant-renewal ceremony postulated by some scholars. Outside the Pentateuch, only seven further renewals of the national covenant are explicitly recorded.[39] Several seem to take place at fairly significant junctures in the biblical narrative.

The first renewal ceremony, taking place just after Israel had entered the Promised Land (Josh. 8:30–35), had been anticipated by Moses on the plains of Moab (cf. Deut. 27 – 28). Admittedly, not all of Deuteronomy 27 – 28 (most notably, Deut. 27:9–10) seems to focus exclusively on a future covenant renewal in the vicinity of Shechem (between Mount Ebal and Mount Gerizim). However, the striking parallels between the latter ceremony (as narrated in Josh. 8:30–35) and Moses' instructions in Deuteronomy 27 – 28 (involving the erection of memorial stones inscribed with Israel's covenant obligations,

---

[39] Arguably there were others, such as under Elijah and Hezekiah, but these lack explicit references to covenant-making or renewal.

the construction details of a Yahwistic altar, the splitting of the tribes between Mount Ebal and Mount Gerizim before the Levitical priests, and public recital of covenant blessing and curse) suggest that the primary focus is on this covenant renewal rather than on whatever ceremony took place earlier on the plains of Moab. Perhaps both occasions had some aspects in common; namely, the recital of covenant blessings and curses, possibly prefaced by the liturgical response to the Levitical declarations (the 'curses' or better 'offences' listed in Deut. 27:15–26). In any case, the narrator twice reminds his readers that this covenant renewal at Shechem had been expressly commanded through Moses, and recorded for posterity in 'the Book of the Law' (Josh. 8:31, 33). While this renewal of the covenant may have re-established Israel's relationship with God after the Ai incident,[40] it seems more likely that it was primarily designed to remind the Israelites about the terms of their tenancy in the land, now that the territorial promise was beginning to find fulfilment. Thus understood, this first renewal ceremony constitutes an acknowledgment and proclamation of the fact that possession of the Promised Land and Israel's faithfulness to her covenant obligations were inextricably related. Hence the material that immediately follows (the covenant made between Israel and the Gibeonites) probably sounds an ominous note for the prospects of the people as a whole.

A further renewal of the national covenant at Shechem took place towards the end of Joshua's life (Josh. 24:1–28),[41] after the first major phase of the settlement in Canaan had been completed (cf. Josh. 23:14–15).[42] The respective emphases of Joshua 23 and Joshua 24

---

[40] So Hess 1996: 172. However, the text seems to suggest that this had already been taken care of by the punishment inflicted on Achan and his family. Moreover, if such a restoration of covenant relationship were needed, one might expect this to have preceded the successful taking of Ai (although, admittedly, this may have proved impossible until Ai was taken care of). The Mosaic instruction regarding covenant renewal in the land had probably been delayed by the fact that until Ai was taken, Israel had not yet established a secure foothold.

[41] Some scholars have discerned ancient Near Eastern treaty patterns in Josh. 24, but while there are certain similarities none of the suggested parallels is exact or conclusive.

[42] While paying careful attention to the text of Joshua should eradicate 'flat' readings of the 'conquest' it describes (see Provan 2003: 148–156), it is nevertheless clear that the promise of land was in some measure realized in the settlement period (cf. Josh. 11:23; 21:43–45; 22:4; 23:1). Clearly, what is in view is subjugation rather than full dispossession, as demonstrated by qualifications elsewhere (e.g. Josh. 13:1–2), the juxtaposition of both positive and negative observations in Joshua 23, and the generally more negative picture portrayed in the book of Judges. Nevertheless, while full possession and retention of the land depended on covenant loyalty, the territorial

may imply a different historical setting for the assemblies described (perhaps further suggested by the naming of the location only in the latter chapter),[43] but thematically these chapters belong together: both focus on Israel's covenant obligation to remain loyal to Yahweh.[44] In any case, the historical context for this particular covenant renewal is doubly significant: (a) it is associated with the beginning of a new stage in Israel's leadership (i.e. from centralized leadership to the more localized variety that marks the period of the Judges); (b) it is associated with the initial fulfilment of God's promise of rest in the Promised Land. Clearly, the issue for Joshua at this juncture was whether or not the Israelites would remain faithful to their covenant obligations now that their leadership was no longer concentrated in one human individual and their situation in Canaan was relatively secure. Responding in the affirmative,[45] the Israelites effectively swear allegiance to Yahweh (Josh. 24:21–22, 27), thus renewing the covenant between Israel and Yahweh.[46] Unfortunately, as their subsequent history shows, Israel's confessed commitment to their covenant obligations was again short-lived (Judg. 2:1–12).

The following covenant renewal ceremonies all take place in the context of national repentance and/or religious reform. The first of these was conducted by Asa, the first of Judah's reforming kings (2 Chr. 14 – 15).[47] Encouraged by the prophet Azariah, Asa removed idolatrous paraphernalia (2 Chr. 15:8; cf. 14:3–5), repaired Yahweh's temple (2 Chr. 15:8), and conducted a covenant ceremony through which he and his subjects wholeheartedly committed themselves to seek after Yahweh (2 Chr. 15:9–15). While not explicitly described as a renewal of the national covenant, it is hard to see how else it would

---

promise made to the patriarchs was at least partially fulfilled under Joshua. However, as the latter forewarned (Josh. 23:12–13), and as Judges so graphically illustrates, Israel's enjoyment of rest in the land was short-lived due to covenant disloyalty. It was not until God's chosen king was installed in Zion that such rest was enjoyed again and more fully. For more on this, see Williamson 2005.

[43] There are also indications of a greater formality in Joshua 24; see Woudstra 1981: 340.

[44] Significantly, both chapters present Israel's covenant obligations as a response to God's faithfulness to his covenant promises.

[45] Joshua's negative rejoinder (Josh. 24:19) is obviously intended as a sombre warning rather than as a statement of absolute fact.

[46] Josh. 24:25 literally reads, 'Joshua made a covenant for the people.' In any case, Joshua is clearly functioning as the human mediator of this divine–human covenant, as Moses had done earlier.

[47] The Chronicler's account of Asa's reign is more comprehensive than the account in Kings which does not explicitly refer to covenant-making.

have been perceived, and the consequent blessing of 'rest on every side' certainly implies a strong connection.

Another such covenant renewal was instigated by the priest Jehoiada, in the context of the demise of Athaliah and the end of a period of idolatry in the southern kingdom (2 Kgs 11:17–18). While not explicitly associated with the national covenant, this covenant, in which both people and king identified themselves as the people of Yahweh (2 Kgs 11:17), marked the beginning of religious reforms (2 Kgs 11:18; cf. 2 Kgs 19:4–16) that are best understood in terms of Israel's covenant obligations under the national covenant.

A somewhat similar, albeit much more significant,[48] renewal of the covenant took place in the reign of Josiah (2 Kgs 23:1–3). Once again, this followed a period of national apostasy, and took place in the context of temple repairs and religious reforms (2 Kgs 22 – 23). On this occasion the immediate catalyst was the discovery of 'the Book of the Law' and the prospect of divine judgment that the latter anticipated. The essence of the covenant was an avowal – on the part of both king and subjects – to submit to Yahweh's lordship ('walk after Yahweh'), wholeheartedly obey Yahweh's commands and fulfil their covenant obligations. Strangely, this renewed commitment proved insufficient to turn back the covenant curses, although this was apparently due to the fact that Josiah had failed to reform the people's hearts and minds.[49] Thus this covenant renewal was simply too little, too late.

Two further covenant renewals are recorded, both taking place early in the post-exilic era, and both involving Ezra (Ezra 10:1–5; Neh. 8 – 10). The first of these (Ezra 10:1–5), with its particular focus on the dissolution of marriages involving foreign women, is clearly linked to the national covenant by its association with 'the command of our God' and 'the law' (Ezra 10:3 my trans.; cf. Ezra 7:10, 26; 9:10–15). Thus, while it evidently served a particular purpose, this was clearly a fresh acknowledgment of all Israel's obligations under the terms of the national covenant.

---

[48] Josiah's covenant renewal is more significant because it emphatically involved the entire nation – all the elders, all the men of Judah, all the inhabitants of Jerusalem, all the people, both small and great were present, and all the people joined in the covenant. It is also more significant because it clearly reflects the teaching of Deuteronomy, and, despite the sincerity of Josiah (at least), this covenant renewal failed to secure a divine 'stay of execution' for the nation.

[49] Hence Jeremiah's accusations of superficiality of the shallowness of the religious reforms amongst the people generally (Jer. 3:10), despite his obvious approval and commendation for Josiah personally (Jer. 22:15–16).

The final covenant renewal (Neh. 8 – 10) follows the rebuilding of the city wall (under Nehemiah) and marks the climax of Ezra's religious reforms. Whether or not some of the material in these chapters originally belonged elsewhere,[50] the present setting suggests that this covenant renewal was the climax of the people's response to Ezra's teaching of the law (Ezra 8). Having acknowledged Israel's history of rebelliousness, as well as Yahweh's righteousness and covenant faithfulness (Ezra 9), all the people and their leaders obligate themselves afresh to the terms of the national covenant (Neh. 9:38; 10:29).[51] They also committed themselves to maintaining Yahweh's temple (Neh. 10:32–39), something more in keeping with the spirit of the Mosaic law than a strict requirement (cf. Exod. 30:11–16; 38:25–26).[52] It is clear from this renewal of the national covenant that these members of the fledgling post-exilic community realized that, in order to enjoy all the covenant blessings Yahweh had promised, faithfulness to the obligations of the covenant was absolutely imperative. However, as the subsequent narrative graphically reminds us, such faithfulness on Israel's part remained fickle (Neh. 13), and so the ultimate fulfilment of God's covenant promises remained unrealized in the centuries that followed.

---

[50] E.g. some scholars suggest that Ezra's reading of the law (Neh. 8) was historically located between the events of Ezra 8 and Ezra 9. While this resolves the difficulty in the inexplicable 13-year gap between Ezra's arrival in Jerusalem and his reading of the law (the principal purpose of his journey; cf. Ezra 7:10), it seems to raise a number of historical problems of its own.

[51] While the idiom used here in Neh. 9:38 is unique (lit. 'we are making a firm commitment'), Neh. 10:29 clearly uses terminology closely associated with covenant-making elsewhere. As Williamson (1985: 333) suggests, the 'curse' was most likely an enacted ritual of a malediction (cf. Jer. 34). Perhaps curse and oath should be taken together (i.e. a sworn curse).

[52] As Williamson (1985: 335) observes, there are a number of verbal echoes that may suggest a deliberate attempt to link Neh. 10:32–39 with Exod. 30:11–16.

Chapter Six

God's royal covenant with David

After Sinai, the next major covenantal development in the outworking of God's purpose comes with the institution of the Davidic or royal covenant. While objections have been raised over the application of covenantal language to Yahweh's dynastic promise to David (2 Sam. 7; 1 Chr. 17),[1] it is generally agreed that – despite the absence of the word *běrît* – these passages recount a covenant-making occasion. Undeniably some features associated with covenant-making elsewhere are missing. For example, unlike all previous covenant initiations, no sacrificial rite or covenant ceremony is described. Admittedly, the immediate literary context speaks of numerous sacrifices being offered (2 Sam. 6:13, 17–18; 1 Chr. 15:26; 16:1–2), yet the temporal gap between the relocation of the Ark and the dynastic oracle (2 Sam. 7:1; 1 Chr. 17:1) seems to imply a dislocation between these two events that renders difficult any attempt to relate the sacrifices associated with the procession of the Ark to the inauguration of the royal covenant. Perhaps the lack of covenant ceremony on this occasion is to be explained by the premise that the royal covenant is simply an extension of the Abrahamic covenant (i.e. Gen. 22), in which case there is no need for the kind of formal ceremony elsewhere associated with the establishment of a covenant.[2]

Continuity with the Abrahamic covenant may also explain the peculiar absence of the Hebrew term *běrît* in these narrative accounts. Indeed, there is no explicit mention in either 2 Samuel 7 or 1 Chronicles 17 of a sworn promise or oath, arguably the key defining characteristic of any biblical covenant.[3] Nevertheless, it is clear from other Old Testament texts that the dynastic oracle delivered by

---

[1] Eslinger 1994: 90. For an incisive critique of Eslinger's rhetorical arguments, see Firth 2005: 81–98.

[2] So T. D. Alexander (in a personal conversation). The absence of a separate covenant sign might also be so explained, although this may simply be a feature of any covenant in which the sworn obligations were unilateral (cf. Gen. 15).

[3] See pp. 39–43 above.

Nathan to David was subsequently understood as constituting a covenant (viz. obligation[s] formally sealed with an oath) (see 2 Sam. 23:5; 1 Kgs 8:23; 2 Chr. 7:18; 13:5; Jer. 33:21; Ps. 89:3, 28, 34, 39; cf. Ps. 132:11–12; Isa. 55:3).[4] Moreover, while the usual word for a covenant may be missing in both 2 Samuel 7 and 1 Chronicles 17, these two parallel accounts recounting the dynastic oracle are not entirely devoid of covenantal concepts and terminology. A key example of the latter is the word *ḥesed* (2 Sam. 7:15; 1 Chr. 17:13), a term sometimes used as a synonym for *bĕrît* and having strong covenantal associations.[5] Following Weinfeld, a number of scholars have also highlighted numerous resemblances between the dynastic promise and the so-called 'covenant of Grant' associated with suzerain–vassal relationships. Gileadi (1988: 158) summarizes these as follows:

1. In response to the exceeding loyalty of the vassal king, the suzerain may bestow on him the unconditional right of an enduring dynasty to rule over a particular city-state.
2. A 'father–son' relationship between suzerain and vassal (also known as the suzerain's 'servant') creates a legal basis for the gift of an enduring dynasty.
3. The suzerain guarantees protection for vassal or his heir by promising to annihilate a common enemy, so long as loyalty to the suzerain is maintained.
4. The suzerain guarantees protection of the vassal's people, with whom a subsidiary agreement is sometimes made.
5. A curse formula is directed against those who violate the rights of vassal or his heirs. If disloyal himself, the vassal will be disciplined by the suzerain, often replaced by a loyal heir.

While suggested parallels with such a land grant have not gone unchallenged,[6] it is nevertheless agreed that genuine analogies between the dynastic oracle and secular treaties do exist that underline the covenantal framework of the Davidic charter. Moreover, as

---

[4] At very least these texts, which undoubtedly allude to this particular occasion in David's life, demonstrate that the dynastic oracle was subsequently understood as a royal covenant, however it was perceived at the time of its institution. For cogent arguments that it was understood as a covenant from its inception, see Firth 2005: 79–99.

[5] Cf. Weinfeld (1977: 258–259). See further the recent discussion of *ḥesed* by Britt (2003).

[6] See Knoppers 1996.

Firth (2005: 79–99) has recently demonstrated through a rhetorical analysis of 2 Samuel 7:1–17, 'a cluster of allusions are developed through form and content that point to the existence of such a covenant'. Thus any discussion of the royal covenant must begin with a detailed examination of 2 Samuel 7 and its parallel text in Chronicles.[7]

The literary and historical context of the dynastic oracle

Both biblical accounts (Samuel and Chronicles) place the dynastic oracle in the immediate context of the settlement of the Ark of the Covenant in Jerusalem. Given the movements of the Ark up until this point, this context is particularly significant theologically: with the coming of the Ark to Jerusalem, Yahweh's self-imposed exile is finally coming to an end (cf. 1 Sam. 4 – 5).[8] Yahweh is once again enthroned in the midst of his people. Thus the sequence of the two chapters highlights the fact that 'Yahweh's kingship must be provided for before the question of Israel's can be taken up' (Dumbrell 1984: 142). Hence one important theological point underlined by the priority of the Ark's relocation in Jerusalem is that David's kingship is subservient to Yahweh's,[9] a fact further expressed by the description of David as Yahweh's 'servant' (2 Sam. 7:5, 19–29) and 'ruler' (2 Sam. 7:8).[10]

In addition, placing the dynastic oracle in the context of the re-location of the Ark of the Covenant serves to bring the royal covenant

---

[7] In addition to these passages that describe the establishment of the royal covenant, McKenzie (2000: 65) notes the following relevant texts: 2 Sam. 23:5; 1 Kgs 8:15–26 (//2 Chr. 6:4–17); 9:1–9 (//2 Chr. 7:12–22); 15:4–5; 2 Kgs 8:19; 1 Chr. 22:12–13; 28:7–10; 2 Chr. 21:7; Jer. 33:14–26; Pss. 89; 132. As McKenzie recognizes, a number of other passages that allude to the royal covenant also warrant discussion; see below.

[8] In the narrative of Samuel the story of the Ark was left suspended after its capture by the Philistines and its subsequent return to the border of Israel. 2 Sam. 6 picks up the theme of the Ark once again, recounting its relocation to Jerusalem, where, apart from a very brief time (2 Sam. 15), it remained until the temple's destruction by the Babylonians. While emphasis on the Ark's pre-Davidic history is not so pronounced in Chronicles, the importance of its isolation during Saul's reign (cf. 2 Chr. 13:3) and its return to centre-stage during David's reign is underlined by the amount of space the Chronicler devotes to its relocation (2 Chr. 13, 15 – 16).

[9] As Robertson puts it, by relocating the Ark to Jerusalem, David 'displayed his desire to see his own rule in Israel related immediately to the throne of God. In this manner, the concept of the theocracy found its fullest expression' (1980: 230).

[10] The use of the Hebrew term *nāgîd* implies that, like all human rulers in Israel, David was vicegerent to Yahweh, Israel's true king (*melek*).

into relation with the national covenant – the covenant with which the Ark was so intimately associated (cf. Exod. 25:10–22; 40:20–21). Such a link is further accentuated by the important Deuteronomic motif of 'rest' highlighted in the Samuel account. While not noted by the Chronicler,[11] the contextual comment in 2 Samuel 7:1 about Yahweh having given David 'rest from all his enemies around him' seems especially significant since this rest appears to have been somewhat provisional and incomplete at this stage (cf. 2 Sam. 7:11).[12] Although some have maintained that the sequence of verbs in 2 Samuel 7:10–11 should be translated in the past tense (as non-converted perfects),[13] there is no compelling reason why these verbs (a weqatal chain following wayyiqtols) should be denied a future (imperfective) force,[14] as is further supported (at least in part) by the Masoretic accents.[15] Admittedly, the narrative sequence here in 2 Samuel most likely reflects theological rather than chronological concerns. Since Hiram, the king of Tyre, reigned approximately 980–940 BC, his collaboration in the construction of the royal palace (2 Sam. 5:11; 1 Chr. 15:1) and hence the dynastic oracle itself (cf. 2 Sam. 7:1) must presumably fall within approximately the last decade of David's reign – that is, after the battles recounted in the immediately following chapters of Samuel and Chronicles had been fought.[16] However, rather than continuing the retrospective look at what Yahweh had already achieved for David, the syntactical shift in the middle of verse 9 is more readily explained if the writer is now anticipating what Yahweh would yet do for David and for Israel. Therefore, the

[11] As several scholars suggest (see Armerding 2004: 39), this omission may reflect the contrast the Chronicler draws between David the 'man of war' and Solomon, his peaceful son.

[12] *Pace* Satterthwaite (1995: 54), who suggests that 2 Sam. 7:10–11 is 'describing the continuance of an already existing state of affairs, not a position that still has to be achieved'. It is difficult, however, to see how the reality of present rest and the prospect of future rest can be reconciled other than in relative terms, and such is certainly implied by the present literary context of the chapter (located between David's past military achievements and his subsequent campaigns).

[13] Kruse (1985: 151) cites Rost (1926: 59 n. 2) and Loretz (1961: 294–296) in support. So too Andersen (1989: 120). Admittedly, the context allows (not 'demands', *pace* Loretz) the past tense. However, the sudden switch from wayyiqtol forms is then incongruous, and surely requires explanation and not mere validation as a grammatically feasible form for a seventh–sixth-century Hebrew writer to employ.

[14] While such a series of weqatal forms is often preceded by an imperfect or imperative form, this is not necessarily so.

[15] Accents placed on the afformatives of weqatal verbs distinguish the consecutive from the non-consecutive form.

[16] David reigned from c. 1011–971 BC.

mainline verbal clauses in 2 Samuel 7:8–11 should be understood as follows:

ʾănî lĕqaḥtîkā	qatal	I took you
wāʾehyê ʿimmĕ ka	wayyiqtol	I have been with you
waʾākritâ ʾet kol ʾōyĕbêka	wayyiqtol	I have cut off all your enemies
wĕʿaśitî lĕkā šēm gādôl	weqatal	I will make for you a great name
wĕśamtî māqôm	weqatal	I will appoint a place
ûnĕṭaʿtîw	weqatal	I will plant them (lit. him)
wahănîḥôtî lĕkā	weqatal	I will give you rest

Thus understood, the rest that David had attained by this stage in his career (2 Sam. 7:1) still fell somewhat short of that which Yahweh had promised. As Dumbrell (1984: 149) puts it, 'On the one hand rest had been given to David, 7:1, on the other hand, rest is yet to come, 7:11.' The theological significance of the rest motif here must not be overlooked, for it signals a salvation-historical watershed. This is suggested not only by how such rest is anticipated in Deuteronomy (cf. Deut. 12:10) – where it is also associated with the establishment of Yahweh's sanctuary (Deut. 12:11) – but also by the reintroduction of the rest motif just prior to the articulation of the dynastic promise itself (2 Sam. 7:11). The 'rest' spoken of in these verses signifies *the* realization (or at least, a very significant fulfilment) of God's promises under the national covenant, and the introduction of the next key stage in the outworking of God's universal purpose: the establishment of a royal line from which the anticipated individual royal seed of Abraham will eventually come.[17]

---

[17] Cf. Gen. 15:4; 17:6; 2 Sam. 7:12. It is worth noting the use of the phrases 'seed after you' and 'go out from your own body' in 2 Sam. 7:12 (my trans.), both of which echo God's promises relating to Abraham's seed.

The promissory focus of the dynastic oracle[18]

The dynastic oracle, prompted by David's express intention of building a house (a permanent residence) for Yahweh, initially comes as something of a surprise. Rather than soliciting such an oracle,[19] David's action – informing Nathan of his intentions to construct a more appropriate building for the Ark – seems designed merely to check that his plans met with prophetic approval, and Nathan's initial reaction confirms that they did. However, what ultimately mattered was divine approval, and this was categorically denied.[20]

The stated rationale behind this negative divine response was threefold: (a) Yahweh had not requested any such edifice for himself, for as long as Israel remained 'on the move', so too must he (2 Sam. 7:5–7);[21] (b) the promised 'rest' had still not yet been fully realized (2 Sam. 7:8–11);[22] and (c) Yahweh had selected another for the task of 'building a house for his Name' in the context of the more secure rest in the future (2 Sam. 7:12–13). A fourth reason for Yahweh's denial is subsequently recounted by David himself; namely, his military exploits had rendered him unsuitable as far as constructing a house for Yahweh was concerned (1 Chr. 22:8; 28:3). Even this, however, may be connected to the same underlying issue: the issue of attaining the 'rest' that Yahweh had promised and before which the construction of a temple for Yahweh was premature (1 Chr. 22:9). Thus

---

[18] The following section will focus primarily on the account in Samuel, drawing attention to the parallel passage in Chronicles only where there are significant differences or where the text in Samuel is exegetically challenging.

[19] David does not seem to be requesting an oracle, nor was Nathan apparently anticipating one either – as is evident from his initial reaction, which was wholly positive.

[20] Many scholars discern the presence of two or more conflicting oracles/traditions on the basis of the different perspectives on temple-building reflected in this chapter. However, the chapter makes perfectly good sense without recourse to such hypotheses. Nathan's change of mind is easily explained by the suggestion that his initial response was merely the expression of his personal opinion rather than a revelatory oracle from Yahweh.

[21] The emphasis in these verses has been variously understood. I am suggesting that the major emphasis is on the fact that Yahweh's circumstances are tied up with those of his people: he cannot 'settle' (*yāšab*) until their settlement – Yahweh's provision of their 'place' (2 Sam. 7:10) – is complete (cf. Deut. 12:10–11). The issue is thus mainly one of appropriate timing, rather than the appropriateness of a temple per se. Armerding (2004) contends that Yahweh was initially opposed to the temple-building idea at any time, but this is difficult to square with the fact that both accounts of the dynastic oracle itself clearly suggest otherwise (2 Sam. 7:13; 1 Chr. 17:12).

[22] Admittedly, this second reason is not stated explicitly. However, in context it is difficult to read these verses – with the emphasis on promises of (more complete) rest – any other way. Moreover, this would appear to be how they were subsequently interpreted; cf. 1 Kgs 5:3–5.

understood, the chief underlying reason for Yahweh's denial lay in the fact that the proper circumstances for the erection of the temple had not yet materialized.[23] Even under David, Israel had still not experienced the rest that Yahweh had promised (2 Sam. 7:9–11).[24] For this reason the promises concerning both David's house and Yahweh's house are prefaced by promises of a more complete rest to come. As Dumbrell (1984: 149) observes, 'The logic of the chapter recognizes that only when this ideal result has been achieved should a sanctuary be built.' Therefore while Yahweh firmly rejected David's plans to build the temple, he did not reject the concept itself. As the subsequent part of this prophetic revelation makes clear, such a temple would indeed be built, although not by David; rather, David's seed and successor would be responsible for constructing this house for Yahweh's Name (2 Sam. 7:12–13). David had been wrong to assume that he should be the one to erect a house for Yahweh (cf. the emphatic 'Are *you* . . .' in 2 Sam. 7:5; cf. 1 Chr. 17:4),[25] but his reasoning – that such an edifice should be constructed once Yahweh had given his people rest – was evidently correct, as confirmed by Yahweh's promise to raise up a successor, establish his kingdom, and delegate to him (the emphatic 'he' in 2 Sam. 7:13; cf. 1 Chr. 17:12) the responsibility of constructing a temple once the anticipated rest had finally been realized.[26] In other words, David was mistaken primarily

[23] This is not to deny the possibility that there may also be a deliberate contrast here between the expectations of Yahweh and those of rival deities, whose royal devotees were expected to express gratitude and/or secure favour by the erection of such a temple. Moreover, there may well have been a number of other issues, such as the appropriateness of initiating and/or erecting such a construction for Yahweh, who could certainly not be confined within such an edifice, and whose blessings stem from grace and not human effort.

[24] Significantly, Yahweh's promises to David (2 Sam. 7:9c, 11b) bracket those applying to Israel (2 Sam. 7:10–11a). Hence David's future and Israel's future are inextricably linked. As Davis (1999: 76) insightfully observes, Yahweh *establishes the Davidic dynasty for the sake of his people . . .* David's kingship is to be the instrument by which Yahweh's exodus redemption reaches its goal, that is, to "plant" (v. 10a; see Exod. 15:17) Israel safely in the land he gave them' (emphasis his). For supporting argument for understanding 'place' (2 Sam. 7:10) as referring to land rather than temple, see Murray (1990).

[25] *Pace* Armerding, who rather sweepingly dismisses 'harmonising Nathan's somewhat ambiguous question in 2 Samuel 7:5 with the clear negative found in 1 Chronicles 17:4' (2004: 40). His reason for doing so (viz. that 2 Sam. 7:5–7 constitutes a 'strong objection to a Temple' per se, only holds true if the emphatic 'you' (2 Sam. 7:5) is effectively ignored.

[26] There may be an intentional Hebrew wordplay between *wāhănîḥōtî* 'I will give rest' (2 Sam. 7:11a) and *wāhăkînōtî* 'I will establish' (2 Sam. 7:12). In any case, the much anticipated 'rest' came in some measure with the establishment of the Solomonic empire.

in the timing, not in the underlying theology of this temple-building enterprise.[27]

Nevertheless, while the opportunity to erect an abode for Yahweh was denied, David's unique role in the outworking of Yahweh's purpose was positively affirmed in the dynastic promise that follows.[28] By means of a subtle wordplay,[29] attention shifts from the house David intends to build for Yahweh to the house Yahweh is going to build for David. As Robertson (1980: 232) observes, 'In both cases, perpetuity is the point of emphasis. David wishes to establish for God a permanent dwelling-place in Israel. God declares that he shall establish the perpetual dynasty of David.' As the wordplay underlines, these two concepts are closely connected, for the permanence of God's 'house' or 'dwelling-place' is contingent upon the permanence of David's 'house' or 'dynasty'. David's rule and Yahweh's presence are bound together: 'God shall maintain his permanent dwelling-place as king in Israel through the kingship of the Davidic line' (Robertson 1980: 233).

Hence the latter house – the Davidic dynasty – will be established forever (2 Sam. 7:13b, 16).[30] Nothing – not even the covenant infidelity of David's successor(s) – will threaten the permanence of David's kingdom and throne.[31] Thus, like some of the ancestral

[27] Significantly, the rationale behind Yahweh's denial in 2 Sam. 7:5–7 confirms this – the premise seems to be that Yahweh cannot have a permanent abode as long as Israel is denied such.

[28] While Nathan's prophetic revelation begins in v. 5, the dynastic promise proper is introduced by the declaration formula in v. 11b. Arguably, it is the latter that marks out this dynastic promise as a covenant, such a divine declaration having the force of an oath (cf. Ps. 110:1, 4).

[29] The same Hebrew term, *bayit*, is used both of the 'house' (i.e. temple) for Yahweh's Name and the 'house' (i.e. dynasty) that Yahweh promises to David.

[30] While even in historical terms, David's dynasty (c. 400 years) was quite remarkable (surpassing even the longest dynasty in Egypt by a century and a half), the full import of the 'forever' qualifying this promise is disclosed in the culmination of the Davidic line in Jesus, Israel's Messiah and David's Son par excellence (cf. Matt. 1:1, 12–16; Rev. 11:15). McKenzie's (2000: 72–75) suggestion that a more limited time-frame was originally envisaged is unconvincing for two reasons: (a) as McKenzie concedes, other texts referring to the Davidic promise 'certainly interpret its eternal nature more or less literally'; (b) it is difficult to see how this promise could engender hope, especially after the collapse of Judah, unless its permanence was assumed.

[31] Although the English text suggests a single successor is in view, the collective Hebrew noun *zera'* may allude to a line of successors. Admittedly, however, the text does seem to focus on one successor in particular, who will also be responsible for the building of the temple. However, unless this particular king's reign is envisaged as lasting forever, the promises of an everlasting dynasty seem to point well beyond the reign of Solomon – as subsequent OT reflection on the dynastic oracle confirms (cf. Pss. 89:30–37; 132:11–12).

promises, the royal promises are couched here in absolute terms.[32] While there is certainly no suggestion that David's successors may act with impunity (cf. 2 Sam. 7:14b), there is an unqualified guarantee that their wrongdoing will never result in a permanent breach in the special adoptive relationship established between Yahweh and the Davidic dynasty (2 Sam. 7:14–16).[33] As Davis (1999: 78) observes, the threefold use of the verb *sûr* (to remove, take away) underlines the absolute security of David's house: 'David's line will never meet Saul's end . . . sin can bring disaster on any current "resident" but cannot demolish the "house" (dynasty).'[34] Thus the major emphasis of the dynastic oracle is that the Davidic dynasty will be firmly and permanently established by Yahweh himself. It is this divine guarantee of an eternal Davidic line that constitutes the essence of the royal covenant.

David's response to the dynastic oracle

While there are several allusions to the dynastic oracle elsewhere,[35] the spontaneous prayer of David himself (2 Sam. 7:18–29) constitutes the earliest theological reflection on the royal covenant. In his submissive, prayerful response David makes several observations:[36]

---

[32] While other texts (see below) expressly qualify the promises made to David, making it clear that they were contingent upon obedience, the certainty of their final realization is nevertheless upheld. For more on this, see below. Arnold (2003: 481) rightly objects, however, to a simplistic conditional/unconditional dichotomy being applied to the biblical covenants, correctly insisting that each covenant involves mutuality, albeit with an asymmetrical focus (e.g. the Davidic emphasizes the promises of the stronger party, God, whereas the Mosaic emphasizes those of the weaker party, Israel).

[33] Interestingly, the Chronicler makes no explicit mention of misbehaviour or divine discipline (cf. 2 Sam. 7:14b), reiterating only the promise of an unbroken relationship (1 Chr. 17:13). As Armerding (2004: 40) observes, this omission is to be explained by the Chronicler's *Tendenz*: 'he has little theological need to concentrate on the potential failures of a son of David; his more immediate concern will be the preservation of the Temple and its worship'.

[34] In a similar vein Knoppers (1998: 100) concludes that 'the Deuteronomist understands the Davidic promises as having conditions and limits. Even though continuity of the dynasty is assured, individual monarchs are subject to the rule of (divinely administered) law and the extent of their domain is not vouchsafed by the basic dynastic promise.'

[35] See below.

[36] As Arnold (2003: 776) observes, 'Perhaps here more than anywhere else we see the contrast between David and Saul.' By the implicit contrast between David and Saul's reactions to Yahweh's prophetic word 'the books of Samuel teach that the king who suitably rules Israel will value Yahweh's prophetic word and obey it faithfully. All future anointed ones will prosper only insofar as they live in consonance with Yahweh's word.'

1. The dynastic promise affirms the special role of David and his successors in the outworking of salvation history (2 Sam. 7:18–21). This seems to be the overarching point in these verses however one understands the notoriously cryptic phrase *wĕzōʾt tôrat hāʾādām* ('and this is the instruction of/for humanity'; 2 Sam. 7:19 my trans.) or the Chronicler's even more opaque, *ûrĕʾîtanî kĕtôr hāʾādām hammaʿălâ* ('you have regarded [favoured?] me as the row/cord of humanity, the ascending'; 1 Chr. 17:17 my trans.). Given its support in the Septuagint, the phrase in Samuel is most probably original, Chronicles possibly reflecting an attempt to clarify its meaning.[37] In any case, the overarching point apparently relates to David's exalted status in the larger scheme of things, arguably the implied meaning of 'this is the instruction of/for humanity',[38] as also suggested by the way the Chronicler's phrase is rendered in the Septuagint: 'you have gazed upon me as a vision/appearance of humanity/a man and exalted me' (my trans.). Thus understood, the dynastic promise has ramifications beyond Israel's borders; it is tied in somehow with God's universal purpose in creation and the prospect of international blessing promised through Abraham (Gen. 12:3) and his royal seed (Gen. 22:18). As Kaiser (1974: 314) puts it, 'it is the plan and prescription for God's kingdom whereby the whole world shall be blessed with the total content of the promise doctrine. It is a grant conferring powers, rights, and privileges to David and his seed for the benefit of all mankind.' By means of this dynastic oracle Yahweh has thus thrust David and his successors centre stage in the outworking of salvation history; it is through the Davidic royal line that Yahweh's ancestral promise of international blessing will eventually be fulfilled.

2. The dynastic promise consolidates the special relationship that existed between Yahweh and Israel (2 Sam. 7:22–24). David's focus shifts in these verses from his own status in the revealed plan of God to that of Israel. But presumably David is still extrapolating here from the promises Yahweh had just given to him through Nathan. Certainly the promise to maintain Israel's divinely chosen dynasty

---

[37] Attempts to 'correct' the Samuel text on the basis of Chronicles and/or a conflated reading are unconvincing; it seems more likely that the Chronicles text reflects an adaptation of a text similar or identical to that in Samuel.

[38] Following Kaiser (1974), several scholars see the phrase in Samuel – meaning something like 'this (the dynastic promise) is the prescription for humanity', alluding to the role David's house will play in human history. There is certainly no grammatical or contextual basis for taking it as an interrogative (as do NIV and NKJV).

had implicit guarantees for Israel itself. Moreover, David is implicitly tracing the significance of the royal promises back to the Sinaitic covenant and the purpose underlying Israel's redemption from Egypt; namely, to be the people through whom Yahweh would make himself known. Clearly, David understands the dynastic promise against this backcloth: Yahweh's earlier promises and their outworking in the experience of Israel. As Arnold (2003: 447) notes, David 'rightly understands that this promise to establish a permanent Davidic dynasty is related to God's great saving acts of old, his deliverance of Israel from Egypt and the conquest of the Promised Land'. Thus, echoing Deuteronomy,[39] Israel's special status is underscored. Not only had Israel a God who was unique (2 Sam. 7:22); Israel had a unique relationship with this God (2 Sam. 7:23).[40] Moreover, as those Yahweh had *established* as his people *forever*, Israel was as permanent as the Davidic dynasty itself (2 Sam. 7:24; cf. 2 Sam. 7:12–16). Like the Davidic king, individual Israelites could certainly forfeit their covenant blessings through unbelief, but the special relationship that existed between God and his people was one that would endure. Yahweh had become Israel's God,[41] and David expresses his confidence that Yahweh would continue to be such. Thus the promise that Yahweh had just made through Nathan is understood in terms of continuity with God's mighty saving acts in Israel's past, consolidating the relationship that already existed between Yahweh and Israel.

3. The fulfilment of the dynastic promise will encourage others to recognize Yahweh's greatness and sovereignty (2 Sam. 7:25–26). Turning from praise to petition, David prays that Yahweh will fulfil his promise. Interestingly, however, what motivates David is not primarily a concern for his own honour (e.g. that the promise relating to his name or reputation, 2 Sam. 7:9, might be realized), but rather a concern for the reputation and acknowledgment of Yahweh (2 Sam. 7:26). 'By making this promise to David a reality, Yahweh will demonstrate his great faithfulness to Israel and show himself different from the whimsical gods of the ancient Near East' (Arnold 2003: 478). Once again, therefore, David ties in the dynastic promise

[39] Cf. Deut. 4:32–39.

[40] Despite the textual and grammatical ambiguity of 2 Sam. 7:23, its overarching point seems clear: as the sole beneficiaries of Yahweh's redemptive acts, Israel is a unique nation.

[41] Note the echo here of the covenant formula; cf. Gen. 17:7; Exod. 6:7; Lev. 26:12.

with Yahweh's universal purpose and the role that the Davidic dynasty will play in its outworking.

4. The dynastic promise evokes confidence and trust but leaves no room for complacency (2 Sam. 7:27–29).[42] Continuing the note of petition, David recalls the essence of the dynastic oracle and, on the basis of Yahweh's trustworthiness, pleads once more for Yahweh to implement his word and fulfil his promise. Framed on either side with reminders of Yahweh's reliability, David's petition underscores nevertheless that there was nothing automatic about the promises God had made – reflecting none of the complacency to which the dynastic oracle (and the related Zion theology) subsequently gave rise. Rather than presuming on God's promises, David made them the basis for prayer, invoking God to put his word into effect.

Subsequent reflection on the royal covenant

As indicated above, subsequent theological reflection on the royal covenant is exhibited in a number of Old Testament texts.[43] With few exceptions, the following discussion is restricted to passages in which the dynastic oracle is unambiguously mentioned.

2 Samuel 23:5

Here, in his future-orientated swansong,[44] David apparently anticipates a righteous ruler whose kingship will result in blessing (vv. 3–4; cf. Ps. 72:6) rather than cursing (vv. 6–7), not just for Israel but for humanity.[45] As Davis (1999: 246) suggests, rather than merely holding up an ideal for Davidic kings (in which case the emphatic stress on divine inspiration seems patently absurd), David is surely anticipating the one through whom God's kingdom will finally

---

[42] The Chronicler renders this last aspect of David's response as an affirmation rather than a prayer, again removing any hint of conditionality evident in the Samuel account.

[43] The following discussion assumes that the events narrated in 2 Sam. 7 formed the basis for subsequent OT reflection on the royal covenant. The direction of literary dependence is a separate issue, and is complicated by the possibility that different biblical authors may have culled their information from a similar independent tradition.

[44] The preceding thanksgiving psalm has looked back on how Yahweh had established the kingdom. Here in David's last official testimony the focus is primarily on how Yahweh will consummate it in the future. Its revelatory nature is emphasized by the repeated use of 'oracle' in the introductory verse and the subsequent stress on the fact that he is communicating Yahweh's word (vv. 2–3).

[45] Note the 'ādām (humanity) in v. 3.

come.[46] This is suggested not only by the rather grandiose description of his kingship (v. 4) but also by the express soteriological purpose of his 'springing up' (v. 5b), metaphorical language significantly used in the Latter Prophets of the future messianic 'Branch' (cf. Jer. 23:5; 33:15; Zech. 3:8; 6:12).[47]

Identifying such a ruler with his own dynasty,[48] David alludes to the oracle of 2 Samuel 7,[49] here describing it in terms of an everlasting or perpetual *covenant*. The substance of this covenant relates to David's 'house',[50] whose identification with this anticipated righteous ruler is equated with the fact that its legitimacy has been divinely sanctioned – 'signed and sealed' by the aforementioned covenant.[51] Thus the basis for Israel's hope in a future Davidic king who would reinvigorate the earth is the present reality of the everlasting covenant established between Yahweh and David.

1 Kings 2 – 11

Within these chapters recounting the reign of David's immediate successor, the dynastic promise is explicitly mentioned several times: in David's charge to Solomon (1 Kgs 2:2–4); in Solomon's self-maledictory oath (1 Kgs 2:24); in Solomon's verdict on Shimei (1 Kgs 2:45); in Solomon's message to Hiram (1 Kgs 5:3–5); in Yahweh's cautionary word to Solomon (1 Kgs 6:11–13); in Solomon's public address (1 Kgs 8:15–21) and dedicatory prayer (1 Kgs 8:23–26) after the completion

[46] Verse 3b literally reads, 'Ruler/ruling over mankind, righteous. Ruler/ruling, fear of God.'

[47] The Jeremiah passages seem especially pertinent to David's oracle here in 2 Sam. 23. Not only is this 'righteous Branch' related to David, but the nature of his reign (i.e. in biblical terms, 'reigning wisely' is synonymous with 'ruling in the fear of God') and the consequences of his coming (i.e. salvation) are similarly expressed. While the texts in Zechariah refer initially to Joshua, it is significant that the key role in which he is involved is the building of Yahweh's temple (cf. 2 Sam. 7:13), foreshadowing an even greater temple-building by a 'greater than Solomon' to come.

[48] The first line of v. 5 should either be taken as emphatic ('Indeed, surely my house is so with God') or, following the MT, as an interrogative ('Indeed, is not my house so with God?'). AV is misleading.

[49] Cf. esp. 2 Sam. 7:12–16.

[50] As Firth (2005: 98) observes, the use of *bayit* (used only once since 2 Sam. 7 in the special sense of 'dynasty'; cf. Nathan's judgment speech 2 Sam. 12:8–10) here is clearly significant. However, rather than indicating that God's justice had by this stage been fully exhausted on the Davidic dynasty (so Firth), it may simply highlight David's confidence that, despite the judgment Nathan had pronounced, Yahweh's covenant love would triumph over divine justice; cf. 2 Sam. 22:51.

[51] Such is the most likely connotation behind the phrase 'arranged and secured in every part' (TNIV). It carries the weight of a legally binding document (so Gordon 1986: 311).

of the temple; in Yahweh's response to Solomon's prayer (1 Kgs 9:4–9); and in Yahweh's judgment on Solomon's apostasy (1 Kgs 11:11–13).[52]

These passages show that Solomon fulfilled the dynastic promise, although only in part. Not only was he the biological son who by succeeding David to the throne establishes the dynasty (1 Kgs 2:24, 45; 3:6–7), but he was also the one who, by divine providence (1 Kgs 5:3–5), was responsible for the construction of the temple in Jerusalem (1 Kgs 8:15–21, 23–26). However, while Solomon's reign constituted the primary fulfilment of the dynastic promise, it did not represent the complete or ultimate fulfilment. Such is clear from the references to subsequent heirs of the dynastic promise (1 Kgs 2:4; 8:25; 9:6), and from the fact that Solomon's reign, however glorious, was relatively short-lived and ended somewhat ignominiously with the imminent prospect of large-scale reduction in its extent and influence (1 Kgs 11:11–13).

This latter passage illustrates one of the recurring refrains throughout the preceding texts: the dynastic promise was in some sense qualified by the covenant fidelity of those it encompassed (1 Kgs 2:4; 6:12–13; 8:25; 9:4–9). On the one hand, such fidelity, to the national covenant (1 Kgs 2:3; cf. Deut. 17:18–20), was incumbent on each king in the Davidic line and was clearly a prerequisite for the ongoing and ultimate fulfilment of the dynastic promise. On the other hand, the absence of such covenant fidelity, hence a failure to reflect Yahweh's righteous rule, would inevitably result in Yahweh's abandonment of his temple and his withdrawal from his people, with all the ominous ramifications for national security that such entailed (1 Kgs 9:6–9).

In many respects the rest of Kings is an extended illustration of this latter point, serving to show how the covenant infidelity of the Davidic kings ultimately brought about the collapse of the kingdom, just as Yahweh had promised.[53] Nevertheless, as well as this negative note, the more positive undercurrent in Kings is never far from sight: despite the failures of Judah's royal house, Yahweh ensured that the Davidic line continued in unbroken succession so that, even after the collapse of the kingdom, the Davidic 'seed' – and hence the prospect held out in the royal covenant – was not obliterated (cf. 2 Kgs 25:27–30).

---

[52] In addition, the dynastic promise is probably alluded to in Solomon's sentence on Joab (1 Kgs 2:33), in Solomon's encounter with Yahweh at Gibeon (1 Kgs 3:6–9), and in the grandiose portrayal of Solomon and his kingdom throughout these chapters (cf. the psalms discussed below).

[53] For the pivotal place of the Davidic covenant in the history of the prophetic word (i.e. the 'fulfilment motif') narrated in Kings, see Robertson 1980: 255–269.

Psalm 89

While it is impossible to ascertain the date of this psalm or the precise historical circumstances to which the psalmist alludes, the underlying issue is not in doubt: the royal covenant has apparently been placed in jeopardy (Ps. 89:39).[54] Having begun by acknowledging Yahweh's enduring faithful love,[55] the psalmist introduces his central theme – the solemnized promise that Yahweh had made to David concerning an everlasting dynasty (Ps. 89:3–4).[56] The following hymn of praise (Ps. 89:5–18) appears to pick up a number of motifs from 2 Samuel 7, namely Yahweh's uniqueness (Ps. 89:6–8) and the acclamation of his name (Ps. 89:12, 15–16), while highlighting his awesome power (hence the absolute reliability of his promises) and subtly reintroducing the main concern – the privileged status of Yahweh's designated king (Ps. 89:17–18). Thus, after more fully rehearsing the terms of the royal covenant (Ps. 89:19–37), the crux of the problem is finally arrived at (Ps. 89:38–45) and the psalmist concludes by imploring Yahweh to rectify the present crisis by demonstrating his faithful love afresh (Ps. 89:46–51).[57]

The importance of this psalm for the present discussion lies in the fact that it elaborates on the promises narrated in 2 Samuel 7.[58] Other than explicitly defining the promise as a covenant/sworn oath, the

[54] If the title implies authorship, it was originally composed in the late Davidic or Solomonic era (cf. 1 Chr. 15:17, 19). Even so, the crisis it addresses could be one of several occasions when the dynastic promise may have seemed under threat (e.g. the rebellion led by Sheba or that led by Jeroboam). For others, the crisis precipitating this psalm was the Syro-Ephraimite attempt to oust Ahaz, the crisis posed by Athaliah's purge, or the empty Davidic throne brought about through Babylonian exile. Whether the language of vv. 40–45 should be interpreted literally or figuratively, the resonance with similar sentiments in Lamentations (e.g. compare v. 40 with Lam. 2:8, and v. 41 with Lam. 1:10, 12; 2:8) may well point to the occasion with which the canonical form of the psalm was associated – especially if, as Kidner suggests (1975: 324–325) the situation depicted in v. 45 alludes to Jehoiachin's circumstances (cf. 2 Kgs 25:27, 29).

[55] For use of both ideas in association with covenant, see Deut. 6:9. The perpetuity or permanence of both is the key motif in the psalm; cf. vv. 5, 8, 14, 24, 33, 49.

[56] Significantly, not only is the dynastic promise described here as a covenant, but is further explicated in terms of a divine oath. See also vv. 28, 34–35, 39, and 49.

[57] The final verse appears to be a colophon for Book III; cf. similar doxologies at the end of the other main sections of the psalter.

[58] The issue of literary priority is complicated by the fact that the canonical form of 2 Samuel probably dates to the early exilic period, long after the demise of Ethan the Ezrahite. Since the canonical psalter is later still, the priority of the text in 2 Samuel is nevertheless possible. However, the suggestion that all three canonical texts (2 Sam. 7; 1 Chr. 17; Ps. 89) borrow – to a greater or lesser extent – from an original, independent source is equally plausible. But whatever the direction of any literary dependency, it is clear that Ps. 89:19–37 constitutes an exegetical interpretation of the dynastic oracle (see Ps. 89:19; cf. 2 Sam. 7:4–5); hence its significance for the present discussion.

initial summary (Ps. 89:3–4) adds little to the dynastic oracle as narrated in Samuel.[59] However, in the central section of this psalm (vv. 19–37) the dynastic oracle is expanded considerably.

As in 2 Samuel 7, emphasis is placed on Yahweh's role in David's remarkable career, with attention focused almost entirely on what Yahweh had promised to do for his anointed servant.[60] In addition to crushing his foes (Ps. 89:22–23; cf. Gen. 22:17), magnifying his name (Ps. 89:24; cf. Gen. 12:2), extending his dominion (Ps.89:25; cf. Exod. 23:31), and appointing him as his own heir (Ps. 89:27; cf. Exod. 4:22–23), Yahweh had promised, most notably, to maintain his covenant with David and his seed for ever (Ps. 89:28–37). Here the irrevocability of the covenant is underlined not only by the frequent use of 'for ever' (Ps. 89:28, 29, 36) and the strong negative particle (Ps. 89:33–35), but also by the entities – the heavens, the sun and the moon – with which its permanent status is reinforced (Ps. 89:29, 36, 37). While the precise nature and role of the 'witness in the sky' (Ps. 89:37b TNIV) is debatable,[61] the underlying point – further emphasizing the enduring nature of the dynastic promise – is not in doubt.

However, all Yahweh's promises to David, and particularly that of an enduring dynasty, had evidently been called into question by the prevailing circumstances: Yahweh has apparently rejected his anointed servant, spurned the royal covenant,[62] and brought humiliating defeat and shame on the Davidic house (Ps. 89:38–45). Significantly, the psalmist acknowledges that the covenant allowed for some measure of divine discipline (Ps. 89:30–32).[63] Indeed, it is clear from his use of plurals here that more than one unfaithful king

[59] However, it is interesting to see that Yahweh's promise to 'establish David's seed forever' is unpacked with a promise to '*build* David's throne from generation to generation' (Ps. 89:4 my trans.). The deployment of this key verb from 2 Samuel is unfortunately lost in the NIV/TNIV.

[60] The psalmist brings together the messages about David given through Samuel and Nathan respectively, as the majority MT reading, 'your faithful ones' (v. 20; English v. 19), suggests – although the latter may also incorporate oracles of assurance given to David personally attested in several of his psalms (so Kidner 1975: 322). One such psalm (Ps. 2) is discussed briefly below (cf. also Ps. 110).

[61] Some have suggested a further simile in v. 37 (i.e. to God's bow in the clouds; Gen 9:13–14), whereas for others the 'witness in the sky' is either the sun or moon, representing the heavenly assembly and functioning as a covenant witness, as in other ancient Near Eastern and biblical texts. For more on the latter, see Mullen 1983: 209–217.

[62] Cf. Lam. 2:7, the only other occurrence of this root in the OT. There the NIV/TNIV reads 'abandoned' and ESV reads 'disowned'.

[63] As Knoppers (1998: 99) insists, like Nathan's oracle in 2 Sam. 7, Ps. 89 contains a bilateral element, and therefore does not stress the absolute nature of the promise at the expense of the obligations placed on its recipients.

in the Davidic line could anticipate such punishment.[64] Nevertheless, the present crisis was obviously of such magnitude that any such royal discipline in Israel's past paled into insignificance.[65] To all intents and purposes it looked as though Yahweh's promises had failed and the divine oath counted for nothing.

Yet despite appearances, the psalmist clings resolutely to his faith and confidence in Yahweh, imploring him to take action before it is altogether too late,[66] and appealing once more to his faithful love as the basis for bringing about a dramatic reversal to the present dire circumstances.

Thus it is clear from this psalm that the dynastic promise was understood in terms of a solemn oath, sworn by Yahweh to David, the essence of which was the permanent and unending nature of the Davidic dynasty. Enduring as long as the heavens themselves, David's throne could not remain defiled, any more than the solemn promise of Yahweh could remain unfulfilled.

Psalm 132

The theme of this psalm, one of fifteen 'Songs of Ascent',[67] is likewise the dynastic promise made by Yahweh to David – although the emphasis here is on 'the close relationship between the dynasty and the sanctuary' (Allen 2002: 275). The psalm neatly divides into two parts,[68] the first concentrating on the efforts (chiefly David's) put into finding a resting place for Yahweh (Ps. 132:1–10), and the second

[64] I.e. the psalmist did not understand the 'seed' of the dynastic oracle to have only one referent (whether Solomon or the ultimate scion of David, as some suggest), but interpreted the word in its collective sense. For Heim (1998: 299–300), however, this is one of several changes the psalmist has made to the original promissory (non-covenantal) oracle. While Heim maintains that these changes go beyond the source text (i.e. 2 Sam. 7), he does not agree with Fishbane's analysis that they go against it (Heim 1998: 301–303).

[65] As Heim (1998: 297–298) avers, 'According to Psalm 89, the covenant stipulations did not exclude military defeat and national catastrophe . . . However, this catastrophe which prompted the lament in Psalm 89 cannot be just *any* defeat, for this would not have provoked the daring complaint of vv. 39–52, where the Lord is implicitly accused of unfaithfulness to the covenant stipulations (especially in v. 50). Most likely, therefore, Psalm 89 is a prayerful response to the historical disaster of the exile' (emphasis his).

[66] In view of the way the Davidic oracle finds its ultimate fulfilment through the death and resurrection of Jesus, the psalmist's question in v. 48 now seems somewhat ironic. Cf. Rev. 1:5.

[67] These pilgrim psalms were most likely sung by worshippers as they made their way up to Jerusalem for the festivals in Israel's annual religious calendar.

[68] So most scholars, although both the exact point of transition and the precise relationship between the two parts is certainly debatable; see Allen (2002: 264–266).

focusing on Yahweh's subsequent promises to David (Ps. 132:11–18). The connection between these two foci (i.e. the respective oaths of David and Yahweh) lies at the very heart of the psalm's principal request – that David's efforts should not go unrewarded in the psalmist's own day (Ps. 132:1).[69]

Rather than constituting an inclusio that brackets the first half (so Allen 2002: 264–266), verse 10 may simply introduce the second part of the psalm. Understood accordingly, the latter section (vv. 10–18) does not constitute some sort of liturgical/oracular response(s) to the prayer, as several exegetes suggest.[70] Instead, these verses are an extension of the prayer, articulating further reasons why Yahweh should respond to the petitioner(s); namely, the promises he has made concerning David and Zion. This interpretation removes the need to discern additional voices within the psalm, such as that of the Davidic king and some cultic official – whether priest or prophet. Other than the cited words of David and Yahweh, and possibly liturgical responses of the worshippers,[71] one main speaker is implied throughout; namely, the psalmist. His concern is with the manifestation of Yahweh's kingship in Zion, as expressed through the representative reign of the Davidic king.[72]

In relation to the royal covenant, this psalm is significant for a number of reasons. Like Psalm 89, it describes the dynastic oracle of 2 Samuel 7 in terms of a 'sworn oath' (Ps. 132:11) and perhaps also a

[69] This rather vague petition of the opening verse is apparently fleshed out in the more specific requests of vv. 8–9, v. 10b, to which there is probably some allusion in the divine promises with which the psalm concludes (vv. 14–18). The verbal parallels (vv. 8–10; cf. 2 Chr. 6:41–42) with Solomon's prayer during the dedication of the temple may suggest the occasion the psalm is commemorating (and the worshippers were reenacting), even if the composition was considerably later. Thus understood, the psalm is a prayer (like the potted version in 2 Chr. 6:41–42) that Yahweh will manifest his presence in Zion and fulfil his covenant with David.

[70] It seems to me that a perceived liturgical arrangement may have been read too quickly into the structure of this psalm, consequently resulting in a skewed interpretation of its contents on the part of many commentators. Rather than reading vv. 14–18 as Yahweh's response to the petition of vv. 8–10, these verses can equally be read as promissory grounds supporting the legitimacy of the psalmist's request(s).

[71] While the first plural forms of address in vv. 6–7 may arguably be ascribed to the worshipping pilgrims, they might equally be understood as the sentiments originally expressed by David and his subjects (cf. 1 Chr. 13:1–3), whether or not they now constitute a liturgical response within the psalm itself.

[72] While the reigning Davidic king had obviously a vested interest in the petition of v. 10, he is not the only Israelite who might conceivably offer such a prayer. Thus, while the king may be the implied speaker, he is not necessarily so, and the plural summons in v. 7 suggests that the psalmist is articulating the sentiments of all the pilgrims involved in what was presumably a ritual re-enactment and procession to Zion.

'covenant'.[73] Interestingly, David's express intent to relocate the Ark to Jerusalem is similarly described as a solemn oath he had sworn (Ps. 132:2), even though there is absolutely no hint of such an oath by David within the Samuel narrative. For this reason, some dismiss the oath language of this psalm as simply cultic elaboration. However, this psalm may well be preserving information derived from a more detailed tradition of the royal covenant's inauguration than that found in the Samuel narrative. In any case, it is clear from this psalm that, whatever may have been the original perception, the dynastic oracle was subsequently understood in terms of a royal covenant.

It is also clear from Psalm 132 that this royal covenant was perceived in absolute terms. Like Psalm 89, the perpetuity of this covenant forms the basis for the psalmist's prayer. The essential argument underlying all the petitions in this psalm is that Yahweh must surely make good on assurances he has given regarding Zion and her divinely chosen king.[74] While stated more categorically than previously,[75] even the conditional statement qualifying the dynastic promise (Ps. 132:12) does not imperil its ultimate fulfilment (cf. vv. 13–18). Otherwise the divine assurances cited in the latter half of the psalm lose considerable force and the psalm's emphasis on Yahweh's promises rather than the covenant fidelity of David's successors makes little sense. Rather, as Kaiser (1995: 89) correctly points out, 'The conditional "if" of Psalm 132:12 cannot affect the certainty of the promise; it can only affect an individual's participation in the benefits of that promise, while the promise itself remains inviolable.'

The most significant contribution of this psalm, however, is the way that it connects the dynastic oracle with the relocation of the Ark and Yahweh's intentions for Zion.[76] Such a connection is made not only by the respective oaths that parallel each other in the psalm's two panels, but also – and more pointedly – by the juxtaposition of the dynastic oracle and Zion's significance within the second half of the psalm: Yahweh's choice of Zion and its consequent blessings (vv.

[73] The latter depends on whether the 'covenant' in view in v. 12 is that associated with David or Moses, an issue over which there is little consensus (see Allen 2002: 268–269).

[74] As Clements has recently observed (2003: 42), 'the assertions of Pss. 89:19–37 and 132:11–12 affirm that even a failure to adhere to this commitment to the divine demands would not lead to the annulment of the covenant'.

[75] I.e. here there is no caveat underlining Yahweh's faithful love despite their disloyalty.

[76] The association between David's intentions for the Ark and Yahweh's assurances to David is already clear in the Samuel narrative. However, here the relationship between the Ark of the covenant and the dynastic oracle is spelt out more fully.

13–16) is bracketed by the dynastic promise (vv. 11–12) and its ultimate fulfilment (vv. 17–18). Indeed, Yahweh's choice of Zion as his perpetual dwelling place is linked causally to the dynastic promise: the former is the basis for the latter. Hence the perpetual nature of the Davidic dynasty is founded on Yahweh's prior selection of Zion as the place where his own kingship will be exhibited. Consequently, Yahweh's commitment to the Davidic dynasty (vv. 11–12) and the future blessing of Zion's people (vv. 15–16) are inextricably linked by Zion's unique status as the place Yahweh has chosen to manifest his kingship (vv. 13–14) through the ultimate Davidic king (vv. 17–18).[77]

Allusions to the dynastic oracle elsewhere in the psalter

While not mentioned explicitly, the dynastic promise seems to be foundational for several other psalms,[78] among which the following two are undoubtedly the most important:

Psalm 2

Highlighting the futility of human rebellion against Yahweh and his anointed king, the psalmist appears to allude to the dynastic promise in his elaboration of the decree that makes such revolt ridiculous (Ps. 2:7; cf. 2 Sam. 7:14).[79] Thus understood, the theological centre of this psalm (vv. 7–9) is a clear reaffirmation of the royal covenant. It is in this context that the language of adoption is employed in the psalm: 'in the OT the king was not by nature "son of God," nor did he enter the sphere of divinity by the nature of things through his enthronement; but at the accession to his kingship he was declared to be the son by the definite will of the God of Israel'.[80] Hence it is futile to rebel against Yahweh's anointed king, because, in view of the royal covenant, his position is absolutely secure: he has been made heir of absolutely everything and his kingship over all the nations has been divinely guaranteed. Thus, instead of rebelling against him, people should give him homage, take refuge in him, and thus experience his blessing rather than his wrath.

---

[77] The identity of this ultimate Davidic king is suggested by the piling up of Messianic motifs in these two verses: the 'horn' (Ps. 89:24; cf. Luke 1:69) whom Yahweh will cause to 'sprout' (cf. 2 Sam. 23:5).

[78] I.e. those in the so-called 'Royal Psalms' category.

[79] As well as the change in tense and personal pronouns, the statements are inverted and the verb 'to bear' is used in the second line by the psalmist. However, despite these changes, an allusion to the dynastic oracle seems probable.

[80] M. Noth, cited in Kraus 1988: 131.

Psalm 72

This is a prayer for the king, possibly originally offered by David on Solomon's behalf.[81] The latter inference makes best sense of both the psalm's title, with its reference to Solomon, and the postscript, ascribing authorship to David. Admittedly, neither phrase is unambiguous, but this seems to be the most straightforward reading strategy, as Heim (1995: 235) suggests. In any case, whatever the original significance of the prayer, its inclusion in the post-exilic collection of the psalter suggests 'a contemporary relevance for succeeding generations' (Heim 1995: 226). Hence this intercession for the present king (initially, Solomon) has in the post-monarchy setting become 'a model prayer . . . for the restoration of the monarchy/kingdom' (Heim 1995: 225).

While the psalmist never actually cites the dynastic oracle, the same underlying kingship ideology is transparent throughout. Moreover, both the psalm's association with David and the opening description of the king as 'the royal son' subtly remind the reader of the Davidic covenant.[82] What is hoped for is clearly the perfect king, the one through whom the dynastic oracle will find complete fulfilment. Accordingly, the prospects anticipated for this ideal king and his reign are replete with imagery used elsewhere in association with the royal covenant and/or its anticipated heir.[83] This is reflected:

1. *In the character of his kingship.* Endowed with divine justice and righteousness (Ps. 72:1), this king will rule justly (Ps. 72:2; cf. 2 Sam. 23:3); the oppressed and afflicted will be delivered from their troubles (Ps. 72:12–14; cf. Ps. 132:15–16); the oppressor will be crushed (Ps. 72:4; cf. 2 Sam. 23:6–7; Ps. 89:23; Ps. 132:18); and the righteous will flourish (Ps. 72:6–7; cf. 2 Sam. 23:4; Ps. 132:15–16).
2. *In the extent of his kingdom.* All geographical boundaries having been removed (Ps. 72:8), this kingdom will know no political limits, (Ps. 72:8–11; cf. Ps. 89:22, 25),[84] and its king will mediate blessing on an international scale (Ps. 72:17b; cf. 2 Sam. 7:19).

---

[81] The most likely context, both historically and liturgically, is the king's coronation, although this is admittedly speculative.

[82] Heim 1995: 235.

[83] Although the NIV uses the indicative mood in vv. 2–14, it seems better to translate all of vv. 2–17 as jussives (as do ESV and TNIV) or, as Heim suggests (1995: 226), to translate vv. 2–7 and 9–11 as indicatives which 'express future events contingent on the fulfilment of the requests in vv. 1 and 8'.

[84] As Heim (1995: 243–244) observes, 'The geographic allocations in v. 10 designate the uttermost ends of the psalmist's world . . . The tribute of people from these remote places shows that they are within his dominion.' As he further observes, v. 11 leaves us

3. *In the permanence of his reign*. This king will have no temporal bounds, but will reign forever (Ps. 72:5, 7; cf. 2 Sam. 7:13; Ps. 89:29, 36–37).[85]

Despite his promising start, this prayer for the royal son was clearly not fulfilled in the reign of Solomon. However, given its foundation in the royal covenant, an affirmative answer to this prayer could never ultimately be in doubt.

The royal covenant in the latter prophets

Isaiah

While the royal covenant is explicitly mentioned or alluded to a number of times in the prophetic corpus,[86] primarily with a view to its final fulfilment in the ultimate Davidic King, it constitutes the dominant subtext in the book of Isaiah.[87] As Clements has recently pointed out, 'two main themes – God's chosen dynasty of kings and the glory of the holy city from which it ruled – form the backbone of the entire Isaiah book' (2003: 65). As noted above, the Davidic dynasty and the Davidic city are inextricably linked in the royal covenant. Therefore it is not surprising that the main focus of this prophetic book should alternate between the city and the monarchy throughout.

In keeping with the main focus of the dynastic oracle, however, the following discussion will concentrate on passages where Yahweh's relationship with the Davidic monarchy seems to be primarily in view. Undoubtedly, the most obvious and important of these are chapters dealing with crises when the reigning Davidic king was under direct threat – those that occurred during the reigns of Ahaz (Isa. 6–11) and

---

in absolutely no doubt, with its twofold 'all' and its chiastic structure (indicating completion). Even if the imagery was originally hyperbole, the deliberate ambiguity and inverted order in Ps. 72:8 (cf. Exod. 23:31) suggests a universal interpretation, which is further supported by how this verse is picked up in Zechariah (Zech. 9:9–10) and by how the latter is cited in the Gospels (Matt. 21:5; John 12:15). See Heim 1995: 244–247.

[85] Admittedly, the MT (v. 5 reading 'they will fear you' rather than Septuagint, 'he will endure') suggests a permanent consequence of this king's rule rather than a permanent endurance, and arguably reflects the best reading (see Heim 1995: 238–243). However, even if the fear of Yahweh is the focus in v. 5, this permanent result may imply a permanent reign, as further attested in v. 7.

[86] Jer. 23:5–6; 33:20–26; Ezek. 37:24–27; Amos 9:11–12; Mic. 5:2–5.

[87] See Clements 2003: 40–65.

Hezekiah (Isa. 36–39).[88] Both passages highlight the necessity of trusting in Yahweh (and, implicitly, in the dynastic promise). While the historical circumstances are less clear in chapters 28 – 33, the underlying issue is apparently the same: the need to maintain confidence in Yahweh and trust in the promises he has made concerning the Davidic dynasty.

In the first of these crises the Davidic dynasty came under threat when Ahaz refused to join a northern alliance that had formed to stave off the growing military threat from Assyria. Thus, having failed to persuade him, the Syro-Ephraimite alliance made plans to oust Ahaz and replace him with one 'ben Tabeel' (Isa. 7:6).[89] While, as Clements (2003:45) rightly insists, the precise identity of this otherwise unknown character remains uncertain, the assurance offered to the king by the prophet seems to make a great deal more sense if ben Tabeel was not in fact of Davidic descent, if a Judean at all. In any case, what was at stake here was Ahaz's position as the legitimate heir of David, something which the prophetic assurance of divine protection strongly affirmed,[90] as did the subsequent birth announcement of a new king upon the throne of David, whose eternal, righteous reign was divinely guaranteed (Isa. 9:6–7).[91] Although Ahaz chose to reject the prophetic assurances and press on with his overtures to Assyria, with disastrous consequences, the location of this prophecy of a new Davidic king 'makes clear that, through Judah's royal dynasty, Israel would rise again to greatness as a nation in spite of the damage that Ahaz's actions had brought' (Clements 2003: 56). This point is further underlined in Isaiah 11, where the

---

[88] For the significance of these two royal narratives in the structure of the book, see Conrad 1988.

[89] Traditionally dubbed 'the Syro-Ephraimite War', it has more recently (and more appositely) been described as 'the Syro-Ephraimite debacle' (Seitz 1992: 480).

[90] As Clements (2003: 46) observes, each of the three children's names in chapters 7 and 8 'affirmed the prophet's assurance that God would protect Ahaz's royal position and that there was no need to fear the enemies ranged against him'. As Schibler (1995: 99) suggests, 'there is much to be said for the opinion that "Immanuel" refers to the new heir to the throne, that is, Hezekiah'. Significantly, 'Immanuel' resonated strongly with the triumphs of the model Davidic king, King David himself. Yet while the initial referent of both the 'Immanuel' child of Isa. 7 and the enthronement text in Isaiah 9 may have been Hezekiah, the exalted language clearly points beyond him to the ultimate king whose reign he merely foreshadowed. For more on the latter, see Provan 1995: 76–85.

[91] 'The location of the prophecy at this point aims to demonstrate that the royal dynasty, and the divine promise on which it rested, were greater than the status and reputation of any one of its representatives' (Clements 2003: 56).

reign of the righteous, spirit-anointed king anticipated by the prophet is described, and he is explicitly associated with David (cf. Isa. 11:1, 10).[92]

The new Davidic king is clearly foreshadowed in Hezekiah, who appears as the positive counterpart to Ahaz in chapters 36 – 39. Like his predecessor, he too faced a major political crisis. Moreover, he too was tempted to look to military alliances for help. However, unlike Ahaz, Hezekiah trusted in Yahweh for deliverance; he sought out prophetic reassurance; and supernatural divine intervention removed the Assyrian threat. But as Isaiah's oracle underlines, the main reason Judah survived on this occasion was because of the special relationship between Yahweh and the Davidic royal house (cf. Isa. 37:35).

However, as the subsequent story illustrates, this particular escape from imminent disaster did not mean that Yahweh would likewise protect Jerusalem from all future threats. The assurances of divine protection were not unqualified, and never had been. Of course, this was a lesson that Jerusalem and her kings were slow to learn, and ultimately learnt the hard way. But, while offering no particular king or generation reason for complacency, it is nevertheless clear that in Isaiah, as elsewhere, the Davidic covenant is understood as irrevocable (cf. Isa. 55:3–5). Thus, whatever disaster might befall Jerusalem and its royal house, the covenant between Yahweh and David would remain forever valid.

Other prophetic books

The royal covenant is cited or alluded to in several other prophetic books: Jeremiah 23:5–6; 33:20–26; Ezekiel 34:23–24; 37:24–27; Hosea 3:5; Amos 9:11–12; Micah 5:2–5. While some of these passages will be discussed at more length in relation to the anticipated new covenant of the future (see chapter 7), it is worth pointing out at this stage that collectively they bear witness to the irrevocable nature of the royal covenant. Despite the extremity of God's judgment that Jeremiah has just highlighted (Jer. 22:24–30; cf. Jer. 17:24–27), he firmly believes in the future fulfilment of the royal covenant (Jer. 23:5–6; cf. Jer. 30:9; 33:20–26). Likewise, Ezekiel has harsh words about the present shepherds of Jerusalem (Ezek. 34:1–10), yet is in no doubt about the prospect of a future Davidic king in whom the royal covenant would find ultimate realization (Ezek. 34:23–24; 37:24–27).

---

[92] Undoubtedly, his description as a 'shoot/root of Jesse' is intended to point not only to the humble origins of the Davidic dynasty, but also to the fact that this coming king will be a new David.

The future envisaged by Hosea is similar, with a period of disruption to the monarchy being followed by the restoration of a Davidic king (Hos. 3:4–5). While more allusive in nature, Amos and Micah reflect a similar conviction. However severe the punishment about to be meted out on Israel, Amos is persuaded that Yahweh will raise up David's fallen tent and restore it (and the people) to former glory (Amos 9:11–12). Similarly, Micah 5:4 anticipates a future ruler whose birthplace (Bethlehem), tribe (Judah) and international significance ('his greatness will reach to the ends of the earth' TNIV) all echo the royal covenant and allude to its ultimate fulfilment.[93]

The royal covenant in the purpose of God

While continuing the trajectory of the national covenant established at Sinai, the Davidic covenant is most closely aligned with the ancestral promises. The chapter in which the establishment of the Davidic covenant is first described (i.e. 2 Sam. 7) is replete with allusions to the divine assurances given to Abraham. For example, both Abraham and David are promised 'a great name' (Gen. 12:2; 2 Sam. 7:9); victory over enemies (Gen. 22:17; 2 Sam. 7:11 cf. Ps. 89:23); a special divine–human relationship (Gen. 17:7–8; 2 Sam. 7:24; cf. Ps. 89:26), and a special line of 'seed' through which their name would be perpetuated (Gen. 21:12; 2 Sam. 7:12–16). In addition, the descendants of both are obligated to keep God's laws (Gen. 18:19; 2 Sam. 7:14; cf. Pss. 89:30–32; 132:12), and a unique descendant of both would mediate international blessing (Gen. 22:18; Ps. 72:17).

Given these clear connections between the Abrahamic and Davidic covenants, there can be no doubt that they are inextricably related. In the Davidic covenant the promises made to Abraham become more focused. The Davidic dynasty inherits the promises Yahweh made to Abraham: the special divine–human relationship and attendant blessings now relate primarily to the Davidic royal lineage. Thus the royal covenant serves to identify at a later stage in Genesis–Kings the promised line of 'seed' that will mediate blessing to all the nations of the earth.

---

[93] Mention could also be made of the messianic hopes reflected in Haggai (Hag. 2:20–23) and Zechariah (Zech. 9:9–10; cf. Zech. 13:1). At very least, these post-exilic texts imply a future for the Davidic dynasty, presumably on the basis of the royal covenant.

Understood in this light, with the royal covenant there is a subtle change in promissory focus; namely, from the promises enshrined within the 'covenant between the pieces' (Gen. 15) to those of the 'covenant of circumcision' (Gen. 17). In the Davidic-Solomonic kingdom the former covenant finds its most extensive fulfilment (2 Sam. 7:1, 23–24; cf. 1 Kgs 4:20–21). With the promise of a 'great nation' now realized, attention shifts from Abraham's national descendants to his royal descendants, the 'kings' to which attention was subtly drawn back in Genesis 17:6, 16. The importance of this royal line, which had already been traced explicitly through Jacob (Gen. 35:11) and Judah (Gen. 49:10), and implicitly through Perez (Gen. 38; cf. Ruth 4:18–22), lay in the fact that its most illustrious descendant would be the individual, conquering 'seed' of Genesis 22:18. Thus the Davidic covenant identifies the royal dynasty from which the anticipated victorious 'seed' of Abraham would eventually come.

Nevertheless, notwithstanding the foreshadowing of the 'blessing of the nations' in the Davidic-Solomonic era, this promise awaited ultimate fulfilment. The history of the Israelite monarchy illustrates why this was so. Despite a few reforming kings, none of the Davidic dynasty – including David himself – fully complied with the crucial criterion for divine–human relationship: irreproachable behaviour. None had, like Abraham, 'obeyed God's voice and kept his charge, his commandments, his statutes, and his laws' (Gen. 26:5). Thus, while the divine promise to bless the nations in Abraham's seed would be fulfilled in a scion of David, ultimately it depended on a Davidic king who would be a son of Abraham in the fullest possible way, and not merely biologically (cf. Ps. 72).

Chapter Seven

God's new covenant anticipated by the prophets

Introduction

For centuries now, it has given us the title for the second major part of our Bible, the New Testament. The latter term is derived from *testamentum*, the Latin translation of the Hebrew word *bĕrît* (covenant). It is not altogether clear who was responsible for this innovation, but it obviously reflects the conviction that Old Testament expectations of a future, everlasting covenant find their ultimate fulfilment in the Christian gospel. Such a supersessionist reading does not necessarily deny that the reconstitution of the Israelite community is the primary focus of such Old Testament oracles;[1] rather, taking its cue from Jesus,[2] it redefines the 'Israel' that is reconstituted. While certainly including biological descendants of Abraham, this new covenant community is not defined by biological ancestry but rather by spiritual descent.

Jeremiah's 'new covenant' text

Somewhat surprisingly, the promise of a 'new covenant' is explicitly mentioned only once in the entire Old Testament (Jer. 31:31). However, to conclude from this that 'The new covenant is simply not a major theme in the Hebrew Bible' (McKenzie 2000: 59) is rather misleading. While the precise terminology is found only here in Jeremiah 31, the actual concept is attested in several other places, and this is arguably the climactic covenant that all other divine–human covenants anticipate and foreshadow.

This passage in which the new covenant is announced by Jeremiah (Jer. 31:31–34) is obviously foundational for our understanding of the

---

[1] *Pace* Brueggemann 1998: 292. For more on supersessionism, see below.

[2] Arguably, such a redefinition is initiated in the OT itself, with prophets like Jeremiah providing 'the necessary transition from Israel as a nation to Israel as a theological ideal' (Dumbrell 1984:173).

concept.[3] Such is patently so for the author of Hebrews, who cites it twice, the first time in full (Heb. 8:8–12) – the longest Old Testament quotation in the New Testament. Fewer than two chapters later this Jeremiah passage is cited again (Heb. 10:16–17) forming an inclusio around this important section of the epistle and underlining its theological significance for this New Testament author at least.[4] Clearly, he believed that these words of Jeremiah are of tremendous importance for understanding the relationship with God that his readers had entered into through Jesus Christ. Moreover, he was not alone in such a belief. While explicit references to the new covenant in the New Testament are perhaps surprisingly few, the echoes and allusions that are present underline its perceived theological fulfilment in Jesus Christ. The new covenant anticipated by Jeremiah clearly lies behind the contrast Paul draws between old (2 Cor. 3:14) and new (2 Cor. 3:6) covenants in 2 Corinthians 3:1–18; here there are numerous echoes of Jeremiah 31:31–34. In addition, it is explicitly related to the death of Jesus in the Lukan and Pauline accounts of the institution of the Lord's Supper (cf. Luke 22:20; 1 Cor. 11:25).[5] There can be little doubt, therefore, that Jeremiah 31:31–34 is a very significant text as far as the apostolic, and hence the Christian, understanding of the new covenant is concerned.[6] And so, in our discussion of the new covenant and its prophetic anticipation, this seems to be the most obvious place to begin.[7]

[3] While one must concede that the new covenant era that Jeremiah himself envisaged was hardly as grandiose as that unpacked by the author of Hebrews, it is misleading to suggest that the NT and/or Christian theology has foisted upon it an interpretation that is 'irrelevant for the meaning of the text' (Carroll 1986: 612; similarly, Brueggemann 1998: 292). While Jeremiah may not have fully appreciated the significance of what he was announcing, it is clear that he had in view the climax of covenant history. Thus Thompson (with others) correctly identifies this passage as 'one of the deepest insights in the whole OT' (1980: 580).

[4] This is clearly so, whether or not one agrees with scholars like Brueggemann who dismiss Hebrews as 'a distorted reading' that 'misreads and misinterprets the text' (1998: 294–295).

[5] These NT passages, along with several others, will be examined in more detail in the following chapter.

[6] As Rendtorff observes (1993: 196), 'The Christian interpreter cannot avoid having in mind the whole Christian tradition, in which the notion of a "new covenant" is of crucial importance. So his or her task is a double one: to read in as unbiased a way as possible what the Hebrew Bible says about the new covenant; and to try to find an appropriate explication of the Christian understanding of the new covenant.' Unfortunately, however, Rendtorff believes that even some NT authors were not particularly interested in the former and were clearly mistaken in how they arrived at the latter. In a similar dismissive vein, Holmgren categorically states that 'The New Testament was written to nourish faith, not to transmit the plain meaning of the scripture' (1999: 104).

[7] For other relevant OT passages, see the discussion below.

The context of Jeremiah's 'new covenant' passage

As Robertson (1980: 273) correctly insists, 'Jeremiah's word concerning the establishment of a new covenant must not be treated in isolation from the historical situation in which this prophecy occurred.' Unfortunately, however, a great many scholars seem unable to see beyond the prophecy's historical and literary setting (i.e. Judah's covenant-breaking and the ensuing Babylonian exile), and so insist on reading this oracle with a single eye to its original context. Thus understood, the prospect held out by this prophetic oracle amounts to little more than the future reconstitution of political Israel and a renewal of the national covenant with a community whose sins will be forgiven and whose circumcised hearts will no longer reject Yahweh's Torah.

Thus Holmgren (1999: 75), while conceding that 'this prophetic text appears to speak of God's decision to establish a new and different kind of covenant with Israel', somewhat typically denies that such is in fact the case: 'The "new covenant" is not completely new or different; it is the Sinai covenant presented ironically under another designation. Jeremiah 31:31–34 was directed to Israel, and the plain meaning of the text found fulfilment in that community.' He elaborates as follows:

> Nowhere in 31:31–34 or in its broader context is there any indication that this announcement of a new covenant is to have its fulfilment hundreds of years later. The oracle is not a vision into the far-flung future. The plain sense of the passage points to a covenant with Israel and Judah, that is, with the people who lived in the general time period in which Jeremiah exercised his prophetic calling ... Throughout the book of Jeremiah, the prophet calls for a return to God which means a turning back to the Sinai covenant (e.g., 7:1–15). There is no indication that he is looking forward to a new, different kind of covenant. Any interpretation of this one passage in 31:31–34, which speaks of a 'new covenant,' must keep this general context in view.

Holmgren's view regarding the precise meaning of the oracle may be somewhat extreme,[8] yet his general stance is fairly typical of those

---

[8] Following Wallis (1969), Holmgren (1999: 90–92) maintains that language suggesting discontinuity (e.g. 'not like' and 'new') is in fact satirical irony, meaning precisely the opposite of what is said, and intended to highlight his audience's spiritual

who refuse to look beyond the oracle's immediate historical setting (however the latter is perceived). Admittedly, a more balanced approach is adopted by others who, while insisting on a primarily historical interpretation (i.e. the new covenant was fulfilled in some sense in the post-exilic restoration of Israel), nevertheless acknowledge a 'depth' dimension; namely, an eschatological fulfilment of Jeremiah's 'new covenant' in Jesus Christ and the New Testament.[9] But however appealing such staged-fulfilments of Jeremiah's oracle may be in view of how its theological significance is understood by New Testament books such as Hebrews, it is important to ensure that such meaning is not simply being imported into the text from elsewhere. Thus a careful examination of the context is required.

These verses fall within a distinct subsection in the book of Jeremiah; namely, chapters 30 – 33, often described as the 'Book of Consolation' or 'Book of Hope' on account of their overarching theme: the future restoration of Israel and Judah to the Promised Land. In other words, these chapters reflect the more positive side of Jeremiah's ministry. The opening chapter of Jeremiah informs us that God had called this prophet to a twofold ministry: he was called both to demolish and to construct, both to tear down and to build (Jer. 1:10). By and large, the previous chapters have focused on the former role, his demolition work, emphasizing that 'there could be no hope of salvation for Judah except through the judgment of exile' (McConville

---

ignorance and warped understanding of their covenant relationship with Yahweh, and shock them into repentance before the nation comes to ruin. However, both the idea of ironic speech here and the notion of last-minute repentance are problematic. Holmgren has apparently identified such rhetorical irony without any obvious cues or signals in the text. Indeed, without Holmgren's premise (i.e. that the new covenant must be equated with the covenant established at Sinai), such an interpretation of the discontinuity language is far from obvious. Furthermore, Holmgren seems to overlook the fact that, for Jeremiah's contemporaries, the die was already cast; the judgment of the nation was now inevitable. Most importantly, Jer. 31:31–34 and the surrounding oracles look beyond exile to restoration ('the days are coming', v. 31; 'after those days', v. 33 ESV). It is thus difficult to see how Holmgren can interpret it as a call to a radical repentance that will avert judgment.

[9] E.g. Lohfink 1991, who sees its ultimate fulfilment – the depth dimension – exclusively in the person of Jesus. Holmgren (1999: 99) takes issue with this on the grounds that such reductionism – limiting the fulfilment of Jeremiah's oracle concerning a community to a single person – is exegetically unwarranted. Others project the ultimate fulfilment of this oracle into the eschaton, when what is said here of the covenant community will be most fully and permanently realized. This latter perspective is reflected also by evangelicals such as Robertson (1980: 297–300), Dumbrell (1984: 174, 182–185) and (more guardedly) McComiskey (1985: 80–93), for whom the historical return of Israel after the exile merely foreshadowed a more consummate realization of Jeremiah's expectation in the person and work of Jesus Christ.

1993b: 79). For McConville, the turning point in the book comes at Jeremiah 25, which serves to link the two parts of the book together. Thus understood, Jeremiah 26 – 29, focusing on Jeremiah's role as a true prophet of Yahweh, serves not only to introduce the new, positive phase of Jeremiah's prophetic ministry, but also to distinguish Jeremiah from his self-serving prophetic contemporaries whose false assurances of hope may have seemed all too similar. In any case, more positive elements appear in these chapters that are unpacked in Jeremiah 30 – 33,[10] chapters that clearly focus on the second aspect of Jeremiah's ministry, the work of reconstruction.

The 'Book of Consolation' begins with a declaration that there will be a return from exile and that all God's people – both Israel and Judah – will be restored to the Promised Land (Jer. 30:3). Such a restoration is further elaborated in the verses that follow; these verses highlight that the time of Jacob's trouble will come to an end, that a new Davidic king will be raised up,[11] and that the benefits of the special relationship between God and his people will again be enjoyed. Moreover, this future restoration will encompass the entire people of God; such is the overarching emphasis of the following chapter, in which this prospect of future restoration is further unpacked. Using exodus imagery, Jeremiah anticipates an analogous saving act of God in the future: Yahweh will accomplish a new exodus, regathering all his scattered people – both Ephraim and Judah; 'all the clans of Israel' – and returning them to their homes where they would experience his promised rest. The present mourning will give place to jubilation, and Israel's fortunes will be restored.[12]

The following passage, in which the new covenant text is embedded, continues the restoration theme of the previous verses. It comprises three subunits, each introduced with 'Behold, the days are coming, Yahweh declares' (my trans.), and each serving to explain Yahweh's more positive stance in the new era. In the first of these (Jer. 31:27–30) Yahweh promises to reverse the judgment announced previously against both humans and animals (Jer. 31:27; cf. Jer. 7:20; 21:6). As Yahweh had been vigilant in bringing about the threatened destruction, so too he would be vigilant in bringing about the promised

[10] These chapters may be further subdivided as follows: Jer. 30 – 31 and Jer. 32 – 33. However, while these constitute distinct subdivisions in terms of scene and tone, the overarching emphasis is the same.

[11] Cf. the assurance of Jer. 23:3–8.

[12] Whatever its precise meaning, Jer. 31:26 clearly constitutes a break between the preceding section and vv. 27–40.

restoration (Jer. 31:28; cf. Jer. 1:10). The rationale for this divine 'about-face' is provided (at least in part) by the following verse; in this new era there will be absolutely no justification for complaints concerning corporate judgment (cf. Ezek. 18:2; Lam. 5:7); this newly planted people of God will be free from the burden of ancestral guilt (this having been dealt with by the judgment of the exile), thus there will be no evading of personal accountability: 'everyone will die for their own sin' (cf. Deut. 24:16; Ezek. 18:3–4). Admittedly, the declaration that 'everyone will die for their own sin' (Jer. 31:30 TNIV) sits rather uneasily with the subsequent promise of absolute forgiveness (Jer. 31:34).[13] Arguably, both concepts may be held in tension if the era in view is not some kind of 'utopian future' (Carroll 1986: 609) but the present age in which, despite the reality of complete forgiveness, personal sin still carries consequences (including premature physical death). However, one should probably not press this statement too literally (i.e. the main point being simply that 'the future will no longer be burdened by the past'),[14] but rather place more stress on the cumulative effect of the points made in the passage: ancestral sin will no longer evoke judgment; personal sin will no longer evoke judgment; consequently, sin and its defilements will no longer evoke judgment![15]

The next subunit (Jer. 31:31–37) discloses how Yahweh will ensure the preservation of his people in the future: he will make with them 'a new covenant' that, quite unlike the covenant he established with their ancestors at Sinai, will be unbreakable (Jer. 31:31–34). Because of this, Israel's future will be absolutely secure. This security is underlined by the two cosmological illustrations that follow: the fixed order of creation (Jer. 31:35–36) and the impenetrability (by humans) of heaven and earth (Jer. 31:37–38).[16]

[13] To explain the anomaly in terms of different authors does not do justice to the intelligence of the final redactor.

[14] Jones 1992: 399.

[15] Cf. Shead's suggestion (2000a: 42) that Jer. 31 presents 'a process of graded reversals' that climax in unconditional forgiveness, and complete cleansing seems to reach a similar conclusion by a slightly different route. Carson (2004: 278), however, maintains that the antitheses in Jer. 31:29–30 and Jer. 31:31–34 both highlight that Israel's tribal and representative system will not be a feature of the new era: 'In both instances, the change is the same. Under the new covenant, *all* will be transformed . . . and under the expectation that the proverb will no longer apply, *all* face judgment without facing judgment inherited from the "fathers".' This, however, does not seem to pay sufficient attention to the progression reflected in this series of oracles.

[16] It is surely significant that trajectories from all the previous divine–human covenants converge in Jeremiah 30 – 33 (the same is true, to a lesser extent, in Ezekiel 36 – 37 and Isaiah 40 – 66), indicating that the new covenant constitutes the ultimate fulfilment of all God's covenants; cf. 2 Cor. 1:20.

The third and final subunit (Jer. 31:39–40) further emphasizes the security that would characterize this future era by focusing on the rebuilding, expansion and consecration of the city. While some of the topography is obscure, the overarching point is clear: areas that were formerly desecrated by dead bodies and sacrificial ashes would in the future be sacred to Yahweh, thus indicating that no area would be defiled as a consequence of sin in the rebuilt city.[17] Hence 'the city will never again be uprooted or demolished' (Jer. 31:40 TNIV). Not only will God's city be rebuilt; it will never again be uprooted or demolished. Rather, like the people of the new covenant, this new Jerusalem will be eternally secure.

Therefore, in its immediate context, Jeremiah's new covenant prophecy serves to explain how God will maintain his relationship with his people in the future and ensure that history does not simply end up repeating itself. This clearly gives Jeremiah's new covenant oracle a climactic significance that must not be ignored in its interpretation.[18]

The essence of the anticipated new covenant

Jeremiah clearly states that this new relationship between God and his people will differ radically from the old one – the relationship that was formally ratified by the national covenant at Sinai.[19] Such discontinuity is highlighted not only by the adjective used to describe this covenant,[20] but also by the contrastive clauses (e.g. 'not like the covenant . . . But this is the covenant' ESV) and the twofold use of 'no

[17] For such defilement in the past, see Jer. 2:7; 7:30–34; 19:13; 32:34–35.

[18] As Robertson (1980: 277) contends, 'It is not only the new covenant; it is the last covenant. Because it shall bring to full fruition that which God intends in redemption, it never shall be superseded by a subsequent covenant.' Cf. Dumbrell's similar (1984: 174) observation: 'In the anticipated return from exile Jeremiah saw the inbreaking of the end.'

[19] It is clear from Jer. 31:32 that the superseded covenant is the national covenant, not the 'Abrahamic-Mosaic covenant' (*pace* Baker 2005: 43). Curiously, Robertson (1980: 281), while acknowledging this explicit contrast, maintains that the contrast is also implicitly made with the Abrahamic and Davidic covenants. This, however, does not automatically follow from the fact that all three covenants are certainly related.

[20] While the Hebrew word (*hādāš*) can also mean 'renewed' (hence, for many scholars, Jer. 31:31 speaks of a covenant renewal), the radical discontinuity stressed in the text (cf. Shead 2000a: 36–37) seems to point to a new covenant rather than merely the renewal of an old one. As Dumbrell observes (1984: 175), this may be further suggested by the use of the verb 'create' (*bārā'*) in association with *hādāš* in the immediate context (Jer. 31:22), a verb that 'always refers to the creative newness of the experience' (ibid.). However, as Dumbrell further acknowledges, this does not necessarily exclude elements of continuity, which may help explain the choice of the Greek term *kainos* in the Septuagint.

longer' (v. 34). Yet one of the striking features of this 'new covenant' is the measure of continuity it seems to reflect: it encompasses the same people (Israel and Judah);[21] it involves the same obligation (Yahweh's law);[22] and it serves to secure the same objective (a divine–human relationship) expressed by the same covenant formula.[23]

So how exactly does this new covenant differ from the old one? Or to phrase the question as it often appears in theological essays or exams, 'What is "new" about the new covenant?'

Some interpreters have rightly noticed the emphasis in the text on the divine initiative: this covenant's unilateral nature is highlighted by the dominant use of the first person throughout these verses: 'I will make . . . I will put . . . I will write . . . I will be . . . I will forgive . . . I will remember' (ESV).[24] While such divine initiative was also the hall-mark of all previous divine–human covenants, there is no hint here of the mutuality expressed in the Mosaic covenant. There is no con-ditional 'if clause' here, as there clearly was back in Exodus 19:5. That is not to say that the people of God have absolutely no obligations under this new covenant; it is surely implicit here that they do; other-wise, why put the law in their minds or write it on their hearts?

[21] As Shead (2000a: 34) notes, the inclusion of both Israel and Judah extends the hope 'beyond the circle of God's people then extant'. As he further observes, this is quite in keeping with the book as a whole, whose use of the terms and whose orienta-tion to the nations (Jer. 1:10) 'point to a reality that goes beyond Israel and Judah as they used to be' (2000a: 39). Clearly, Jeremiah, like Ezekiel (cf. Ezek. 37:15–23), is at pains to underline the comprehensive scope of the restoration in view here (cf. Jer. 30:3; 31:1). While the 'Israel' with whom this future covenant was to be made would cer-tainly include biological descendants of Abraham, like the covenant it superseded (cf. Exod. 12:38) it would include others also (Jer. 12:14–17; cf. Isa. 19:18–25).

[22] While this is generally accepted, some interpreters have suggested otherwise. E.g. Huey (1993: 286) maintains on the basis of Gen. 26:5 and 1 Cor. 9:21 that the 'my law' specified in v. 33 refers to something more basic or foundational than its specific mani-festation in the Mosaic law. However, this seems to be introducing a dichotomy that is not only questionable exegetically, but also that Jeremiah would have found difficult to comprehend. It seems better to understand both Gen. 26:5 and 1 Cor. 9:21 as sum-marizing the essence of God's Torah, as reflected in the Mosaic law and throughout Scripture.

[23] See too Jer. 24:7; 30:22; 32:38. Cf. Jer. 7:23; 11:4; also cf. Gen 17:7–8; Exod. 6:7; 29:45; Lev. 26:12; Deut. 26:17–18. For a fuller discussion of the covenant formula, see Rendtorff 1998: 57–94 and Sohn 1999: 355–372.

[24] Holmgren (1999: 83) castigates biblical commentators who 'have too often liter-alized the "God alone" language of the Bible' in this way, accusing them of having 'pressed religious speech too hard'. However, while some of his examples illustrate that not all God's actions are one-sided, he seems to be missing the point when he equates a text that speaks of God circumcising human hearts (Deut. 30:6) with others (Deut. 10:16; Jer. 4:4) that encourage people to do so. Indeed, it would appear that Holmgren's insistence on human 'free will' (1999: 94) has led him to deny divine sovereignty.

Clearly, the people of God are still under obligation to conform to the will of God and live as those who are indeed God's people.[25]

But it is equally clear here that God himself is going to facilitate such obedience, and this clearly constitutes one of the major differences with respect to this future covenant. God is going to put his law – the expression of his will – in their minds;[26] God is going to write his word on their hearts, rather than on tablets of stone (cf. Exod. 31:18; 34:28–29; Deut. 4:13; 5:22). As Brueggemann (1998: 293) puts it, 'the commandments will not be an external rule which invites hostility, but will now be an embraced, internal identity-giving mark, so that obeying will be as normal and as readily accepted as breathing and eating'. Thus a major difference between the old covenant and the new is that the obligations of the covenant will be internalized in the new covenant community (cf. Jer. 24:7; 32:39).[27] Consequently, the primary objective of the earlier covenant (a permanent divine–human relationship) would now be attainable.[28]

More significantly, as is highlighted by the following verse (Jer. 31:34), such radical transformation involving the internalizing of Yahweh's law would affect the *entire* covenant community. It is perhaps this, more than anything else, that constitutes the most radical distinctive of the new covenant. Internalization of the law was not a radically new concept (Deut. 11:18; cf. 30:14), nor was the associated idea of circumcision of the heart (Deut. 10:16; cf. 30:6).[29] But such had certainly not been the collective experience of the covenant community. Rather, such had been the distinguishing mark of individuals in the community who constituted Israel's righteous remnant.

[25] As Dumbrell (1984: 178) insists, 'The tendency to see the covenant of Jeremiah as a new covenant because it replaces obligation by promise drives a wedge between promise and law. This division is not consistent with the relationship of those entities in prior Old Testament covenants such as the Sinaitic . . . Covenant simply confirms promise, recognizes the existence of a relationship to which promise and obligation are attached.'

[26] The Hebrew verb here appears to be a 'rhetorical perfect' – i.e. a Qatal perfect describing a future reality considered a certainty from the speaker's rhetorical viewpoint (Arnold and Choi 2003: 55).

[27] This internalization of God's will is described by Ezekiel (cf. Ezek. 11:19; 36:26) in terms of spiritual heart surgery performed by God's Spirit (Ezek. 36:27; 37:14). For the NT terminology, see John 1:10–13; 3:1–10; Titus 3:5; 1 Pet. 1:3, 23; 1 John 4:7; 5:18.

[28] As Thompson observes in relation to the covenant formula, 'Its actualization had escaped Israel' (1980: 581). This is clearly reflected in v. 32, which, as Shead (2000a: 39) plausibly argues, may constitute the formula's negative counterpart: 'they broke my covenant [i.e. they did not act like my people], though I was their husband/master'.

[29] However, as Shead (2000a: 38) correctly notes, God acts as the agent only in Deut. 30:6, a text that also addresses the post-exilic experience.

The majority – as Jeremiah himself had clearly underlined (cf. Jer. 17:1) – had hearts engraved with sin and were thus spiritually uncircumcised (cf. Jer. 9:26; 16:10–13). However, the law would be internalized by everyone who belonged to the covenant community of the future. As Shead (2000a: 38) observes, 'the law is written not only inwardly, but universally'.[30] Thus in this coming era there would no longer be any need for personal exhortation as far as knowing Yahweh was concerned (cf. Hos. 6:3), for everyone would know him, 'from the least of them to the greatest'.[31] Knowledge of Yahweh and conformity to his revealed will are inseparably connected (cf. Jer. 22:16). It was the lack of such knowledge that had precipitated divine judgment, first for Israel (Hos. 5:4; cf. Hos. 2:20),[32] and subsequently for Judah (cf. Jer. 2:8; 4:22). But as Jeremiah insists here, under the new covenant the situation will be very different: the entire community will reflect such knowledge of Yahweh. Thus understood, 'the prophet is not speaking of theoretical knowledge but of the inward, personal relationship with God inherent in the word *know*' (McComiskey 1985: 86–87).[33] Therefore, rather than necessarily

[30] Whether or not such is implicit in the use of singular nouns (lit. 'their midst' and 'their heart'), it is clearly highlighted in the following verse: 'all of them shall know me, from the least of them to the greatest' (Jer. 31:34 my trans.).

[31] As Huey (1993: 285) correctly observes, 'It is exhortation rather than instruction that is to be rendered superfluous by the new covenant. Having the law written on one's heart is not so much a matter of immediate knowledge as transformed attitudes and behaviour (22:16). The result is said to be not just the knowledge of the law but the knowledge of the Lord, i.e., a relationship with the Lord of the covenant by faith, the goal of all the earlier covenants.' So also McComiskey 1985: 86–87. Cf. Dumbrell 1984: 181–182.

[32] Knowledge of God (*da'at 'ĕlōhîm*) is a significant theme in Hosea, a book that seems to have influenced Jeremiah significantly (for Hosea's influence on this passage in particular, see Robinson 2001: 184–193). In Hos. 6:6 knowledge of God is more important than cultic observance. In Hos. 4:6 the people perish for lack of knowledge (see also Hos. 5:4; 8:2; and 13:4). The knowledge of God seems to refer to the faithful acceptance of what God has revealed of himself in his saving acts. This is clear in Hos. 13:4 where they are said to know only Yahweh as God, since he alone demonstrated his existence and power to them through saving them from bondage in Egypt. 'Knowing God' is 'Hosea's formula for normative faith, the apprehension of Yahweh's history with Israel in the classical era before her life in Canaan' (Mays 1969: 63). Significantly, in Hos. 2:20 it is said the people will 'know the Lord' (ESV; NIV/TNIV's 'acknowledge' obscures the meaning) in the restoration era. Apparently, it is just such knowledge of Yahweh that Jeremiah also has in mind here in Jer. 31:34, a knowledge based on the reality of divine forgiveness.

[33] Similarly, Kaiser sates that 'Jeremiah does not mean possessing intellectual data only, but in accordance with his usage in Jeremiah 22:15, 16 it is a knowledge which results in appropriate action and living' (1972: 20 n. 46). For others, it is more a question of covenant mediation (i.e. the role of Moses, levites, priests and prophets): 'the most natural interpretation in context would point to the fact that the new covenant situation would

implying the redundancy of teachers in the new covenant era,[34] the text may suggest simply that in the future there will be no need to exhort other members of the covenant community to know (i.e. obey) the Lord. This will be the natural response of all whose minds have been renewed and whose hearts have been inscribed with Yahweh's Torah. That such knowledge issuing in obedience will be reflected in the entire covenant community ('they will all know me, from the least of them to the greatest' TNIV) is clearly one of the most distinctive features of the new covenant. Therefore, 'what is "new" about the new covenant is not the covenant partner but the quality of the community created by God's amazing acts' (Dearman 2002: 287).

As the following clause apparently suggests,[35] this universal knowledge of Yahweh would result from the fact and extent of Yahweh's forgiveness, 'presented by Jeremiah as providing the basic substructure for the new covenant relationship' (Robertson 1980: 283). The basis of such forgiveness is not stated. While the context may imply that God's wrath has been fully exhausted in the judgment of the exile (Jer. 31:28),[36] it is difficult to see how this could secure the forgiveness of future sins, if such are in fact envisaged (cf. Jer. 50:20).[37] In any case, apparently this is not an issue of concern to Jeremiah, who seems content simply to highlight that all these new covenant blessings would result solely from the gracious initiative of a God who would forgive the iniquity of his people and refuse to act on it again.[38] It is this latter aspect that clearly distinguishes

---

be one in which the need for people to mediate the covenant would disappear' (Robertson 1980: 293). D. A. Carson's suggestion (2004) that there will no longer be any need for 'mediatorial instructors' (rather than theological teachers per se) is along similar lines.

[34] See Dumbrell 1984: 181–184. Admittedly, however, these new covenant promises attain their ultimate fulfilment in the eschaton, when personal teaching of any kind (whether exhortation or instruction) will presumably become truly redundant.

[35] The final *kî* clause appears to give the reason for the fact that 'they will all know me' (TNIV), and possibly all the foregoing (so Brueggemann 1998: 294).

[36] As Brueggemann (1998: 290) observes, 'the five negative verbs [in Jer. 31:28] have all been fully enacted. There is no more threat in them. God has monitored . . . the fulfillment of all the negatives and has kept track ("watched") until the promise of destruction has been fully actualized'.

[37] It is not immediately clear whether Torah-inscribed hearts eradicate sin altogether, or simply deal with it in the appropriate manner (i.e. via sacrifice), and whether the forgiveness described in Jer. 31:34 is a once-for-all action, or an ongoing feature of the new covenant era. However, the radical discontinuity of the new covenant ultimately points to the former on both counts.

[38] Such is the significance of Yahweh 'remembering their sin no more'. The act of remembering means more than mental recall; it often entails taking the appropriate and obligatory action (cf. Jer. 14:10).

the two covenants. While the Mosaic covenant certainly made elaborate provision for the forgiveness of sin, the repetitive nature of the sacrificial ritual underlined that sin was not in fact removed but merely passed over. However, 'by saying that sins would be remembered no more, Jeremiah anticipates the end of the sacrificial system of the Old Testament' (Robertson 1980: 283). This future reality of complete forgiveness would issue in the knowledge (i.e. the obedience of faith) of Yahweh, the distinguishing mark of this new covenant community.

Consequently, unlike the old covenant (v. 32), there will be no possibility of breaking this new covenant. Indeed, 'the ability of sin to disrupt the relationship is made obsolete by the astounding announcement that God will not remember sins and their effects on the relationship' (Dearman 2002: 287). And it is surely this that especially highlights the 'newness' of the new covenant – the fact that, unlike the old covenant, this covenant is unbreakable. Unlike the old covenant, this new covenant will not, and indeed cannot, be broken. Sin cannot imperil the divine–human relationship guaranteed by this new covenant, for sin will not be brought into account: God 'will forgive their wickedness and will remember their sins no more' (Jer. 31:34 TNIV). Hence 'it is the quality of the covenant bond between God and his people that gives the essential "newness" to the coming new covenant' (Dearman 2002: 287).

The fulfilment of Jeremiah's new covenant hope

It is difficult to see how Jeremiah's hopes concerning the new covenant were climactically fulfilled by the events that took place immediately after the Babylonian exile. While a small remnant of Jews were permitted to return to Palestine, this was hardly the grandiose reunification and restoration of all the clans of Israel repeatedly insisted on by the prophet. Moreover, in the years that followed, while the returnees may have renewed their covenant with Yahweh (Neh. 8 – 10), the community's ongoing difficulty with the implementation of Yahweh's Torah receives ample illustration. Most significantly, if Jeremiah's hopes focus exclusively on the reconstitution of the nation after the exile, then his authenticity as a true prophet of Yahweh must surely be challenged, for his prophetic expectations – especially his insistence that Yahweh would no longer remember their sins (Jer. 31:34) and that 'the city will never again be uprooted or demolished' (Jer. 31:40 TNIV) certainly proved false.

Thus it would appear that, unless we naively dismiss Jeremiah as a false prophet, the new covenant he anticipates here is a reality that finds its ultimate fulfilment and its full theological significance far beyond the bounds of the oracle's immediate historical setting. In this it is not alone, as attested to by the prophetic anticipations of a future covenant elsewhere.

Other anticipations of a future covenant

Although the concept of a 'new covenant' is especially associated with Jeremiah 31:31–34, several other Old Testament texts allude to an everlasting covenant that will be established between God and his people in the future: Cf. Hosea 2:14–23; Jeremiah 32 – 33 (in particular, Jer. 32:40); Jeremiah 50:5; Ezekiel 11:16–20; 16:60; 34, 36–37 (in particular, Ezek. 37:26), Isaiah 40 – 66 (in particular, Isa. 42:6 and Isa. 49:8, where covenant language is applied to the enigmatic 'servant of Yahweh', a figure whose mission closely parallels the 'seed' of Abraham and David; Isa. 54:10, where God's 'covenant of peace' is mentioned in the context of 'everlasting kindness' [TNIV] and the fulfilment of promises associated with various covenants; Isa. 55:3, where the promise of an 'everlasting covenant' associated with God's promises to David is given; Isa. 56:5–6, which highlights both the inclusive and exclusive nature of the new covenant community; Isa. 59:21, where God's covenant is explicated in terms of the conferral of his Spirit and the perpetual proclamation of his words; and Isa. 61:8, where the promise of an everlasting covenant is again associated with the fulfilment of God's international purpose).[39] Given the difficulties involved in the dating of these prophetic texts, they will be discussed in their canonical rather than their perceived chronological order.[40]

[39] Other OT texts that seem to anticipate new covenant realities could also be added (e.g. Joel 2:18–32). However, in the interests of economy, the following discussion is restricted to passages that explicitly use covenant vocabulary.

[40] Organizing these texts chronologically is complicated by the fact that there is no consensus over the date of publication / final redaction of these prophetic books. This is especially so for the latter half of Isaiah (i.e. Isa. 40 – 66). A further complication arises from the fact that, even if the Isaianic material is dated early (i.e. pre-exilic), it is undeniably written with an exilic and early post-exilic situation in mind. Thus, while a compelling case can be made for the Isaianic authorship of Isa. 40 – 66 (e.g. see Webb 1996; cf. also Motyer 1993; 1999; Oswalt 1986, 1998), the contextual scenarios depicted by the prophet in these chapters did not develop historically until after the ministry of both Jeremiah and Ezekiel. Given such complexities, it seems best simply to arrange the following discussion according to the canonical order of these prophetic books.

Isaiah

Like the other prophets, covenant is the theological foundation upon which Isaiah's message is built. As highlighted above, this is especially true in relation to the royal covenant.[41] However, it is not until the latter part of the book, dealing with restoration and future hope, that covenant becomes a major topic.[42] While earlier covenants are certainly alluded to,[43] Isaiah's primary focus is on the everlasting covenant of peace that would be established in the future.

A 'covenant for the people' (Isa. 42:6; 49:8)

The first two references to 'covenant' in Isaiah 40 – 66 are closely associated with the mission of the enigmatic Servant figure. The Servant's mission is unfolded in at least four passages (Isa. 42:1–9; 49:1–13; 50:4–11; 52:13 – 53:12),[44] collectively known as the 'servant songs'.[45] Both the identity of this ideal figure, and the meaning of his description as a 'covenant for the people' are disputed.[46] While some have identified the Servant as Israel (i.e. the nation, whether in whole or in part),[47] it is more likely (given his ideal, perfect character) that the

[41] See pp. 141–143 above.

[42] The only explicit reference to a divine–human covenant in the first part of the book is Isa. 24:5, most likely a reference to the Noahic covenant.

[43] The Noahic, Abrahamic and Sinaitic covenants are all alluded to in Isa. 54, and the royal covenant is alluded to in Isa. 55. The eschatological context of Isa. 56:6 suggests that the covenant referred to there is the new covenant.

[44] The first servant song is traditionally identified as Isa. 42:1–4. However, the following verses (vv. 5–9) seem to unpack the Servant's mission. Cf. Isa. 49:7–13, which similarly unpacks the Servant's work after the Servant's reintroduction in vv. 1–6. Most understand the second song to end at v. 6, identifying the subject of the 'you' in vv. 7–8 as Israel. In this case the Servant's calling as 'a covenant to the people' is continued through the restored covenant community (so Webb 1996: 194–195). However, the following verses (vv. 7–13) appear to be describing the Servant's work (so A. Motyer; Oswalt), and the 'people' seem to refer primarily to Israel. Hence there is no compelling reason for identifying Israel, rather than the Servant, as the 'covenant to the people' in Isa. 49:8.

[45] To the traditional four 'servant songs', Webb (1996: 170 n. 37) adds a fifth; viz. Isa. 61:1–3. Unquestionably, some relationship between the speaker in Isa. 61:1–3 and the Servant is implied by the similarities in description and role (see Oswalt 1998: 562–563).

[46] For a concise summary and critique of major interpretations of this phrase, see Dumbrell 1984: 193.

[47] For a useful summary and critique of the various interpretations of the Isaianic Servant, see Hugenberger 1995:106–138. Rather than pitting royal, priestly and prophetic interpretations of this figure against each other (as is partly done by Hugenberger with his insistence that the 'prophet like Moses' trajectory predominates), it seems better (esp. in view of the NT's interpretation of this figure as Jesus and its portrayal of him as prophet, priest and king) to see all three trajectories fusing together in the Servant.

enigmatic subject of these songs is an individual who would accomplish the mission Yahweh had given Israel by bringing salvation to all nations.[48] The means by which the Servant will accomplish this task is disclosed progressively in these four 'servant songs', but the goal of his mission is made clear from the outset, and it is implicit in his role as 'a covenant for the people' (Isa. 42:6; 49:8). As the context of both these texts makes clear, the Servant's role as 'covenant for the people' is closely tied to his national and international mission.[49] This individual will be the very embodiment of God's covenant; hence the agent and guarantor of God's covenant love and blessing to all people.[50]

A 'covenant of peace' (Isa. 54:10)

Following on the fourth servant song (Isa. 52:13 – 53:12), in which the Servant's saving work and the basis for forgiveness is most fully revealed, the present chapter significantly announces God's eternal covenant of peace (Isa. 54:10).[51] As Oswalt observes, while there is little by way of direct connective links between these passages (i.e. the fourth servant song and Isa. 54 – 55), the change of atmosphere reflected in the latter chapters presupposes the immediately

---

[48] In some passages the Servant is clearly Israel (e.g. Isa. 41:8–9; 42:18–19; 44:1–2; 45:4; 48:20). However, in the so-called servant songs the servant seems to be distinct from Israel. As Webb (1996: 170–172) suggests, 'the servant . . . seems to be a figure who embodies all that Israel ought to be but is not. He is God's perfect servant . . . a real person who is God's answer to their [Israel's] weakness and failure . . . It is through him that God's purposes for this world will be realized.'

[49] It makes little difference whether 'people' is taken to refer in the first instance to Israel (the most likely referent, as the immediate context of 49:8 suggests) or, as the parallelism in Isa. 42:6 might imply, to the nations generally. The Servant's mission, and hence his role as an embodiment of the covenant, ultimately applies to both. For a concise discussion of this exegetical conundrum (the identity of 'the people'), see Oswalt 1998: 118.

[50] By tying these texts too rigidly to a perceived historical setting (i.e. the end of the exile and the imminent return to Palestine), McKenzie (2000: 62) rejects any idea of a prediction of a new covenant in the distant future. However, this not only overlooks the unique significance of the Servant figure, but also the climactic and eschatological focus of these chapters. Thus, while some of the imagery used in these passages is that of restoration (cf. Isa. 49:5, 6a, 8–9), the international emphasis (cf. Isa. 42:1, 4, 6; 49:1, 6b, 7b, 12) clearly points to a release from captivity (Isa. 42:7) on a much greater scale; cf. 2 Cor. 6:2, where Paul applies the prospect held out in Isa. 49:8 to the messianic age. Note also the language of Jubilee (Isa. 49:8–9; cf. Lev. 25:8ff.), again picked up in Isa. 61:1–3. Cf. Luke 4:16–21.

[51] Peace is the recurring motif that links this chapter and the next; cf. Isa. 54:10, 13; 55:12. Earlier in the book it is associated with the Messiah (Isa. 9:6, 7), those who trust in Yahweh (Isa. 26:3, 12), and the good news of salvation that will be proclaimed (Isa. 52:7).

preceding material: exhortations to confidence in Israel's future restoration have given place to exhortations to 'bask in that reality' (1998: 413). Thus understood, the success of the Servant's mission provides the basis for Yahweh's 'steadfast [i.e. covenant] love' (Isa. 54:10a; cf. 'everlasting love' in Isa. 54:8) expressed in his permanent 'covenant of peace' (Isa. 54:10b).[52] The latter concept (a 'covenant of peace'), is mentioned in several other Old Testament texts (cf. Num. 25:12; Ezek. 34:25; 37:26–27), all linked by a common motif (albeit implicit in some cases); namely, the cessation of divine wrath. That such a connotation is intended here seems clear from the surrounding context (cf. Isa. 54: 9, 15–17). However, as Oswalt (1998: 423) underlines, '*peace (šālôm)* in Hebrew is much more than the absence of hostilities: it describes a condition of wholeness'. Thus understood, it connotes the 'sum total of covenant blessing, the full enjoyment of all that God has promised' (Webb 1996: 214). The latter is underscored in this chapter (and the next) by the piling up of covenantal echoes: the Abrahamic covenant is alluded to in verses 1–3 (cf. Gen. 22:17); the Sinai covenant is picked up in verses 4–8; the Noahic covenant comes into focus in verses 9–10; and the Davidic covenant is introduced in Isaiah 55:3–4. Together this suggests that this 'covenant of peace' (or in the case of the next chapter, the 'everlasting covenant') constitutes the climactic covenant in which all the major divine–human covenants find their ultimate fulfilment. Through the work of the Servant (cf. Isa. 53:5), therefore, people are brought into relationship with God (Isa. 54:13a),[53] resulting in unprecedented (and unending) peace (Isa. 54:13b).

An 'everlasting covenant' (Isa. 55:3; 61:8)

The invitation to celebrate the salvation wrought by the Servant becomes an invitation to embrace it in Isaiah 55. Once again, the invitation is framed in covenant language, articulated in terms of the promise of 'an everlasting covenant' in which the earlier Davidic covenant will also find fulfilment (Isa. 55:3–4).[54] It would appear,

---

[52] Similarly, Heim 1998: 310.

[53] Significantly, the essence of this divine–human relationship is described in terms of discipleship, being 'taught by Yahweh'; cf. Jer. 31:34.

[54] For the suggested dependence of Isa. 55:1–5 on Ps. 89 and the democratization here in Isa. 55 of the Davidic covenant, see Heim 1998: 306–314. Heim rightly insists that what we have here is not a transferral of the original promises from the Davidides to Israel, but rather an extension (in keeping with the overarching message of hope in Isaiah) that by no means excludes the Davidic dynasty.

therefore, that whereas Jeremiah anticipated a 'new covenant' that would supersede the Sinai covenant (Jer. 31:31–34), Isaiah anticipated an 'everlasting covenant' that would have its basis in the Davidic. Thus, as Oswalt (1998: 438) observes, 'for Isaiah the new covenant seems to be inseparably linked to messianic hopes'.[55] This clearly lends credence to the view that Isaiah's enigmatic Servant and the Davidic Messiah are one and the same.[56] In any case, David's calling to be 'a witness to the peoples' (Isa. 55:4) would now be mediated through the one described in the following verse (Isa. 55:5).[57] Thus understood, Isaiah's Servant Messiah assumes the role earlier delegated to David (cf. Isa. 42:1–4; 49:2–3; 50:4), and in turn becomes the focal point of any subsequent witness to the surrounding nations.

In Isaiah 61 the promise of an 'everlasting covenant' (Isa. 61:8) follows the proclamation concerning the ultimate year of Jubilee.[58] As previously (Isa. 54:10; 55:3), the prospect in view incorporates the national hopes of Israel. However, although the language of physical restoration is employed in part (Isa. 61:4–7), and the 'double portion' of blessing (Isa. 61:7) answers to the 'double for all her sins' (Isa. 40:2), the restoration in view here clearly transcends national hopes, incorporating 'all who mourn' and not simply 'those who mourn in Zion' (Isa. 61:2–3). By now the reader associates the 'everlasting covenant' (cf. Isa. 55:10; cf. 42:6; 49:8; 54:10; cf. also Ezek. 37:25–26) with the person and work of the Servant/Messiah. By means of his death (Isa. 53), this figure has satisfied the requirements of the old covenant and ratified a new, everlasting covenant, guaranteeing 'everlasting joy' (Isa. 61:7) and a recognizable offspring who would bear witness to Yahweh's salvation blessings before all the nations (Isa. 61:9, 11). In this manner the divine mandate given to Abraham and his seed (Gen. 12:2d–3) and God's plan for international blessing would at last be fulfilled.

---

[55] Given the central importance of the Davidic house in the first part of Isaiah, this is not surprising.

[56] See Motyer 1993: 13–14; Schultz 1995: 154–159; Heim 1998: 306–314.

[57] The use of 'Behold' at the beginning of each verse describing these respective tasks invites comparison (so Oswalt 1998: 439). While the identity of the first agent (i.e. David) is fairly straightforward (even though the term 'witness' is never applied to him or his leadership role elsewhere; although cf. Pss. 9:11; 18:49; 57:9–11; 108:3–4; 145:21; note also the simile in Ps. 89:37), the identity of the second agent is less obvious. While some identify the subject of v. 5 as Israel, this may be so only in a secondary sense, the primary referent being the Servant/Messiah (so Oswalt 1998: 439; similarly, Motyer 1999: 345).

[58] Isa. 61:1–3 is almost certainly an allusion to the Year of Jubilee; cf. Lev. 25:8–55 (esp. v. 10).

An inclusive and exclusive covenant (Isa. 56:5–6)

As Oswalt cogently argues, the last major section of Isaiah (i.e. Isa. 55 – 66) is clearly intended as a necessary supplement to the preceding material. Many scholars refuse to ascribe this supplement to Isaiah himself, although without any compelling reasons for doing so. Unfortunately, this has resulted in fruitless speculation over the historical setting of this material.[59] A more important and productive enterprise is to consider the theological contribution this section makes to the book as a whole. Oswalt (1998: 453) helpfully summarizes this as follows: 'the internalization of the law by means of an intimate relationship with the God who alone can enable people to live holy lives'. This opening pericope (Isa. 56:1–8) addresses the question of the scope of this new covenant community. Clearly, it is both inclusive and exclusive; inclusive in that it incorporates foreigners and eunuchs (Isa. 56:3),[60] but exclusive in that the covenant community only includes those who 'hold fast to the covenant' (Isa. 56:5–6), which seems to mean maintaining covenant obligations (Isa. 56:1–2).[61] The singling out of sabbath-keeping for particular emphasis (cf. Isa. 56:2–3, 6) probably reflects that the root of the matter is a life made up of worship in every part; keeping sabbath is the positive counterpart to avoiding evil, and both are an expression of worship.[62] Thus in answer to the implied question 'Who is included in the new covenant community?', this passage answers, 'Everyone who gives expression to a genuine relationship with God.' Not surprisingly, the following section (Isa. 56:9 – 57:13) lays particular stress on human inability and the absolute necessity of divine grace.

A word-defined covenant (Isa. 59:21)

As just noted, the present chapter further highlights the extent of human depravity and thus the necessity of divine intervention for God's revelatory purpose to be fulfilled. So, in the light of abject human failure (Isa. 59:2–15a), God himself comes as the divine

---

[59] As Oswalt avers (1998: 451 n. 22), the plethora of historical reconstructions (ranging from early exilic to the time of the Maccabees) suggest the data are insufficient for historical reconstruction in any case.

[60] Significantly, all the latter and some of the former were excluded under the Mosaic covenant; cf. Deut. 23:1–8. Clearly, such exclusion would not apply to the future reality that the OT people of God foreshadowed.

[61] Human inability to do so in their own strength is underlined in the section that follows (Isa. 56:9 – 57:13; cf. also Isa. 59:1–20), which further emphasizes human depravity and the need for divine intervention.

[62] So Oswalt 1998: 456.

warrior to deal with the problem of sin and make himself known throughout the world (Isa. 59:15b–21). Accordingly, the anticipated covenant is described in prophetic terms, in terms of the Spirit empowering the people to speak God's words (Isa. 59:21).[63] In this way, therefore, the mission originally given to Israel (i.e. to make Yahweh known to the nations) will be fulfilled.

Jeremiah

In addition to the famous new covenant passage discussed above, there are at least two other texts in Jeremiah that explicitly refer to the prospect of a future divine–human covenant:[64]

Jeremiah 32:40

Like Jeremiah's new covenant passage, Jeremiah 32:40 belongs to the Book of Consolation (Jer. 30 – 33). Set in the context of a prophetic sign-act (buying real estate in Palestine to indicate the certainty of Israel's future when human logic dictated otherwise) and Jeremiah's prayer for heavenly reassurance,[65] the divine oracle to which this verse belongs (i.e. Jer. 32:27–44) sets out the prospect of restoration beyond exile. While exile was the immediate and inevitable outcome of Israel's history of rebellion, it was a temporary measure that would serve merely as the prerequisite to Yahweh's ultimate objective: the restoration of a spiritually renewed Israel whose relationship with Yahweh will be forever maintained through an 'everlasting covenant' (v. 40).

While not referred to here as a 'new covenant', the same reality is apparently being described. This may be inferred, not only from the similar description of spiritually renewed Israel (vv. 39, 40b), but also from the similar blessings associated with this everlasting covenant (vv. 37–38, 40a, 41). See table on next page.

As Jones (1992: 418) observes, 'The truth which stands out from both passages is that the new era of peace and life cannot be secured

---

[63] Cf. 1 Sam. 10:6; 16:13; Isa. 11:2–4; 61:1–2; Ezek. 2:2.

[64] While not mentioning 'covenant' explicitly, Jer. 24:7 is also relevant; focusing on the prospect of Israel's future restoration, the prophet anticipates the subsequent new covenant annunciation of spiritual transformation ('I will give them a [new] heart' ESV), a new knowledge of God ('to know that I am the LORD' ESV), wholehearted commitment to God ('they shall return to me with their whole heart' ESV), and the realization of the covenantal objective ('they shall be my people and I will be their God' ESV).

[65] It would appear that, despite his tremendous faith in God's promise (as demonstrated in his model obedience to God's instructions here), Jeremiah was not without his doubts or bewilderment – hence his request for reassurance. This interpretation seems preferable to that which understands the prayer simply as a rhetorical device to reinforce the prophet's message (for the latter, see Jones 1992: 410–411).

without a fundamental change in the human personality; and this change, only God can give.'

Jeremiah 31:31–34	Jeremiah 32:37–41
v. 31 I will make a new covenant with the house of Israel and with the house of Judah	v. 40a I will make an everlasting covenant with them [i.e. the people of Israel and Judah cf. v. 30]
v. 32 It will not be like the covenant . . . they broke	v. 40c they will never turn away from me
v. 33a I will put my law in their minds and write it on their hearts	v. 39 I will give them singleness of heart and action
	v. 40b I will inspire them to fear me
v. 33b I will be their God, and they will be my people	v. 38 They will be my people, and I will be their God
v. 34a they will all know me	v. 39b they will always fear me
v. 34b I will forgive their wickedness	vv. 40b, 41 I will never stop doing good to them
And will remember their sins no more (TNIV)	and will assuredly plant them in this land with all my heart and soul (TNIV)

The following chapter (Jer. 33) elaborates further on the hope of restoration held out in this prospect of an everlasting covenant. Here the expectation of a complete reversal of Israel's fortunes in the wake of Babylonian captivity (described [vv. 6–13] in terms of the people's healing, cleansing, forgiveness, repatriation, prosperity, security and spontaneous worship, the city's reconstruction and significance among the nations, and the harmonious relationships that would characterize the land)[66] is reinforced by God's faithfulness to his covenant promises: Yahweh will fulfil his 'good promise' to the house of Israel and the house of Judah; the central promises of the royal covenant and the priestly covenant will indeed be realized (Jer. 33:14–18; cf. 1 Sam. 2:35; 2 Sam. 7:15–16) – for these covenants are as secure as God's covenant with creation itself (Jer. 33:19–26; cf. Gen. 8:22–9:17).[67]

[66] The pastoral imagery in vv. 12–13 is most likely metaphorical; cf. the negative image reflected in Jer. 23:1–2 and Ezek. 34:1–6 with the future prospect depicted in Jer. 33:14–16; Ezek. 34:11–31; and Ezek. 36:37–38; cf. also Ezek. 37:15–28.
[67] With Jones (1992: 424), I take the allusion here to be to the Noahic covenant (for more on this, see earlier material on the question of a creation covenant). As Jones

Moreover, it is through the descendants of David and the Levites that Yahweh will fulfil his oath to Abraham (Jer. 33:22, 26; cf. Gen. 17:6; 22:17–18). Hence the future reversal of Israel's fortunes is absolutely certain, for it is inextricably linked to the outworking of God's ultimate purpose of international blessing through Abraham's royal seed.

Jeremiah 50:4–5

Part of a collection of oracles concerning the anticipated downfall of Babylon, these verses focus on Israel's forthcoming deliverance from her Babylonian oppressors. As before, the prospect of restoration is held out here to all Israel (i.e. both 'the people of Israel and the people of Judah' v. 4a), and it is associated with the forgiveness of sins (Jer. 50:20). Here, however, it is also linked to repentance and a new covenant commitment to Yahweh (vv. 4b–5).[68] While the relationship between this 'everlasting covenant' and the 'new covenant' (Jer. 31:31–34) is not spelt out, the fact that both are set in the context of Israel's restoration and both are described as having perpetual effects (Jer. 50:5; 31:34; cf. Jer. 32:40) suggests that the same reality is in view.[69] Thus understood, while the emphasis in Jeremiah 31:31–34 is on Yahweh's part, and the emphasis here in Jeremiah 50:4–5 is on Israel's new covenant commitment, the covenant in view is one that will guarantee the divine–human relationship in an absolute sense.

Ezekiel

Although only some of the following texts in Ezekiel refer explicitly to the making of a future covenant, their relevance to the discussion is not in doubt: whereas Jeremiah speaks of an internalization of the Torah, Ezekiel speaks of an inner renewal involving a heart transplant and the conferral of a new spirit.

---

notes, the same word is used here for 'breaking' a covenant (*prr*) as in Jer. 31:22; thus a contrast is probably intended (cf. Jer. 31:35–37). In any case, the covenants with David and the Levitical priests are clearly encompassed within Jeremiah's new and everlasting covenant. As Carroll (1986: 639) comments, 'Permanent royal leadership and perpetual levitical sacrifice will characterize this future.'

[68] As Jones (1993: 525) comments, 'Their weeping is no longer that of lamentation in disaster, but the sign of a true and godly penitence.' It makes little difference whether v. 5b is translated, 'They will come and bind themselves . . .' (NIV/TNIV), or 'Come, let us join ourselves . . .' (ESV). In either case, such action is the catalyst for restoration.

[69] The suggestion that what is in view is a covenant renewal is undermined by the fact that the prophet speaks of '*an* everlasting covenant' rather than '*the* everlasting covenant'.

Ezekiel 11:16–20

Coming near the end of a section that has sketched out Yahweh's staged withdrawal and its inescapable consequences for Jerusalem, this passage answers Ezekiel's expressed anxiety over the complete annihilation of Israel's remnant (Ezek. 11:13). Whereas the Jerusalemites had evidently written off the exiles as divine rejects (Ezek. 11:15), Yahweh disabuses them of any such notion with the reassurance of future restoration to the land (Ezek. 11:17). However, as well as repatriation, Yahweh speaks in terms of regeneration;[70] physical restoration will be accompanied by spiritual renewal (Ezek. 11:19; cf. Jer. 24:7; 31:33; and esp. Jer. 32:39) that has as its goal a new attitude to God's revealed will (Ezek. 11:20a; cf. Ezek. 11:18) and a genuine divine–human relationship (Ezek. 11:20b).[71] The latter is expressed by the covenant formula, here introduced by Ezekiel for the first time.[72] The use of the formula marks the covenantal significance of this new scenario that Ezekiel here envisages. However, lest any of the exiles should be tempted to take all this for granted, the warning with which the oracle ends (Ezek. 11:21) is a salutary reminder that even the blessings of the new covenant will not follow automatically, but are contingent upon genuine repentance and faith.[73]

Ezekiel 16:60–63

These verses conclude Ezekiel's bold allegory highlighting the unfaithfulness of Jerusalem. Despite the outrageous nature of his people's behaviour, Yahweh has made it clear that after he has vented his wrath (Ezek. 16:42) he will restore the fortunes of his people –

---

[70] While the language of regeneration belongs to the NT, the concept of such a radical inner transformation is undoubtedly in view here and in similar OT texts; hence Nicodemus' rebuke by Jesus (John 3:10).

[71] The *lĕmaʿan* at the beginning of Ezek. 11:20 introduces a purpose clause (cf. ESV).

[72] This formula is a prominent refrain in both Ezekiel (cf. Ezek. 14:11; 34, 30–31; 36:28; 37:23, 27) and Jeremiah (cf. Jer. 7:23; 11:4; 24:7; 30:22; 31:1, 33; 32:38). Most probably derived from ancient legal terminology in the marriage ceremony, it reverberates throughout the OT (cf. also 2 Cor. 6:16; Rev. 21:3). For a comprehensive discussion, see Rendtorff 1998.

[73] Admittedly, the subjects in this verse ('those whose hearts are devoted to their vile images' TNIV) are somewhat ambiguous. However, while they could arguably be those against whom the earlier charges were laid, coming as it does after the announcement of the new covenant, it seems primarily directed at Ezekiel's immediate (exilic) audience (so Block). In any case, as Block solemnly reminds us, 'True spirituality is not expressed by claiming the promises of God or parroting theological dogma. Those who lay the greatest stock in these externals may be those whom God rejects. For the true Israelite the claim to covenant relationship with God is matched by genuine piety . . .' (1997: 356).

both Israel and Judah (Ezek. 16:53–55). His basis for doing so is spelt out in verses 60–63: in contrast to his negligent covenant partners, Yahweh will remember the covenant he made with them in their youth (Ezek. 16:60a) and will establish for them an eternal covenant (Ezek. 16:60b). While some contend that the latter speaks not of a new covenant being established, but of a previous covenant being maintained,[74] this seems unlikely for the following reasons:

1. The two clauses in verse 60 (i.e. 'I will remember my covenant with you' and 'I will establish an eternal covenant for you' my trans.) are not necessarily synonymous in meaning.
2. The indefiniteness of the covenant mentioned in the second clause ('an eternal covenant', rather than 'my eternal covenant' or even 'the eternal covenant') suggests that this covenant differs from that of the previous clause.
3. Given the undeniable echoes of Jeremiah's 'new covenant' passage here,[75] Ezekiel's 'eternal covenant' and Jeremiah's 'new covenant' would appear to be synonymous.[76]
4. Ezekiel's subsequent reference to an eternal covenant of peace that Yahweh would make with his people (Ezek. 37:26) seems also to anticipate the establishment of a new covenant as opposed to the maintaining or fulfilling of a pre-existing one.

It is preferable, therefore, to understand the relationship between the two clauses in verse 60 consequentially: because Yahweh will remember the covenant he made with the nation in its youth he will establish an eternal covenant with it in the future. This latter covenant would permanently replace or supersede the covenant that Israel had so flagrantly violated.

[74] E.g. Greenberg 1983: 291; Block 1997: 516–517; Duguid 1999: 215. While acknowledging that *hēqîm běrît* may describe the institution of a covenant, Block (1997: 516) prefers to understand the idiom (citing the following texts in support: Gen. 6:18; 9:9, 11, 17; 17:7, 10, 19, 21; Exod. 6:4; Lev. 26:9; Deut. 8:18) as signifying the fulfilment of a pre-existent covenant, which he identifies as the Mosaic on the basis of the two passages lying behind this paragraph, Lev. 26 and Jer. 31:31–34. Block takes the latter text likewise to refer to a renewal of the Mosaic covenant. However, the fact the more common idiom for covenant initiation (*kārat běrît*) is employed there surely militates against his argument for insisting that *hēqîm běrît* means 'fulfil a covenant' here in Ezek. 16:60.

[75] See Block 1997: 517.

[76] Obviously, the weight of this argument cuts both ways. If, with Block and others, one understands Jer. 31:31–34 to refer to a covenant renewal, then this eternal covenant must also be such.

The results of this eternal covenant are spelt out in verses 61–63:

1. *A quickening of memory (v. 61a).* Israel will remember her ungrateful response to Yahweh's grace in the past.
2. *An intense sense of shame (v. 61b).* Such shame would flow, not only from the memory of her sinful past, but also from the experience of God's gracious acts in the future, when Sodom, Samaria and their dependencies would be subordinated to Jerusalem (cf. vv. 53–55).[77]
3. *A profound recognition of Yahweh (vv. 62–63).* The recognition formula used throughout Ezekiel is here paired with the establishment of Yahweh's covenant (presumably the aforementioned eternal covenant), and followed by a purpose clause which unpacks the profound effect that this recognition of Yahweh should have: the people will remember and be ashamed, and forced into an embarrassed silence.[78]
4. *A full atonement for sin (v. 63b).* While coming at the climax of this pericope, this purging of Jerusalem's sin clearly lies at the heart of the covenant: the other results described here refer to the effects of this covenant on the people, whereas this act of atonement is something Yahweh does on their behalf. Remarkably, the usual sequence of shame leading to repentance and the removal of sin is here reversed. Thus here (cf. Jer. 31:34) atonement for sin serves as the basis or catalyst for the people's new perspective in relation to both Yahweh and themselves.

It would seem, therefore, that Ezekiel here follows Jeremiah in announcing that, in the coming era of salvation, Yahweh was going to replace with an eternal covenant that would be unbreakable the covenant Israel had broken. While the terminology may differ significantly, the essence of the covenant anticipated by Ezekiel is the

---

[77] The precise meaning of the final phrase of v. 61 (lit. 'not from your covenant') is unclear, but the context seems to suggest that this subordination will take place, not because there was any obligation, but simply as an act of divine grace (i.e. it will transcend the terms of the original covenant). Alternatively, it may indicate that Sodom and Samaria will be fully incorporated within the (eternal) covenant (cf. ESV footnote).

[78] It is not altogether clear what is meant by 'you will no longer have an opening of the mouth on account of your disgrace' (v. 63b my trans.), but it seems to allude to silencing verbal speech, possibly the unjustified bragging about superiority over Sodom described in Ezek. 16:56 (so Greenberg 1983: 292; Allen 1994: 246). Alternatively, Block (1997: 519) suggests it alludes to the end of ritual complaints against Yahweh for having failed his people.

same: God's new work of grace, which would involve the removal of Israel's sins, would lead to a new recognition of Yahweh, and a new attitude towards themselves and their former shameful behaviour.

Ezekiel 34:25–31

Coming at the end of a chapter in which the issue of Israel's abuse at the hands of their corrupt leadership is dealt with, this final subsection announces the prospect of a 'covenant of peace' between Yahweh and those rescued by him and blessed with a truly Davidic king – one who would prove to be the shepherd that Yahweh intended (v. 25; cf. Ezek. 37:26–27; Isa. 54:10).[79] As mentioned above, all four texts that mention such a 'covenant of peace' are linked by a common motif (albeit implicit in some cases); namely, the cessation of divine wrath. However, as is illustrated by the verses that follow here in Ezekiel 34, in which this promised *šālôm* is unpacked, 'The term obviously signifies much more than the absence of hostility or tension. It speaks of wholeness, harmony, fulfilment, humans at peace with their environment and with God' (Block 1998: 303).[80] What is envisaged here is the harmony of creation restored, with the people of God enjoying a life of peace, blessing and security. All this results from and attests to the harmonious relationship between the people and Yahweh, which is fittingly expressed in terms of a variation of the age-old covenant formula (Ezek. 34:30–31; cf. Lev. 26:12).

Ezekiel 36:22–38

Like Ezekiel 11:16–20, there is no explicit mention of a covenant in these verses. However, its restoration setting, clear echoes of Jeremiah's new covenant passage and its use of the covenant formula (Ezek. 36:28), clearly point to the significance of this oracle in relation to the eternal covenant anticipated by Ezekiel elsewhere.

Chapter 36 has two main parts: verses 1–15 and verses 16–38 (the latter is made up of three distinct sub-units: vv. 16–32, vv. 33–36 and vv. 37–38). The first oracle, verses 1–15, is a companion piece to the oracle against the mountains of Edom in the preceding chapter (Ezek. 35), with the focus being on the transformation of the land. Verses 16–38 constitute a distinct unit introduced by the message reception formula of verse 16, and containing three separate salvation oracles –

---

[79] Elsewhere the only explicit mention of a 'covenant of peace' is that associated with Phinehas: Num. 25:12.

[80] As Block further observes, Ezekiel's idyllic picture of the messianic age recalls Isa. 11:6–9, but bears even closer resemblance to Hos. 2:18–23 and Job 5:23.

all introduced by the messenger formula (cf. vv. 22, 33 and 37). Verses 17–21 seem to be an historical explanation that introduces the first oracle (so Allen 1990) or all three oracles (so Block 1998).[81]

The first oracle (vv. 22–32) focuses on the transformation of the people.[82] The mountains will no longer be hostile, barren and unfruitful, but fruitful, populated and friendly to their inhabitants. The people will no longer have stony hearts, but hearts of flesh, renewed by the Spirit. The final two oracles of Ezekiel 36 (vv. 33–36 and 37–38) stress the effect that this will have on both the nations round about and on Israel itself. Both will know that Yahweh is God (see vv. 36, 38). Thus the theme of these verses is Yahweh's vindication of his Name; he will restore his honour by fulfilling his covenant promises – restoring his spiritually cleansed and transformed people to the Promised Land.

As Allen (1990: 178) suggests, there is a particularly close connection between the historical review (vv. 17–21) and the first oracle (vv. 22–32). The first oracle begins in verse 22 by echoing the closing words of the review in verses 20–21. That is, the review highlights the problem to be solved (the profanation of Yahweh's name) and the first oracle (vv. 22–32) announces what Yahweh will do to resolve this issue (i.e. to vindicate his name among the nations).[83] The action Yahweh will take is described once again (cf. Ezek. 11:17–20) in terms of physical restoration and spiritual renewal.

The first (restoration to the land) addresses the taunt of verse 20. Yahweh's restorative work begins where it must, with the regathering of his people. Their return from exile is portrayed as a new exodus – a prominent motif in Ezekiel's restoration oracles.[84]

---

[81] Block's outline helpfully shows how the unit, for all its disjointedness, hangs together:

The Formulaic Introduction	(v. 16)
a. The Crisis for Yahweh's Honor	(vv. 17–21)
b. The Recovery of Yahweh's Honor	(vv. 22–32)
(1) Yahweh's Name-Sanctifying Goal	(vv. 22–23)
(2) A Catalogue of Yahweh's Name-Sanctifying Actions	(vv. 24–30)
(3) Yahweh's Name-Sanctifying Goal	(vv. 31–32)
c. The Vindication of Yahweh's Honor	(vv. 33–38a)
(1) Among the Nations	(vv. 33–36)
(2) In Israel	(vv. 37–38a)
The Formulaic Conclusion	(v. 38b)

[82] This oracle – cast as a divine speech to be relayed by Ezekiel to his audience – opens with the charge to speak to the house of Israel (addressed in the second person throughout) and is framed by 'not for your sake have I acted' (so Block).

[83] The prominence of the Lord as the subject of the verbs in vv. 24–30 is striking.

[84] Cf. Ezek. 11:17; 20:34–35, 41–42; 28:25; 29:13; 34:13; 37:12, 21; 39:27). Here in 36:24, Ezekiel's terminology is influenced by Deut. 30:4.

The second action (spiritual renewal) addresses the issue of defilement raised in verse 17. Using the language of ritual purification (cf. Exod. 30:17–21; Lev. 14:52; Num. 19:17–19), Yahweh promises to reverse the people's defilement through spiritual cleansing – 'sprinkling clean water' on them (v. 25). But in addition to such spiritual cleansing, radical internal change is required (v. 26; cf. Ezek. 11:19): nothing short of spiritual heart surgery is needed to solve the problem of Israel's fossilized organ (cf. Ezek. 2:4–11; 3:4–11),[85] and nothing short of the infusion of Yahweh's Spirit is necessary to evoke the obedience that Yahweh commands.[86] Such an infusion of Yahweh's Spirit, prompting inner transformation (i.e. regeneration), was apparently neither a novel concept nor distinctly eschatological (as Jesus' rebuke of Nicodemus clearly shows).[87] Rather, the problem for Ezekiel was 'ecclesiological – this transformation was not occurring on a national scale. The issue was one of scope' (Block 1998: 361).

Thus this infusion of Yahweh's Spirit will produce the proper response to Yahweh's instruction. As elsewhere, the underlying issue is that of permanence or irreversibility. These verses (26–28) show how Israel's past history of covenant failure will be prevented from simply repeating itself (cf. Lev. 26:3), and how God's ancient ideal (expressed by the covenant formula of v. 28) will at last be realized. As Block contends, there is obvious Jeremianic influence here (cf. Jer. 31:33), infusion with the Spirit of Yahweh taking the place of an internalization of the divine Torah (apparently the same inner change described differently).

As highlighted by the subsequent verses, regeneration of the people's hearts will be followed by rejuvenation of the land, hence the removal of Israel's disgrace and the restoration of Yahweh's honour among the surrounding nations. However, as the final two verses underline (vv. 31–32), this will come about in spite of Israel rather than because of her. Indeed, given her track record, the only fitting response to Yahweh's magnanimous grace is one of shame.[88]

---

[85] The solution here is even more radical than that of Deut. 30:6–8, the textual foundation for Ezekiel's message.

[86] As Block (1998: 356) suggests, it would appear that both the new heart and the new spirit are explicated in vv. 26b and 27a respectively: thus, the 'new heart' is a 'heart of flesh' and the 'new spirit' is 'my [i.e. Yahweh's] Spirit'. But even if 'new spirit' and 'new heart' are understood in synonymous terms, the basic idea is the same: Israel must undergo radical inward transformation.

[87] So Block 1998: 360–361. This does not detract from the fact that such endowment with the Spirit was a sign of the messianic age (so Taylor 1969, who cites Isa. 42:1; 44:3; 59:21; Joel 2:28–29; cf. Ezek. 37:14; 39:29).

[88] As Wright (2001: 301–302) insightfully comments, this chapter offers profound reflections on the proper place of shame in the life of the believer: 'Israel was not to feel

Ezekiel 37:24–28

Ezekiel 37 continues the theme of Israel's future hope of restoration. In the first section, Ezekiel's vision of dry bones (vv. 1–14),[89] hope is held out that Israel will be 'resurrected'. The second section, narrating and interpreting the last of Ezekiel's prophetic sign-acts, focuses primarily on Israel's reunification (vv. 15–28). As in the previous chapter, the prospect of Yahweh's Spirit indwelling them (v. 14) and the imagery of ritual cleansing (v. 23) describe the people's transformation into God's new covenant community.[90] Significantly, the effect of this radical transformation will be conformity to Yahweh's law (v. 24b; cf. 11:19–20; 36:26–28; Jer. 31:33), and the realization of the hopes held out in previous covenants (vv. 24–28).[91] The most striking feature of this anticipated realization of Yahweh's covenant promises is its permanence.[92] The 'covenant of peace' (v. 26; cf. Ezek. 34:25) associated with this future hope will be 'everlasting' (v. 26; cf. Ezek. 16:60; Isa. 24:5; 55:3; 61:8; Jer. 32:40; 50:5), as will the blessings (a permanent home,[93] a permanent Davidic ruler, and a permanent

---

ashamed in the presence of the other nations (15), but they were to feel ashamed in the presence of their own memories before God (31–32). Similarly, there is a proper sense in which believers who have been forgiven by God for all their sins and offences may rightly hold up their heads in company . . . the believer can face the world, certainly not with pride, but equally certainly without shame . . . But on the other hand, the same person, alone with God and the memories of the past, can quite properly feel the most acute inner shame and disgrace. It is not, however, a destructive or crushing emotion. Rather, it is the core fuel for genuine repentance and humility and for the joy and peace that flow from that source alone. When *I* remember my sins I know that *God* does not . . . For this is not the memory that generates fresh accusation and guilt – that is the work of Satan the accuser . . . No, this is the memory that generates gratitude out of disgrace, celebration out of shame. It is the memory which marvels at the length and breadth and depth of God's rescuing love that has brought me from what I once was, or might easily have become, to where I am now, as a child of his grace' (emphasis his).

[89] Block subdivides the material in vv. 1–14 more precisely as follows: there is a break at v. 11, where the vision gives way to a series of interpretative comments. Thus a vision report (1–10) is followed by a disputation address (11–14) with two proof sayings (12–13, and 14). Verse 11 is a bridge. It interprets the imagery of the vision and introduces the disputation that follows.

[90] The use of the covenant formula (Ezek. 37:23, 27; cf. vv. 12–14) is most significant.

[91] The ancestral, royal and national covenants are all reflected in these verses, and one could arguably detect an allusion to the universal covenant in the anticipated 'covenant of peace' (cf. Isa. 54:9–10).

[92] As Block (1998: 415–416) observes, particular stress is placed on the permanence of the restoration through the reiterated use of 'ôlām: 'With his fivefold affirmation of the eternality of the restoration, Yahweh transforms this oracle into a powerful eschatological statement, envisaging an entirely new existence, where the old historical realities are considered null and void, and the new salvific work of God is perceived as final' (1998: 416).

[93] Note the repeated 'they . . . will live in the land' (v. 25) and the emphatic 'they, and their children and their children's children . . . for ever' (my trans.).

divine presence[94]) it guarantees. Through this anticipated covenant, all previous covenants will thus be climactically fulfilled and God's universal purpose – international blessing – will eventually be realized.[95]

Other possible allusions to the anticipated 'new covenant'

Daniel 9:24–27

While an announcement of a future covenant is found here in Daniel's notoriously enigmatic prophecy concerning the 'seventy sevens' (Dan. 9:24–27), the identity of the covenant maker – the one who 'shall make a strong covenant with many' (ESV) in the seventieth week is hotly disputed.[96] The immediate antecedent is 'the prince who is to come' (v. 26b ESV), although the 'he' of v. 27a could arguably hark back to the 'anointed one who shall be cut off and have nothing' (v. 26a my trans.). In favour of the latter are the following observations:

1. The 'seventy sevens' chronography is probably best understood against the background of Jewish sabbatical years,[97] and the Jubilee year in particular (cf. Lev. 24:8; 25:1–4; 26:43; cf. 2 Chr. 36:21). Thus understood, the seventy sevens constitutes ten jubilee years, the last (the seventieth seven) signifying the ultimate Jubilee (cf. Isa. 61:2). Given the Jeremianic context that prompted this revelation (Dan. 9:2; cf. Jer. 25:11–12; 29:10), some explicit association between this climactic Jubilee and the anticipated new covenant is not unexpected.

[94] Clearly, the permanent divine presence reflects a permanent divine–human relationship, as underlined by the covenant formula (v. 27).

[95] Admittedly, this is more than Ezekiel explicitly states in v. 28. However, the fact that the promised restoration will affect the rest of the nations clearly hints at God's ultimate objective of international blessing.

[96] Interpretations include the following: (a) Antiochus IV, the Greek king whose treacherous hostility towards the Jews resurfaces in Dan. 11 and whose atrocities certainly included the suspension of the sacrificial system; (b) Jesus Christ, whose inauguration of the new covenant is closely associated with putting an end to sacrifice and offering; (c) the Roman general Titus, whose destruction of the temple in AD 70 spelt the end of the sacrificial ritual; (d) the final Antichrist, whose hostility towards the people of God is allegedly foreshadowed by the actions of Antiochus.

[97] With others, Lucas (2002: 248) rightly concludes that chronography is a preferable term to chronology, as suggested by the symbolic nature of the figures employed.

2. The events associated with the final seven (cf. v. 24, 26a, 27a) correspond closely to eschatological realities associated elsewhere with the new covenant. Indeed, the use of a verb typically applied to the ritual of covenant ratification (i.e. *kārat*) may connect the 'cutting off' of this anointed one with the subsequently mentioned 'making firm a covenant with many' (my trans.).[98]

3. The Hebrew syntax in verse 27 seems to support distinguishing between the subject of the first two clauses (i.e. the 'he' who makes the covenant and brings an end to sacrifices) and the subject of the final two clauses (i.e. the desolator who makes desolate). This ties in with the similar distinction found in the previous verse between the 'anointed one who is cut off' (v. 26a) and the desecrating and destructive 'people of the prince who is to come' (v. 26b ESV). Thus understood, the first half of each verse concerns the 'anointed prince', and the second half focuses on the 'desolating prince'.

4. The events and achievements associated with this 'anointed prince' seem to tally with the person and work of Jesus Christ. It is in him that the prospects anticipated in verse 24 become realities; he is cut off just before the destruction of Jerusalem; and he does make strong [ratify?] a covenant with many, and climactically puts an end to sacrifice and offering (Heb. 9:26; cf. 7:11; 10:8–9).[99]

Admittedly, dogmatism over the interpretation of this enigmatic text would be rather naive. However, a strong case has been made for interpreting Daniel's seventieth seven as yet another explicit anticipation of the future, everlasting covenant between God and his people. Moreover, the correlation between the realities anticipated here and prospects associated with the new covenant elsewhere cannot be ignored.

Hosea 2:14–23

Sandwiched between Hosea's marriage (Hos. 1) and remarriage (Hos. 3),[100] the oracle recorded in Hosea 2:2–23 picks up the

[98] So Riddlebarger 2003: 154. Riddlebarger contends that the use of the verb *gbr* in v. 27 indicates the confirmation of an already-existing covenant, which he goes on to identify as the Abrahamic. This, however, is not necessarily the case; the only other use of the hiphil verb form is in Ps. 12:4 (MT v. 5), where the sense is simply 'prevail' or 'establish strength'. Hence most English versions suggest, 'he will make a strong/firm covenant'.

[99] Moreover, the imagery of this passage (Dan. 9:27a) is picked up in Revelation, where the era of the church militant is associated with a 'time, times and half a time' (Rev. 12:14 TNIV).

[100] *Pace* Stuart (1987: 64–69), I am assuming here that the same woman, Gomer, is referred to in both chapters.

imagery of the unfaithful wife but applies the language primarily to Israel rather than to Gomer. The flow of the oracle is analogous to the flow of the domestic situation that unfolds in chapters 1 and 3: unfaithfulness leading to rejection, and love leading to reconciliation. There are two main sections, the first (2:2–13) outlining Yahweh's intended response to Israel's infidelity; and the second (2:14–23) outlining Yahweh's programme of restoration.[101]

Possibly threatening divorce (v. 2a), the plaintiff (Yahweh, the aggrieved husband) wants his spouse (Israel, the adulterous wife) to change her outward appearance (to take the most basic step of reform) or face the consequences (vv. 3–4). The reason underlying this threat is spelt out in verse 5: Israel as a whole has become spiritually corrupt, acknowledging her lovers (the baals) as the source of her material blessings. Yahweh will therefore judge her appropriately, cutting her off from her lovers (v. 6).[102] While initially even this enforced chastity will fail to check her promiscuity (v. 7a), eventually Israel will desire to return to her true husband, Yahweh (v. 7b).[103] Before any restoration, however, Israel would have to be truly humbled (vv. 8–13). Yahweh would therefore withhold the blessings allegedly conferred by the baals, whose impotence would thus be amply demonstrated.

Yahweh, however, would not forget his people. Rather than the anticipated announcement of their fate, he unexpectedly promises to rescue them all over again (vv. 14–15). He will once more lead Israel into the desert, woo her afresh, and restore to her the blessings of the Promised Land.[104] Israel will respond (not 'sing' as in NIV; although see Stuart 1987: 62) as she did initially – in true commitment and faithfulness (cf. Jer. 2:2).

As indicated by the recurring motif 'In that day' (vv. 6, 18, 21), this vision transcends the forthcoming judgment and speaks of restoration beyond it. Such restoration will involve the eradication of the last

---

[101] Alternatively, one could see the major break coming at v. 16. However, while vv. 16–23 share an eschatological motif (i.e. 'In that day . . .', vv. 16, 18, 21), vv. 14–15 clearly mark (admittedly, somewhat abruptly, given the introductory 'therefore'; cf. vv. 6, 9) the turning point to weal from woe.

[102] Most probably an allusion to exile.

[103] Commentators disagree over whether or not this repentance was genuine. Certainly, the thrust of the following verses would suggest that at this point it was somewhat superficial.

[104] The Valley of Achor (meaning 'trouble') alludes to the original conquest, in particular to the Achan incident that threatened to undermine its success (Josh. 7:24).

vestiges of Baal worship,[105] and be marked (v. 18) by two parallel blessings: peace and harmony with the animal world (cf. Ezek. 34:25, 28, Isa. 11:6–9, 35:9, which also reflect this eschatological harmony) and peaceful relations with other human beings (the absence of war).[106] For Stuart (1987: 58), 'both blessings are reversals of curses . . . and are manifestations of the general restoration blessing of covenant renewal'. However, the fact that various aspects of this oracle in Hosea appear to underlie Jeremiah's anticipation of a 'new covenant' may well suggest that more than mere 'covenant renewal' is in view here. Admittedly, the only covenant explicitly mentioned (v. 18) seems to be of a rather different order – a covenant made with (i.e. an obligation imposed upon) creation for the benefit of Yahweh's people. Nevertheless, as other 'new covenant' texts also illustrate, this could simply be a case of a covenant trajectory (in this case, the universal covenant) – which Israel's behaviour had placed in jeopardy (cf. Hos. 4:1–3) – finding its ultimate fulfilment in the context of the anticipated everlasting covenant of the future. That such a covenant is in view here is certainly implied by the following verses (Hos. 2:19–20), in which the metaphor is that of betrothal – the final stage in the courtship process. Here Yahweh promises to betroth Israel, but in this case the relationship is established in/with righteousness, justice, covenant love (ḥesed), mercy and faithfulness. While it is unclear whether these qualities are Yahweh's alone or are conferred on Israel also,[107] the situation portrayed here appears in any case to be unassailable and irreversible. Thus the covenant envisaged here,[108] in which Israel would 'know Yahweh' (v. 20), is not one that would subsequently be broken (cf. Jer. 31:31–34).

Therefore 'in that day' (vv. 21–22) Yahweh would ensure that the

[105] As Achtemeier (1996: 26; although cf. Stuart 1987: 57) observes, 'Verse 16 implies that Yahweh had been worshipped as a baal god . . . the presence of Yahweh had been invoked with the name "My Baal", a practice expressly forbidden in Exodus 23:13. Now the very mention of the name of Baal will be lost to Israel's vocabulary, v. 17.'

[106] As Dell (2003: 116) observes, 'Hos. 2:18 seems a kind of reversal of the picture we get in Hos. 4:1–3 which indicates that the behaviour of the people of Israel has a direct impact on the life of the land.'

[107] It is not clear whether the preposition should be translated 'in' or 'with' here. Grammatically, either is possible; taken in the first sense, these qualities will accompany the marriage, characterizing both Israel's and Yahweh's response. Taken in the second sense, it is with these qualities that Yahweh betroths Israel (i.e. these are the bride price). Stuart suggests that the ambiguity is intentional, and that both senses are to be understood in these verses.

[108] While the envisaged relationship is not explicitly said to be covenantal, the text is permeated with covenant language and metaphors, and ends with a restatement of the covenant formula.

land would yield its blessing to his people and so, in a dramatic reversal, the three symbolic names of Hosea's children are turned around in this restoration oracle to speak of the new covenant (v. 23).[109] As Stuart (1987: 54) aptly concludes:

> In this allegory, Yahweh 'courts' Israel in two senses. He takes Israel to court in the accusation of a crime – adultery. But as the passage unfolds, it is clear virtually from the outset (v 5 [3]) that the actual purpose will be to 'court' Israel in the sense of inviting her back to faithfulness after she has done penance for her sin. Yahweh will never lose his beloved nation. He will renew it. Playing all the decisive roles, judge, jury, prosecutor, police, he can put an end to her promiscuity by seeing that Israel, collectively and individually, is taken from her lovers and made chaste again. The legal metaphor thus stands alongside the love parable. Yahweh will indict and convict as the evidence dictates. But after serving her sentence, Israel has hope for the distant future even more glorious than was the distant past. That future is not to be fulfilled until after a sentence of exile and debasement. It will be truly fulfilled only in a new age, one we know to have been ushered in by Christ (Rom 11:28–32).

Malachi 3:1

The reference in Malachi 3:1 to 'the messenger of the covenant in whom you delight' (ESV) raises a number of challenging exegetical questions,[110] and thus any conclusions reached here must be considered tentative. Hill (1998: 269–270, 289) makes a good case for identifying the covenant in question as the future covenant announced by Jeremiah and Ezekiel:

1. Malachi's audience has already alluded to the new covenant in their complaint regarding divine justice (Mal. 2:17; cf. Jer. 31:29; Ezek. 18:3).
2. The eschatological context of this fourth disputation oracle (cf. 'day of his coming' Mal. 3:2 ESV) suggests that the new covenant is in view.

[109] In v. 23 the verb 'sow' (MT v. 25, 'and I will sow her', *ûzĕraʿtîhā*) now interprets 'Jezreel' (*yizrĕʿeʾl*) by a wordplay – the latter contains the same root (*zrʿ*).

[110] The identity of this messenger, his relationship to the Lord (in the parallel line), the specific covenant with which he is associated and the rationale behind the people's 'delight' are all unclear.

3. The people's expectant desire for divine intervention is certainly in keeping with new covenant hopes.[111]
4. The allusion to Ezekiel 43:1–5 and the return of Yahweh's presence to the temple points to the new covenant era.

Thus understood, Malachi is warning those whose perception of new covenant realities was somewhat skewed; like those of an earlier era (cf. Amos 5:18), 'popular expectation for the outcome of the Day of Yahweh is tragically mismatched with the reality of the event' (Hill 1998: 271). As emphasized by the subsequent oracles, only those marked by penitence and godly fear would experience deliverance on that Day.

Drawing the various strands together

Because there are so many different passages that herald this new covenant, and because of its future, visionary character in the Old Testament, drawing together the various threads is rather more complex in this case than with previous covenants. Even so, the following points can be discerned.

The new covenant will be both national and international

The descriptions of both Jeremiah and Ezekiel are primarily nationalistic (cf. Jer. 31:36–40; 33:6–16; Ezek. 36:24–38; 37:11–28). Against the historical backdrop of the Babylonian exile, such an emphasis is to be anticipated; the catastrophe of 587 BC raised significant questions in relation to the fulfilment of God's earlier promises concerning the nation and its king. Therefore, it is unsurprising that the repatriation of a reunified Israel in a renovated land with a Davidic king should be a dominant motif in the prophetic hope associated with the new covenant.

However, the scope of this new covenant clearly transcends national and territorial borders. While Jeremiah and Ezekiel both allude to the international significance of the new covenant (Jer. 33:9; Ezek. 36:36; 37:28), its universal scope is depicted most clearly in Isaiah. Ostensibly nationalistic horizons are still envisaged (cf. Isa. 44:28; 45:13). Nevertheless, this covenant will extend to the ends of

[111] This is especially so if we assume that the Isaianic material lies at the basis of the people's expectations. As noted above, Isaiah connects the future covenant with the Servant/Messiah figure, and clearly anticipates the kind of scenario that Malachi and his audience are expecting in their respective ways.

the earth, ultimately encompassing all nations (Isa. 42:6; 49:6; 55:3–5; 56:4–8; 66:18–24). Thus the new covenant projects the ultimate fulfilment of the divine promises on to an ideal Israel (i.e. a community of faith) located in a rejuvenated universe (Isa. 65:17; 66:22).

This ideal Israel is not, however, a novel concept foreign to the intent of the original promises. Rather, from the beginning of the nation's history it had been made clear that ethnic descent from Abraham was neither sufficient (Gen. 17:14) nor essential (Gen. 17:12, 13) for inclusion among the people of God. Moreover, ethnic Israel is clearly depicted in the Bible as foreshadowing the new covenant reality: the 'Israel of God' (Gal. 6:16). Thus, while the restoration of the Jews in the Promised Land marked the beginning of the fulfilment of the new covenant promises, this was merely the beginning. The best was yet to come, when the 'rest' foreshadowed in Joshua would find its ultimate consummation in the new heavens and the new earth.

The new covenant will involve both continuity and discontinuity

Several features underline the new covenant's continuity with previous divine covenants: its emphasis on the divine Torah (Jer. 31:33; Ezek. 36:27; Isa. 42:1–4; 51:4–8); its focus on Abraham's 'seed' (Jer. 31:36; Ezek. 36:37; Isa. 63:16), particularly his royal 'seed' (Jer. 33:15–26; Ezek. 37:24–25; Isa. 55:3); its use of the covenant formula, 'I will be their God, and they shall be my people' (Jer. 31:33; Ezek. 37:23, 27; cf. Isa. 54:5–10). Thus, although some sort of break with the past is clearly understood, 'the newness of the new covenant must not stand in absolute contradiction to the previous covenants. A factor of continuity must be recognized' (Robertson 1980: 281).

Yet the newness of the new covenant must not be underestimated; it incorporates novel dimensions that reflect a radical discontinuity with the past (cf. Jer. 31:32): a complete removal of sin (Jer. 31:34; Ezek. 36:29, 33); an inner transformation of heart (Jer. 31: 33; Ezek. 36:26); an intimate relationship with God (Jer. 31:34a; Ezek. 36:27). Significantly, all these aspects of the new covenant underline its most important novelty: its indestructibility. Unlike previous covenants, there will be no possibility of the new covenant being broken unilaterally. This suggests, therefore, the following.

The new covenant will be both climactic and eternal

In some sense previous divine covenants find their culmination in this new covenant, for this future covenant encapsulates the key promises made throughout the Old Testament era (e.g. a physical inheritance; a divine–human relationship; an everlasting dynasty; blessing on a national and international scale), while at the same time transcending them. Thus the new covenant is the climactic fulfilment of the covenants that God established with the patriarchs, the nation of Israel, and the dynasty of David. The promises of these earlier covenants find their ultimate fulfilment in this new covenant, and in it such promises become 'eternal' in the truest sense.

Chapter Eight

God's new covenant inaugurated through Jesus

Introduction

As noted previously, the term covenant (*diathēkē*) occurs some 33 times in the New Testament, distributed as follows:

1. *Gospels and Acts*: Matt. 26:28; Mark 14:24; Luke 1:72; 22:20; Acts 3:25; 7:8
2. *Letters of Paul*: Rom. 9:4; 11:27; 1 Cor. 11:25; 2 Cor. 3:6, 14; Gal. 3:15, 17; 4:24; Eph. 2:12
3. *Hebrews*: Heb. 7:22; 8:6, 8, 9 (2×), 10; 9:4 (2×), 15 (2×), 16, 17, 20; 10:16, 29; 12:24; 13:20
4. *Revelation*: Rev. 11:19 ('ark of the covenant')

In addition to these passages in which the word is used, there are admittedly other texts that echo the covenant idea or allude to its fulfilment in Jesus and the international community.[1] Ideally, therefore, an examination of the theological significance of covenant in the New Testament should not restrict itself to texts that explicitly employ the term. As in the Old Testament, the covenant concept is much wider than that.[2] However, in the interests of economy, the present chapter will focus primarily on passages where covenant terminology is explicitly used, while incorporating other relevant material where necessary.

[1] According to Tan (2005: 151–152), Luke's use of the cognate verb (*diatithēmi*) with respect to the kingdom of God (Luke 22:29) is especially significant, given its association with covenant ratification elsewhere (cf. Gen. 15:18; 21:27, 32; Exod. 24:8; Deut. 5:2; 2 Kgs 10:19; Acts 3:25; Heb. 8:10; 9:16, 17; 10:16). If this is indeed the connotation of *diatithēmi* here, this verse may lend exegetical support to the idea of some form of covenant arrangement involving the Father and the Son. However, the verb may arguably be used here simply to mean 'confer', as is reflected in most English translations.

[2] E.g. as Tan (2005) suggests, more subtle allusions to new covenant realities include the redrawing of the boundaries of the people of God, foreshadowed by Jesus' selection of the Twelve and his portrayal as a new Moses. See also Gräbe 2006: 82–107.

The new covenant in the Gospels

Although the 'new covenant' is mentioned explicitly only in connection with the Last Supper,[3] the Gospels are replete with associated ideas. Indeed, from his opening genealogy to his concluding paragraph, Matthew declares that the Old Testament's covenant promises find their fulfilment through Jesus. While the other evangelists may not place quite as much emphasis upon fulfilment,[4] they nevertheless bear eloquent testimony to the fact that Jesus is the anticipated Messiah, the one through whom salvation comes not only to Israel, but to all who submit to him in repentance and faith.

Other than in accounts of the Last Supper, the only occurrence of the word *diathēkē* in the Gospels (i.e. Luke 1:72) is found in Luke's birth narrative, a narrative saturated with the idea of Old Testament hopes being fulfilled: (a) Gabriel's description of Zechariah's unborn son (cf. Luke 1:13–17; esp. v. 17); (b) Gabriel's annunciation of Jesus' birth (Luke 1:26–33; esp. v. 33); (c) Mary's song of praise (Luke 1:46–55; esp. vv. 54–55); (d) Zechariah's prophecy (Luke 1:68–79; esp. vv. 69–75).[5]

Given its use of explicit covenant terminology (vv. 72–73), as well as the number of covenant allusions it contains, this last text is especially significant.[6] Zechariah's song is made up of two distinct parts; the first (vv. 68–75) rehearses God's covenant faithfulness to the present; the second (vv. 76–79) anticipates the climax of covenant history in the coming visitation from on high.[7] It is clear that Zechariah understood God's present activity as the culmination of his covenant promises, the most foundational of these being the 'oath that he swore to . . . Abraham' (ESV).[8] While the immediate context

---

[3] See below.

[4] While the fulfilment motif is especially pronounced in Matthew, such a motif – as Wilson has recently underlined (2005: 159–177) – is significant in Luke also. In particular, Wilson notes Luke's emphasis on forgiveness (for him the major promise of Jer. 31) as a central aspect of Jesus' ministry (2005: 172–177).

[5] The fulfilment theme continues in the next chapter; cf. the Isaianic allusions in the angelic praise (Luke 2:14) and in Simeon's response to the baby Jesus (Luke 2:29–32; cf. vv. 25–26).

[6] Covenant allusions are discernible in the use of Israel (v. 68), exodus language (vv. 68, 71, 74), a Davidic Saviour figure (v. 69), and the word of the prophets (v. 70). In addition, there are clear echoes of anticipated new covenant realities (vv. 69, 74b–75, 77, 79).

[7] As Wilson (2005: 168) observes, 'The use of the important term *episkeptomai* (to visit) in verses 68 and 78 appears to form an *inclusio* around the prophecy.'

[8] This is obviously in keeping with the idea that Israel's history begins with the call of Abraham.

for Zechariah's prophecy is the birth of John, the reference to 'a horn of salvation . . . in the house of his servant David' (ESV) indicates that Zechariah's thought is more sharply focused on Mary's unborn child than on his own newborn son (cf. Luke 1:31–33). This is further underlined in the second part of the song, which, while acknowledging the unique role of the Messiah's forerunner, looks beyond John to the fulfilment of God's promised blessings of salvation, forgiveness, light and peace.

According to the New Testament's witness, the new covenant was ratified by the sacrificial death of Jesus. While the textual evidence casts doubt over the originality of the word 'new' in Matthew and Mark's account of the institution of the Lord's Supper,[9] the presence of the adjective in 1 Corinthians 11:25 (perhaps our earliest account of the Last Supper) and Luke 22:20 suggests it was at least implicit in what Jesus said.[10] In any case, Jesus was clearly referring to something other than the covenant with which his Jewish disciples would have been most familiar (i.e. the Mosaic). The allusions to both the forgiveness anticipated by Jeremiah (Matt. 26:28; Jer. 31:34) and the blood associated with the establishment of the original Mosaic covenant (Luke 22:20; Exod. 24:7) further underline that Jesus understood his death as the inauguration of the new covenant.[11]

In keeping with this premise, the Gospels present Jesus as the climax of the Old Testament's covenantal promises.[12] Through Jesus the promises made to Abraham find their ultimate fulfilment (Matt. 1:1, 17; 3:9; 8:11–12; cf. Luke 1:55, 72–73; John 8:31–59). He is the one anticipated in the Pentateuch, and in whom the obligations of the Mosaic covenant have been both fulfilled and transcended (Matt. 3:15; 5:17–48; 9:16–17; 11:28–30). He is the royal son of David

---

[9] The adjective is missing in several important early witnesses, suggesting that it has been inserted into Matt. 26:28 and Mark 14:24 from the parallel accounts; cf. Luke 22:20; 1 Cor. 11:25. The omission of Luke 22:19b–20 from some manuscripts (i.e. Codex Bezae) is most likely the result of a scribal error or misunderstanding (with respect to the second cup), and can thus be discounted as far as text criticism is concerned.

[10] While the text-critical question is fairly straightforward, the historical question to which it gives rise is more difficult: which account, if any, accurately reflects the words of Jesus? For McKenzie (2000: 88), 'it is unlikely that the word new, if original to the saying, would have been omitted . . . Thus, Jesus himself probably never actually spoke of a "new covenant." ' While this may be so, Isaianic echoes in the Synoptic accounts suggest at least an implicit connection with the covenant anticipated by Isaiah.

[11] For a more detailed analysis, see Gräbe 2006: 68–107.

[12] For a superb discussion of this, see Holwerda 1995: 27–145.

(Matt. 1:1; 3:17 [cf. Ps. 2:7]; 4:15–16 [cf. Isa. 9:1–10]; 15:22; 16:16; 21:5; 22:41–46; cf. Luke 1:69–70), who will shepherd the people of God (Matt. 2:6; 9:36; 15:29–39 [cf. Ezek. 34:11–16]; cf. John 10:1–16). He is further portrayed as the remnant, the 'true Israel' through whom salvation will come to the nations (Matt. 2:15; 4:1–11; 5:13–16; 8:11; 12:18–21; 13:47; 21:42–44; 24:14; 25:32–34; 28:19; cf. Luke 2:14, 32), and in whom 'new covenant' blessings such as cleansing and forgiveness are experienced (Matt. 1:21; 8:1–4, 17; 9:1–8; 11:2–15).

However, as well as this positive emphasis in the Gospels on the fulfilment of covenant blessings, there is also a more negative theme: the fulfilment of covenant curses (judgment) on unbelieving Israel (Matt. 8:12; 13:12–14; 21:43; 23:37–39; cf. Luke 16:19–31). In order to inherit the covenant promises, more was required than mere biological descent (Matt. 3:9)!

The new covenant in Acts

The term 'covenant' appears only twice in Acts (3:25; 7:8), both times with reference to God's covenant with Abraham. Peter's reference to the patriarchal covenant (Acts 3:25) appears to quote the promissory oath of Genesis 22:16–18,[13] a text with great significance as far as the international dimension of God's promises to Abraham is concerned. Clearly, Peter sees the fulfilment of this covenant in the benefits offered through the death and resurrection of Jesus; namely, the blessing of salvation ('sins blotted out' and 'times of refreshing') that could be experienced through repentance and faith in him (Acts 2:18–20).

The passing reference to 'covenant' in Stephen's speech (Acts 7:8) is less significant; Stephen seems to have in view here simply the giving of the *sign* of the covenant; hence his expression 'the covenant of circumcision'. His focus does not appear to be on the covenant or its fulfilment, and therefore is of little consequence for the present discussion.

However, while Acts may use the word 'covenant' on only these two occasions, it clearly presents Jesus as the fulfilment of the Old

---

[13] While the word 'families' (*patriai*) does not appear in any of the Septuagint Genesis texts in which this aspect of the ancestral promise is explicitly mentioned, Gen. 22:18 (subsequently cited in Gen. 26:4) ties the international blessing to Abraham's seed rather than to Abraham (Gen. 12:3; 18:18) or to both the ancestor (Jacob) and his seed (Gen. 28:14).

Testament's messianic hope and the church as the people of God, the genuine heirs of the covenant promises in the Old Testament (cf. Acts 2:30, 39; 3:25; 7:52; 13:16–39; 15:14–17; 26:6, 23). Significantly, this new covenant people includes not only believing Jews, but also believing Gentiles (see esp. Acts 10:1 – 11:18; 15:1–29), thus again reflecting the international dimension of Old Testament hope.

The new covenant in Paul

Somewhat surprisingly, in the Pauline corpus the term *diathēkē* is used explicitly only nine times (Rom. 9:4; 11:27; 1 Cor. 11:25; 2 Cor. 3:6, 14; Gal. 3:15, 17; 4:24; Eph. 2:12). However, as well as these texts that explicitly use the term 'covenant', there are other passages where associated ideas are brought into focus (e.g. Rom. 4, 15). Moreover, while Sanders (1977: 420–421) may well have overstated the case for Second Temple Judaism in general, one must nevertheless recognize that the concept might sometimes be assumed even where the terminology is lacking. Thus, given the weight Paul attaches to the concept where it is mentioned, covenant – particularly the new covenant and its implications for the place of the law – is undoubtedly more foundational and pervasive in Pauline theology than a mere word study might suggest. Indeed, since the publication of Sanders's seminal monograph, enormous scholarly effort has been invested in rethinking the significance of covenant (in particular, the relationship between covenant and righteousness) in Pauline theology.

Arguing that Second Temple Judaism was not in fact the religion of 'legalistic works-righteousness' reflected in subsequent Talmudic Literature, Sanders insisted that a more accurate picture could be reconstructed from earlier sources (dating between 200 BC and AD 200). The 'pattern of religion' that Sanders drew from this material and dubbed 'covenantal nomism' was summarized by him (1977: 422) as follows:

> (1) God has chosen Israel and (2) given the law. The law implies both (3) God's promise to maintain the election and (4) the requirement to obey. (5) God rewards obedience and punishes transgression. (6) The law provides for means of atonement, and atonement results in (7) maintenance or re-establishment of the covenantal relationship. (8) All those who are maintained in the covenant by obe-

dience, atonement and God's mercy belong to the group which will be saved.

Thus understood, first-century Judaism was not, as traditional Protestant scholarship had suggested, a 'religion of works' undergirded by a 'theology of merit'; rather, it was a religion in which obedience to the law was simply the means of maintaining the covenant (i.e. staying in relationship with God), not a means of entering the covenant (i.e. establishing a relationship with God); the latter, Sanders contended, was purely on the basis of God's gracious election.

While a fuller discussion of Sanders's concept of 'covenantal nomism' and its impact on New Testament scholarship lies well outside the scope of the present study,[14] the following observations are particularly pertinent to our understanding of covenant in Paul:

1. 'Covenantal nomism', even if not full-blooded merit theology,[15] is still antithetical to the theology of Paul. As several critics of the 'New Perspective' have observed,[16] Sanders and his disciples have succeeded merely in correcting an understanding of Judaism as Pelagian with an understanding of Judaism that is semi-Pelagian.[17] As such, it was still something to which Paul was diametrically opposed.

2. 'Covenantal nomism', even if it were the universal 'pattern of religion' reflected in Second Temple Judaism,[18] does not seem to square with the teaching of Paul. O'Brien (2004: 260–272) notes the following irreconcilable differences: (a) Paul's teaching on election and the definition of Israel does not fit Sanders's paradigm; (b) Paul stresses the priority of grace in salvation, not the exclusivity of grace

---

[14] For a penetrating critique, see Gundry 1985. For a much more comprehensive discussion, see Carson, O'Brien and Seifrid 2001, 2004. For something more concise, but with a helpful bibliographical review, see Waters 2004.

[15] Sanders's construct seems to encompass a significant amount of merit theology. See Carson, O'Brien and Seifrid 2001: 545.

[16] This term, coined by Dunn (1983), has been adopted as the nomenclature for recent approaches to Paul that share and develop Sanders's concept of 'covenantal nomism'.

[17] E.g. see Waters 2004: 57–58, 152, 186–187.

[18] Sanders's critics contend that the extent to which this alleged pattern of religion is in fact supported in Second Temple literature has been vastly overstated. It is not that he is altogether wrong; rather, it is that he is not altogether right, and this undercuts his essential premise: that Second Temple Judaism must be understood in terms of covenantal nomism. See Carson, O'Brien and Seifrid 2001: 543.

suggested by Sanders; (c) Paul's critique of misplaced Jewish confidence on the grounds of election-based privileges reflects an altogether different 'pattern of religion'; (d) Paul's insistence on works as the divinely produced evidence of faith is very different from interpreting such as the grounds of one's perseverance; (e) Paul insists that divine grace undergirds salvation from start to finish, not that the latter results from a synergism between divine grace and human effort; (f) Paul's anthropological presuppositions (e.g. his insistence on human depravity and its ramifications) were starkly different from those of Palestinian Judaism (e.g. the presupposition of free will and its ramifications).

3. 'Covenantal nomism', while raising the profile of 'covenant' in Pauline thought, does so at the expense of other doctrines (e.g. justification by faith) which are radically reinterpreted to fit the underlying premise (i.e. that 'good works' are in some sense instrumental in salvation) or are dismissed altogether (e.g. the imputation of Christ's righteousness to the elect). Thus 'righteousness' is understood in a highly reductionist manner; in divine terms it is defined as 'God's covenant faithfulness', whereas in human terms it is equated with 'being in the covenant'. However, as critics have pointed out, apart from the fact that these two concepts ('covenant' and 'righteousness') are seldom linked in the Old Testament,[19] it is wholly misleading to reduce 'righteousness' to the realm of relationships; the basic nuance of the righteousness word group is 'accordance with a norm', and such is arguably the most appropriate understanding of the concept in Paul.

Therefore, however much 'covenantal nomism' is a discernible pattern of religion in Second Temple Judaism, it is of little help in understanding the role of covenant in Paul.

Rather than considering the relevant Pauline texts in chronological sequence,[20] the present canonical sequence will be adhered to in the following discussion. Accordingly, the first explicit mention of covenant in the Pauline corpus (Rom. 9:4) encompasses all the covenants relating to national Israel,[21] presumably including every-

[19] See Seifrid 2001.

[20] The most likely historical sequence, assuming an early date for Galatians, is as follows: Galatians; 1 Corinthians; 2 Corinthians; Romans; Ephesians.

[21] While some important witnesses attest to the singular, the plural ('covenants') is preferable: the plural form of *diathēkē* is rarely used in both the Septuagint and the NT, and copyists are more likely to have assimilated the plural to the predominant use of singulars in this particular list (cf. the attestation of analogous assimilation with respect to 'promises' at the end of the verse) than vice versa.

thing from the covenant of Genesis 15 to the prospect of a new covenant anticipated by the prophets.[22] Paul's point is that these covenants were one of several privileges enjoyed by Israel as God's special people (cf. Eph. 2:12, where the same point is stated negatively with respect to the privileges from which Gentiles were formerly excluded),[23] which raise the spectre that Paul addresses in these chapters: the possibility that God's word and purposes for Israel have somehow failed (cf. Rom. 9:6; 11:1–2, 28–29).[24]

When covenant is next explicitly mentioned (Rom. 11:27) in this important discussion of Israel's place in God's plan of salvation, it is not the covenants generally, but the new covenant that is brought into focus. Whatever else the apostle is saying in these chapters, he is certainly insisting that all true Israelites will indeed be saved, for God's covenant word is his bond. What is less clear, however, is whether 'all Israel' encompasses Abraham's spiritual seed in its entirety (i.e. Jews and Gentiles),[25] or exclusively connotes those who are his biological descendants as well.[26]

The latter premise – that Paul consistently employs 'Israel' in an ethnic sense in these chapters – has led some to find support in Romans 9 – 11 for a 'two-covenant' theology (i.e. rather than replacing God's covenant with ethnic Israel, God's covenant in Christ with

---

[22] Whether or not the new covenant should be included here is debatable. However, since the new covenant was promised primarily to Israel, and it is clearly the focus in Paul's subsequent mention of covenant in these chapters (Rom. 11:27), I see no reason for excluding it.

[23] The fact that Paul differentiates here between 'covenants' and 'promises' is certainly suggestive, although it would probably be unwise to press too much out of the distinction at this point.

[24] These chapters (Rom. 9 – 11) constitute a distinct unit within the epistle and address in particular God's relationship to ethnic Israel in the new covenant era.

[25] So Wright 1991: 250. While no longer popular today, this interpretation boasts a long antiquity, and has been defended by many (following Calvin) in Reformed circles.

[26] For a non-technical defence of this interpretation, see Motyer 1989: 148–159. Motyer argues that 'all Israel' in Rom. 11:26 comprises all elect Israelites (i.e. the group formerly distinguished from mere ethnic Israelites in Rom. 9:6). Rather than anticipating a large-scale conversion of ethnic Israelites at the climax of salvation history, however, Motyer argues that the salvation of these elect ethnic Israelites is an ongoing phenomenon, taking place from the first coming of Christ (alluded to in Rom. 11:26a) through to the end of the present era (alluded to in Rom. 11:25b). While holding to a similar interpretation of 'all Israel', many other exegetes understand Rom. 11:26 in terms of the second coming, and/or anticipate a climactic spiritual revival among ethnic Israelites as the immediate precursor to the parousia. A detailed investigation of the interpretative issues involved lies well outside the parameters of the present study. For concise discussions, see Holwerda 1995: 147–176 and Riddlebarger 2003: 183–194. For a survey of recent scholarly debate at a more technical level, see Moo 1996: 710–739 and 2004: 196–205.

the church exists alongside the former).[27] Indeed, some advocates of such a 'two-covenant' theology interpret the key verses (11:25–27) as predicting an eschatological salvation of Jews that is based on adherence to Torah or some other 'special way' (German: *Sonderweg*) rather than faith in Christ.[28] However, as Moo (1996: 725–726) observes, while holding obvious appeal for those living in a 'post-Holocaust' and pluralistic era, such an interpretation is absolutely foreign to the apostle Paul: 'Paul teaches that salvation can be found in one place only: within the one community made up of those who believe in Jesus Christ . . . Jews, like Gentiles, can be saved only by responding to the gospel and being grafted into the one people of God.' Thus, however these notoriously difficult verses in Romans 11 are understood with respect to the salvation of ethnic Israel – whether in terms of an ongoing ingathering of elect Jews through time, or a climactic ingathering of elect Jews at the end of time – the basis of such salvation can only be faith in Jesus Christ.

If, as Wright suggests, the overall purpose of Romans is to encourage unity in the church by demonstrating how God has been faithful to his covenant promises to Abraham (see Wright 1992: 234), the emphasis in Romans 9 – 11 is surely on the fact that God's covenantal promises vis-à-vis Israel will indeed be fulfilled, but only in the genuine heirs of the covenant(s), Abraham's spiritual descendants (whether Jew or Gentile; cf. Eph. 2:11–22). Thus Paul highlights the fact that, although ethnic Israel had enjoyed some tremendous spiritual privileges (Rom. 9:4–5), God had never promised that *all* Abraham's physical posterity would inherit the covenant promises (Rom. 9:6–13). Rather, through Jesus God has done exactly what he had promised Abraham (Gen. 12:3) and later reiterated through the prophets; namely, extending blessing to all the nations of the earth. Thus Romans 9 – 11 graphically reinforces the point that Paul made earlier in this epistle (cf. Rom. 4:16–19) – that the gospel is the means by which the covenant promise made to Abraham is realized: Abraham's 'fatherhood of many nations' and multitudinous descendants relates to the extension (beyond ethnic Israel) of the people of God.

However, Paul is also at pains to stress in Romans 9 – 11 that this extension of the people of God to include Gentiles did not negate or

---

[27] Such a two-covenant approach has been embraced by some in the context of post-Holocaust ecumenical dialogue that finds any notion of Christian 'supersessionism' embarrassing and/or objectionable.

[28] For a penetrating critique of this *Sonderweg* viewpoint, see Hvalvik 1990.

abrogate the fulfilment of the covenant promises in relation to ethnic Israelites. Unfortunately, this important caveat has been implicitly denied in many supersessionist readings of Scripture, which suggest that Israel has been entirely replaced by the church as the people of God.[29] As Horton has recently argued (2006: 131–132), rather than seeing the church as simply replacing Israel, it is more in keeping with Scripture to see the church 'as Israel's fruition'. Thus understood, the church is the continuation and extension of Israel as the people of God, encompassing both elect Jews and elect Gentiles who, together, make up 'the Israel of God' (Gal. 6:16).[30] Therefore biological descendants of Abraham were in no way disadvantaged under the new covenant, as some of Paul's protagonists were apparently suggesting (cf. Rom. 11:13–22). Rather, they (like the Gentiles) could respond positively to the gospel message – and evidently Paul was convinced that through God's mercy many would (whether this would take place throughout the present era and/or just prior to the parousia is in one sense immaterial) – 'and in this way all Israel [i.e. all elect Israelites; cf. Rom. 9:6–8] will be saved' (Rom. 11:26 TNIV).[31]

[29] Sometimes referred to as 'replacement theology', supersessionism has been categorized by Soulen (1996: 30–34) as follows: punitive or retributive supersessionism explains Israel's displacement as God's judgment for Jewish rejection of Jesus and the gospel; economic supersessionism views the history of national Israel merely as a symbol or type of the eternal antitype (the church); structural supersessionism treats distinctive Israelite elements in Scripture as mere background to its main focus – a salvation history of universal proportions. While none of these is devoid of biblical and theological merit (*pace* Blaising), such replacement theology has arguably become the seed-bed for the anti-Semitism that has unfortunately blighted Christian history. However, it is clear from Paul's discussion in Rom. 9 – 11 that any antipathy towards ethnic Israel is not only unwarranted, but expresses gross arrogance and a lack of mature theological reflection (Rom. 11:11–24). Therefore, while the apostolic interpretation of the OT undoubtedly does involve some degree of 'supersessionism' (contra Blaising, for whom 'supersessionism lives in Christian theology today purely on the momentum of its own tradition' 2001: 436), this concept needs to be carefully nuanced lest an overemphasis on the church as the people of God leads to the exclusion of ethnic Israel. However one interprets the 'all Israel' of Rom. 11:26, it must obviously incorporate elect, biological descendants of Abraham; moreover, it is clear from the overall thrust of Paul's argument that the extension of God's grace to Gentiles did not signal the fact that he had consigned ethnic Israel to perdition.

[30] The meaning of this text is also controversial, but the preceding argument (i.e. that the children of Abraham are identified by faith in Christ rather than circumcision) seems to warrant reading 'the Israel of God' in its redefined sense.

[31] This interpretation of 'all Israel' seems to fit best with the flow of Paul's argument in these chapters. With others Motyer notes two major difficulties with the interpretation of 'all Israel' as 'all elect Jews and Gentiles' (i.e. the whole people of God): (a) 'Israel' must bear two different meanings within the same sentence. (b) To maintain that the whole church will be saved seems to be beside the point, in which the primary focus is on the status and fate of ethnic Israelites (cf. Rom. 9:2; 10:1; 11:1, 25, 28–31).

Hence the covenant promises had been inherited not by Israel in an exclusively ethnic or biological sense, but by all Abraham's true descendants – those united to Abraham through faith in Jesus Christ.

Significantly, the inheritance of the latter appears to include even the territorial promise, albeit in a cosmic sense (Rom. 4:13; cf. Matt. 5:5). Thus understood, the promise of land, while including the territory of Canaan, ultimately encompasses much more; namely, the 'new heaven and the new earth' anticipated by the prophets (Rom. 8:17–25; cf. 2 Pet. 3:13).

In any case, Paul's discussion of covenant in Romans serves primarily to bolster confidence in God's faithfulness to his ancient promises and the fulfilment of these in an Israel that, while not encompassing every biological descendant of Abraham, certainly incorporates all ethnic Israelites who, whether in the present or in the future, turn from their unbelief, and thus, along with their Gentile brothers, enter into the promised inheritance.

The Corinthian passages in which the 'covenant' is explicitly mentioned (i.e. 1 Cor. 11:25; 2 Cor. 3:6, 14) are important because of their associated use of the adjectives 'new' and 'old'. This clearly alludes to the contrast between the old and new covenants reflected in Jeremiah, and suggests that the new covenant anticipated by the prophet has now been inaugurated. Indeed, the Eucharistic text (1 Cor. 11:25) attests to the fact that Paul, presumably following Jesus himself,[32] identified Christ's death on the cross as the sacrificial rite by which this new covenant was solemnly ratified.

Similarly, in the defence of his apostolic ministry (2 Cor. 2:14 – 7:16), Paul identifies the 'new covenant' as the gospel of Jesus Christ (2 Cor. 4:3–6),[33] and the Christian community as those in whom the blessings of the new covenant have been realized (2 Cor. 3:3; cf. Jer. 31:32–33; Ezek. 11:19; 36:26–27). Given the implicit contrast in 2 Corinthians 3 between two conflicting views of the new covenant, it seems that Paul's Judaizing opponents also claimed to be 'ministers of the new covenant'.[34] However, as far as Paul is concerned, these

[32] See the above discussion on the use of 'new' in the Eucharistic traditions reflected in the Gospels.

[33] Clearly, these verses unpack the life-giving, liberating and more glorious 'ministry of the Spirit' (2 Cor. 3:8) associated with 'ministers of a new covenant' (2 Cor. 3:6); cf. the continuing use of key words from the previous passage such as 'veiled', 'image' and 'glory' and the obvious parallel between the removal of the veil and its effects (2 Cor. 3:16–18) and the spiritual illumination described in 2 Cor. 4:6.

[34] McKenzie (2000: 102) infers this from the fact that 'new covenant' is modified in 2 Cor. 3:6 by 'not of the letter but of the Spirit'. However, while this does not

opponents had seriously misunderstood the import of Jeremiah 31 by concentrating on 'the letter' rather than 'the Spirit'. He thus elaborates on this contrast between the death-dealing letter and the life-infusing Spirit in the following verses (2 Cor. 3:7–18). The 'letter' is clearly identified with the Mosaic code, which was 'carved in letters on stone' (2 Cor. 3:7 ESV). While admitting that this epoch (the administration of the law) was inaugurated with divine splendour (2 Cor. 3:7), Paul insists that such splendour (associated with a ministry of condemnation) is far outweighed by the surpassing glory associated with the ministry of righteousness inaugurated by Christ (2 Cor. 3:8–9).[35] Moreover, the inferiority of the Mosaic era is further reflected in the fading nature of its splendour (2 Cor. 3:7), contrasting starkly with the glory associated with what is permanent (2 Cor. 3:11). Paul's argument, therefore, is not that the letter associated with the old covenant is bad or inherently flawed. Rather, it is that it is vastly inferior to the life-giving Spirit associated with the new covenant. As McKenzie (2000: 103) observes, 'Paul . . . takes on Moses not to demean him or his work, but to point out that the "ministry" under him, though necessary for its era, was imperfect and that blindly following him makes no sense in light of the availability of something far superior.' The problem, however, as the apostle highlights in the following verses (2 Cor. 3:12–18), is that the eschatological reality has been obscured by a veil. Such a veil, initially introduced by Moses himself to hide the glory that was fading,[36] remains metaphorically in place (2 Cor. 3:15), preventing those blinded by hardened minds from seeing the glory of God until they turn to the Lord.[37] Only then will they see, with unveiled faces, his superior and transforming glory (2 Cor. 3:16–18). Thus Paul argues

---

necessarily follow, the immediate context does seem to suggest that Paul is dealing with two conflicting concepts of Christian ministry; thus his opponents almost certainly claimed to be ministers of the new covenant – perhaps explaining Paul's use here of unusual terminology. Alternatively, the contrast may be understood as simply between the new dispensation and the old (e.g. see Barnett 1997: 175 n. 23). However, even in this case, Paul is clearly addressing a fundamental deficiency in the understanding of his Judaizing opponents.

[35] While Paul does not elaborate here on either 'condemnation' or 'righteousness', it is clear from elsewhere how these terms are understood: 'the law inevitably led to condemnation because it was impossible to keep completely, but the new covenant brings justification [righteousness] through faith in Christ' (McKenzie 2000: 103).

[36] Lit. 'the end (*telos*) of [the glory] that was being abolished'. As Barnett (1997: 190 n. 6) suggests, this mention of 'end' or 'goal' carries significant eschatological weight.

[37] Clearly, 'the Lord' here is Jesus himself (2 Cor. 3:14; cf. 1 Cor. 15:45; 2 Cor. 4:5), and to 'turn to the Lord' denotes the penitence and faith associated with Christian conversion.

that, by insisting on keeping the letter of the law in accordance with the old covenant, his Judaizing opponents obscure the new covenant reality – the age of the Spirit in which the glory of God is perfectly revealed 'in the face of Jesus Christ' (2 Cor. 4:6 ESV). He thus urges his Corinthian readers to maintain their confidence in this eschatological reality (cf. 2 Cor. 5:17; 6:2),[38] lest they 'receive the grace of God in vain' (2 Cor. 6:1 ESV).

It is clear, therefore, from Paul's use of 'covenant' in the Corinthian epistles, that Paul understands the new covenant to have been inaugurated through Christ's death and to have superseded the old covenant, which was vastly inferior.

Paul's use of covenant terminology in Galatians serves primarily to establish the significance of the Abrahamic over against the Mosaic covenant. Once again (cf. Rom. 11), however, the crucial point to note is that Abraham's genuine 'heirs' are not simply those who can claim biological descent from the patriarch, but rather 'those who believe' (Gal. 3:7 NIV). The latter, as Scripture had foreseen (Gal. 3:8–9; cf. Gen. 12:3), incorporated not only Jewish but also Gentile believers; thus it was this company of believers – those who, like Abraham, were justified before God by faith rather than by the law (Gal. 3:6, 11) – that constituted Abraham's sons and heirs of the blessing (Gal. 3:9).

This chapter is particularly important in view of its discussion of how the covenant promises are inherited. Paul is adamant that it is through faith in Christ, not through 'works of the law' (Gal. 3:10–14 ESV). Indeed, such reliance on 'works of the law' results not in blessing, but in curse (Gal. 3:10). This latter statement has traditionally been understood by the unstated premise that no-one can keep the law perfectly, and thus works-righteousness is impossible. While accepting that such a premise is true, Dumbrell (2004) has recently argued that it is beside the point here. Rather, for Dumbrell the underlying premise here is that with the death of Jesus, the mechanism of atonement (i.e. sacrificial ritual) for law-breakers under the Mosaic covenant has been removed. Thus 'in the "now" of the new covenant age, all the Jews who rely on obedience to the law in order to stay in the covenant are under the curse of the law, since the Mosaic covenant which offered atonement through sacrifice ceased with the cross' (Dumbrell 2004: 303). However, apart from the fact

[38] While the language of 2 Cor. 5:15 – 6:2 is primarily that of 'creation', a comparison between old and new covenants may also be implicit, as the new covenant anticipated by the prophets clearly encompasses the idea of new creation.

that his premise must equally be assumed, Dumbrell's suggestion fails to give adequate weight to the emphasis Paul (following the Septuagint) seems to place on the word 'all', and, more importantly, to the fact that Jesus' death is explicitly presented here as the remedy for this curse rather than its catalyst (Gal. 3:13).

Having emphasized that the covenant blessings are (and always have been) inherited by faith, and therefore cannot be secured through works of the law, Paul introduces the covenant concept explicitly (Gal. 3:15–18). Here it is widely accepted that Paul uses a legal analogy that plays on the different nuances of *diathēkē*: thus its initial occurrence (Gal. 3:15) is translated in most English versions as 'will' or 'testament', whereas it is subsequently used (Gal. 3:17) in its traditional biblical sense; hence translated as 'covenant'. This interpretation, however, has not won universal support. Most recently, it has been strongly challenged by Hahn, who argues that if *diathēkē* is understood in Galatians 3:15 as 'testament', 'the legal background for Paul's statement and the logic of his argument in vv. 15–17 are obscure' (2005a: 79). Thus Hahn suggests taking it in its usual Pauline sense of 'covenant' throughout this pericope. In support, Hahn marshals the following arguments:

1. Within Hellenistic Judaism, *diathēkē* (initially meaning a 'disposition') did not evolve as elsewhere to mean a 'final testamentary disposition' (i.e. a last will and testament), but a legally binding relationship of obligation ratified by an oath (i.e. in Hebrew terminology, a *běrît*) – thus explaining the otherwise anomalous translation of the latter term by *diathēkē* rather than *synthēkē* in the Septuagint.
2. Everywhere else in Paul, the New Testament,[39] the Septuagint,[40] and the Apostolic Fathers *diathēkē* is employed in its normal biblical sense of 'covenant'.
3. The introduction of a Hellenistic 'testament' in Galatians 3:15 would undermine the coherence of Paul's argument and lack rhetorical force or relevance for either Paul or his opponents.

[39] Hahn acknowledges the possible exception of Heb. 9:15–22, but maintains (cf. Hahn 2004) that here too 'covenant' is the preferred understanding. For more on this, see the discussion below.

[40] In the Septuagint 270 of the 286 occurrences of *běrît* in the MT are translated by *diathēkē*.

4. If *diathēkē* is understood as 'testament' in Galatians 3:15, Paul's claim that 'no-one adds to or annuls' such an entity is erroneous.[41] However, such *is* undeniably true in the case of a 'covenant' (cf. Josh. 9:3–27; 2 Sam. 21:1–14; Ezek. 17:11–18; Mal. 2:14–15), and thus, understood in this way, Paul's statement makes excellent sense.

5. As a legal means of extending kinship privileges to outsiders, 'covenant' is a particularly apt illustration here in Galatians 3:6–18 (where the extension of such privileges is of particular concern).

6. In the ancient world (as attested in biblical and extra-biblical texts), covenants transmitted blessings and curses; thus are particularly germane to the preceding discussion (Gal. 3:10–14).

7. The presence of legal terminology in Galatians 3:15 is equally well suited to 'covenant' (a legal instrument) as to 'testament'.

8. The introductory clause 'Humanly speaking' does not introduce 'an example from everyday life' (TNIV), but rather an *a fortiori* argument (i.e. if according to human standards altering covenant obligations is illegal, how much more so according to divine standards) in which the central term *diathēkē* must bear the same meaning throughout.[42]

It would seem, therefore, that rather than introducing an alien idea (i.e. a 'last will and testament') into the discussion, Paul is introducing the biblical concept of a covenant here in order to illustrate his main point: just as a human covenant, once ratified, could not be altered or annulled, neither could a divine covenant. Therefore, the covenant that God had ratified with Abraham, through which God's promises to Abraham and his 'seed' had been solemnly guaranteed, could not be annulled by the law (i.e. the Mosaic covenant),[43] which had come 430 years later (Gal. 3:16–18).[44]

[41] Obviously, this depends on the meaning of 'ratified'; if the death of the testator is implied, obviously no changes to the 'testament' are legally possible. However, there is certainly no explicit suggestion of death in the text, and the analogy with God in Gal. 3:17 seems to make such unlikely.

[42] Longenecker (1990: 127) labels it as an *a minori ad maius* type of argument (i.e. arguing from what is true in the human sphere to what is true in the divine economy), but Hahn's point remains valid nevertheless.

[43] McKenzie (2000: 99) denies that 'the law' here equates with the Mosaic covenant, but surely the overarching context (esp. Gal. 4:21–31) suggests that there is no such dichotomy in Paul's thinking.

[44] Incidentally, Paul's argument seems to reinforce the idea that the covenant ratified in Gen. 15 must be distinct from the covenant announced in Gen. 17 and ratified by oath in Gen. 22. The subsequent introduction of human obligations into what had previously been an unconditional covenant seems to go against the whole grain of Paul's argument here – one that obviously raises the important question of the

As Hahn further suggests, the patriarchal covenant Paul seems to have in mind is that ratified by divine oath in Genesis 22.[45] Here alone all three characteristics highlighted in Paul's discussion are present.[46] Moreover, Paul's conflated quotation earlier in this passage (Gal. 3:8; cf. Gen. 12:3; 22:18) may be a deliberate allusion to the covenant oath associated with the Aqedah incident,[47] as may the quotation from Deuteronomy (Gal. 3:13; cf. Deut. 21:23; Gen. 22:9),[48] followed directly by what is apparently a reworking of the oath (Gal. 3:14; cf. Gen. 22:18). Moreover, the fact that this covenant is immediately preceded by the ratification of the first human covenant recounted in Scripture (Gen. 21:22–34) is certainly suggestive in view of the *a fortiori* argument Paul employs here.[49] Therefore, a plausible case can be made for identifying the covenant spoken of here (Gal. 3:17) as that ratified by divine oath in Genesis 22.

While Hahn's argument is generally compelling, there is one weak link to which he pays insufficient attention.[50] The key phrase ('and to your seed'; Gal. 3:16 TNIV) is not used in Genesis 22. However, although this clause does appear in earlier texts (i.e. Gen. 13:15; 15:18; 17:8), in each of these it relates primarily to a single promise: the promise of land. While this promise was certainly ratified by a divine oath (cf. Gen. 24:7),[51] Paul speaks of *promises* (Gal. 3:16), and

---

relationship between the Abrahamic and the Mosaic covenants. Not surprisingly, therefore, the apostle addresses this issue in the following verses (Gal. 3:19 – 4:7).

[45] In support of interpreting Gen. 22 as a second divine covenant with Abraham, Hahn (2005a: 89) notes the following texts: Luke 1:72–73; Acts 3:25; *Assumption of Moses* 3:9; *Fragmentary Targum* of Lev. 26:42. All of these, he argues, reflect 'an interpretive trajectory [i.e. a shift from 'covenant' to 'oath'] begun in the Hebrew Scriptures themselves' (Hahn 2005a: 90–91).

[46] I.e. the covenant is *ratified by God* (Gal. 3:17), includes both *Abraham and his seed* (Gal. 3:16, 18), and guarantees divine *blessing to the Gentiles* (Gal. 3:14). While the first two elements are present, the third is clearly absent in Genesis 15. In Gen. 17 there is no ratification by God, although (*pace* Hahn) international blessing is implied (see Williamson 2000a: 154–162).

[47] I.e. the 'binding' (Heb. *'āqad*, 'to bind') of Isaac in Gen. 22.

[48] As Hahn (2005a: 93–94) notes, such an echo has been discerned by Jewish scholars also (e.g. G. Vermes and J. Levenson).

[49] Hahn also notes that a further pericope from Genesis 21 (i.e. the expulsion of Ishmael; Gen. 21:8–21) is picked up by Paul in the following chapter (Gal. 4:21–31). Thus understood, Paul's allegorical argument in Galatians 4 is not nearly so abrupt as might otherwise be the case.

[50] Cf. Hahn 2005a: 95 n. 75.

[51] The wording of Gen. 24:7 quotes Gen. 15:18 almost verbatim (in the MT the only difference is that Gen. 15:18 uses a qatal form of the verb, whereas the yiqtol is used in Gen. 24:7). Given that such an oath is intrinsic to covenant, there can be little doubt that Abraham is alluding here (Gen. 24:7) to the covenant of Genesis 15.

such a plurality of promises ratified by divine oath appears only in Genesis 22. Significantly, when Yahweh reiterates the promise of territorial inheritance to Isaac, it is included within the parameters of the oath sworn to Abraham in the context of the Aqedah incident (Gen. 26:3–5).[52]

If, as has been suggested, the divine covenant in view in Galatians 3 is that ratified by divine oath in Genesis 22, it is not surprising that Paul should interpret Abraham's 'seed' in terms of Jesus Christ and those who, through faith, are united to him (Gal. 3:16–17, 29). While Paul's exegesis in verses 16–17 has often been dismissed as somewhat fanciful or midrashic, careful examination of the patriarchal covenants, and in particular the twofold use of 'seed' in Genesis 22 (see chapter 4), lends exegetical credibility to the logic Paul applies here: as Abraham's royal, conquering seed, Jesus Christ uniquely mediates blessing to all who, through belonging to him, become 'heirs according to promise' (Gal. 3:29 ESV). Appeal can also (or alternatively) be made (with Hahn 2005a: 96) to an Isaac/Christ typology, already apparent in Galatians 3, which may explain Paul's emphasis on Abraham's singular 'seed'.[53] In any case, it is clear from Paul's identification of Abraham's 'seed' as both Jesus and those united to Abraham through faith in Christ (Gal. 3:29) that he recognizes that 'seed' (*zera'*) is a collective Hebrew noun, and hence may signify both an individual descendant and a plurality of descendants. That the noun might be used in both senses even within the Abraham narrative itself is a possibility that cannot be ruled out and, as argued above, makes good sense in the original context.

Furthermore, as Hahn (2005a: 97–98; emphasis his) perceptively observes:

> Understanding the covenant oath of the Aqedah as the background for Gal 3:6–18 clarifies Paul's argument concerning the relationship of the Abrahamic and Mosaic covenants, as well as their fulfilment in Christ's curse-bearing death on the 'tree' . . . Paul sees the historical *priority* of the Abrahamic covenant vis-à-vis the Mosaic covenant as revealing the

---

[52] Both the promises alluded to and their association with Abraham's obedience point unmistakably to Gen. 22:16–18.

[53] Hahn notes the emphasis in Gen. 22 on Isaac being Abraham's 'one and only son' (i.e. his sole heir, Ishmael having already been expelled), whose abortive sacrifice was ultimately completed in the cross of Christ, through which the promised blessing of the nations was actualized.

theological *primacy* of God's sworn obligation to bless all nations, over and against Israel's sworn obligation to keep the Sinaitic Torah (v. 17). In other words, Paul argues that since the Mosaic covenant is *subsequent* to the Abrahamic, God's purpose in binding Israel at Sinai to keep the Law (i.e. as Abraham's seed) must be legally *subordinated* to his purpose in binding himself at the Aqedah to bless all the nations (i.e. through Abraham's seed). What God promised to Abraham was not negated by what happened at Sinai . . . The oath of the Aqedah ensured the success of God's plan to bless all the nations through Abraham's seed despite their backsliding. By swearing the oath, God subjected himself to a curse, should Abraham's seed fail to convey that blessing to the nations.

Thus understood, the covenant curse-bearing consequences of Christ's death are brought into sharp focus by his hanging on a tree (Deut. 21:23). As had been prefigured by Isaac, Jesus' consent to curse-bearing impalement 'on a tree' signified 'what God alone must do to bring about "the blessing of Abraham" for Israel and the nations' (Hahn 2005a: 99).

Paul reintroduces covenant language in the following chapter (Gal. 4:21 – 5:1), albeit in what he identifies as an 'allegorical' manner (*allegoroumena*; Gal. 4:24).[54] Here Abraham's wives, Hagar and Sarah, are interpreted as representing two different covenants. The first of these (represented by Hagar) is identified as the Mosaic covenant ('from Mount Sinai . . . in Arabia' Gal. 4:24–25 ESV), which, like the slave woman, bears children for slavery (Gal. 4:24–25). The second covenant (represented by Sarah), while not explicitly identified, is clearly associated with Mount Zion and the promises of the new covenant (Gal. 4:26–27; cf. Isa. 54:1). Thus Hagar represents a covenant of enslavement (to the law), corresponding to 'the present Jerusalem' (Gal. 4:25 ESV), whereas Sarah represents a covenant of freedom and promise connected with 'the Jerusalem above' (Gal. 4:26 ESV). Clearly, Paul associated himself and his readers with the latter (Gal. 4:28, 31), whereas – by their hostility toward those 'born according to the Spirit'

[54] There is some debate over precisely what Paul means by 'allegorically' (Gal. 4:24), many interpreters understanding it more in the sense of 'typology' (i.e. the identification of analogical correspondence between OT type and new covenant antitype), rather than 'allegory' in the strict sense (i.e. where the historical reality is ignored entirely and an interpretation is imposed on the text that is totally alien to the original meaning).

(Gal. 4:29 ESV) – the Judaizers have aligned themselves with 'the son of the slave woman' who has been disinherited (Gal. 4:30 ESV). The point Paul is making through this analogy is similar to that found elsewhere (e.g. 2 Cor. 3); namely, that as heirs of the new covenant, Christians are free from the letter of the law associated with the Mosaic covenant.[55] As such, they must not 'submit again to a yoke of slavery' but stand firm in the freedom they enjoy through Christ (Gal. 5:1 ESV).

In the final explicit mention of covenant in Paul (Eph. 2:12),[56] the apostle is recounting the former disadvantages of his Gentile readers. The five deficiencies listed relate to their being outside God's chosen people (Israel).[57] As such, among other things, they had been 'strangers to the covenants of promise' (Eph. 2:12 ESV; cf. Rom. 9:4). This latter clause clearly implies that the entire series of covenants between God and Israel (i.e. the patriarchal covenants; the national covenants; the royal covenant; the anticipated new covenant) shared a major point of commonality. This 'promise', presumably the foundational promise by which God articulated his programmatic agenda to Abraham (Gen. 12:1–3), has now been fulfilled in Christ, through whom the former disadvantages of the Gentiles have been completely removed (Eph. 2:13–22) and they have become 'fellow citizens with the saints and members of the household of God' (Eph. 2:19 ESV). Thus, while formerly Gentiles were 'strangers to the covenants of promise', now, through union with Christ, they have been incorporated into the covenant community, and so enjoy full rights as heirs (Eph. 3:6; cf. Eph. 1:11–14).

In summary, therefore, Paul understood the new covenant to have been inaugurated by Christ, and ratified by his death on the cross. The heirs of God's promises were not primarily Abraham's biological descendants, but rather those who were his true 'seed' through faith in Christ. As children of promise who had been born of the Spirit, they were free from the letter of the Mosaic covenant, which was

[55] As Barnett (1997: 202–203) observes, in 2 Cor. 3:17 'it is a "freedom" from "the letter"; "letter" is the antithesis of "the Spirit" (v. 6) . . . The new covenant as promised by the prophets was not a covenant of lawlessness, but a covenant under which the people would be moved by the Spirit to "follow [God's] decrees and be careful to keep [his] laws (Ezek 36:27), to have "his] law in their minds . . . [written] in their hearts" (Jer 31:33).'

[56] The Pauline authorship of Ephesians is here assumed. For a recent critique of the arguments against Pauline authorship and a persuasive defence of the traditional view, see O'Brien 1999: 4–47.

[57] The five are as follows: (a) isolated from Christ; (b) alienated from the commonwealth of Israel; (c) strangers to the covenants of promise; (d) without hope; (e) God-forsaken in the world.

vastly inferior to the light of the transforming glory they now had in the face of Jesus Christ.

The new covenant in Hebrews

The most developed 'new covenant theology' in the New Testament is found in Hebrews. Indeed, this is a subject to which the writer returns repeatedly (cf. Heb. 7:22; 8:6 – 10:31; 12:18–24; 13:20), even employing the Jeremiah text as an inclusio (8:8–12; 10:16–17).[58] These references are concentrated in the central section of the epistle (Heb. 8 – 10), in which the superiority of the new covenant is the over-arching point.

The superiority of the new covenant has already been highlighted in the previous passage (Heb. 7:22), where it stems from the nature of Jesus' priesthood. Being a priest after the order of Melchizedek, Jesus was superior to the Levitical priesthood on several counts: (a) this priesthood had been honoured by Abraham, hence implicitly, by Levi also (Heb. 7:4–10); (b) this priesthood was not based on legal require-ment but on divine oath (Heb. 7:11–21); (c) this priesthood was both effective and everlasting (Heb. 7:23–28). Thus, having established the point that Jesus is 'guarantor of a better covenant' (Heb. 7:22 ESV), the writer elaborates on this in the following chapters.

Rather than fulfilling his high-priestly ministry on earth, Jesus carries out this function in heaven, the reality that Israel's cultic worship simply foreshadowed (Heb. 8:1–5). As such, the ministry he exercises is clearly superior, as is the associated covenant (Heb. 8:6).[59] As the reference to 'better promises' and the subsequent quotation from Jeremiah's prophecy implies, the two covenants contrasted here are the Mosaic covenant (Heb. 8:9) and the new covenant anticipated by Jeremiah and mediated by Christ. The former covenant was

[58] Though not explicitly using covenant terminology, Heb. 6:13–17 highlights the continuity between God's promissory oath to Abraham and his oath to 'the heirs of the promise' (ESV; i.e. the new covenant community). However, while the writer of Hebrews does not explicitly describe the Aqedah incident (Heb. 6:14; cf. Gen. 22:17) as the making of a 'covenant' – a term he reserves for the Mosaic covenant and the new covenant inaugurated by Christ – the express function of the oath here is clearly syn-onymous with that of a covenant – solemnly guaranteeing the promise or obligations of one or both parties involved.

[59] The new covenant serves here to reinforce the writer's main point – the superior-ity of Christ's high-priestly ministry as reflected in the contrast between the heavenly and earthly sanctuaries.

[60] Some manuscripts imply that the fault lay with the covenant itself rather than with the people (reading 'for finding fault he says to them' rather than 'for finding fault with

seriously impaired (Heb. 8:7a) by the human partners (Heb. 8:8a),[60] and thus had to be superseded by another (Heb. 8:7b; cf. Heb. 8:13). In saying that the new [covenant] makes the first one obsolete (Heb. 8:13), the writer of Hebrews is clearly suggesting the idea of supersessionism rather than mere covenant renewal. Admittedly, as McKenzie (2000: 117–118) suggests, the extent of such supersessionism may be elaborated by what immediately follows:

> in chapters 9 – 10 Hebrews goes on to explain that what is obsolete about the first covenant is its ritual activities, specifically sacrifices, precisely because these cannot perfect or purify the conscience of the worshiper (9:9, 14), as could the once-for-all sacrifice of Christ . . . The moral laws, and in fact God's will for humanity, have hardly been superseded, because in the view of the author of Hebrews it is the foundation and essence of the covenant under Moses as well as the one under Jesus.

However, it is difficult to see how limiting obsolescence to the ceremonial legislation of the Mosaic covenant truly reflects the full force of the statement in Hebrews 8:13,[61] or accurately expresses the extent to which supersessionism applies in the new covenant era.[62]

The following chapter elaborates further on the superiority of Christ's high-priestly ministry and the new covenant for which, as high priest, he is the mediator. In sharp contrast to the temporary cultic ritual prescribed under the first covenant (Heb. 9:1–10), Christ, through the greater and more perfect tent (Heb. 9:11) entered heaven itself (Heb. 9:12, 24) once and for all time (Heb. 9:12) to offer a better sacrifice (Heb. 9:12a, 23b) that secured an eternal redemption (Heb. 9:12b–14). In this way, Jesus has become 'the mediator of a new

---

them he says'). Admittedly, this tallies better with the imprecise wording of the previous verse ('covenant' does not actually appear in the Greek text of Heb. 8:7a, but is clearly implied). However, the following quotation from Jeremiah squarely places the blame on the people (Heb. 8:9b). It would appear, therefore, that the writer intends to qualify his statement about the imperfection of the first [covenant] by highlighting precisely where the fault lay.

[61] The internalization of God's requirements, the universal knowledge of God, and the complete forgiveness of sin (i.e. the 'better promises' on which the new covenant is founded; Heb. 8:6) render *the letter* of the Mosaic covenant obsolete in its entirety (cf. 2 Cor. 3).

[62] Attempts to deny or downplay supersessionism in an effort to foster Jewish–Christian dialogue are surely misguided. For a helpful overview and critique, see Holwerda 1995.

[63] The opening clause in Heb. 9:15 (*kai dia touto*) signifies a strong causal relationship between these two paragraphs (i.e. Heb. 9:11–14 and Heb. 9:15–22).

covenant' (Heb. 9:15),[63] his death having secured the promised eternal inheritance by dealing with the basic problem with the first covenant: human transgression.

It is widely assumed that at this point (Heb. 9:16–17) the writer introduces into his argument the Hellenistic concept of a *diathēkē* (i.e. a last will and testament).[64] In favour of this interpretation it may be noted that (a) the necessity of 'the death of the one who made it' (Heb. 9:16) suggests 'will' rather than 'covenant'; and (b) the fact that it takes effect only at death and is not in force as long as the maker is alive (Heb. 9:17) certainly applies to a 'will', but not normally to a 'covenant'.

Critics, however, have highlighted the following difficulties:[65]

1. What the writer says in Hebrews 9:17 does not conform to any known legal practice (Hellenistic or otherwise) with respect to the validation or ratification of a will.[66]
2. If referring to testamentary practice, the clauses in both Hebrews 9:16b and 9:17a are grammatically awkward.
3. Elsewhere the author uses *diathēkē* – clearly an important word in this epistle – only in its Septuagintal sense of 'covenant'.
4. The syntactical flow of Hebrews 9:11–22 strongly suggests that the writer's tight-knit argument progresses logically, making the introduction of *diathēkē* in an entirely different sense rather unlikely.
5. The model of the secular Hellenistic testament is incongruous with the wider context (e.g. the author's view of inheritance and his emphasis on cult).[67]

---

[64] So most English translations (NASB is an exception) and some of the major commentaries (e.g. Attridge 1989: 253–256; Ellingworth 1993: 462–463; Koester 2001: 418, 424–426).

[65] Hahn 2004: 417–426 groups these under the following headings: Legal Issues; Textual Issues (subdivided into grammatical, lexical, syntactical and contextual). While ignoring his headings, the following summary is drawn from his synthesis and analysis.

[66] The testamentary interpretation assumes that the key terms in Heb. 9:17 are synonyms for 'executed'; following Hughes (1976–7), however, Hahn maintains that 'no such meaning or usage is attested for either term' (2004: 418).

[67] As Hahn (2004: 422) explains, 'consistently in Hebrews, it is the heir rather than the testator who must die before the inheritance is bestowed'. Furthermore, 'the mediation of both covenants [contrasted here; i.e. old and new] is primarily cultic . . . In contrast to this, a secular "testament involves neither cult nor liturgy, mediator nor priesthood, sacrifice nor sanctuary, cultic law nor transgression thereof . . . One is at a loss to know how the author or his audience would have seen a relationship between a "testament" and the cultic contours of the covenant developed in the epistle' (2004: 424–425).

In view of such problems,[68] a minority of scholars have argued that *diathēkē* is used here (Heb. 9:16–17) in its normal biblical sense of 'covenant'.[69] Rather than introducing a different type of *diathēkē*, the writer is alluding to ancient covenant-making rites, which involved a self-maledictory oath that was ritually enacted by animal death and dismemberment.[70]

For those who understand these verses to be alluding to this ancient covenant-making practice in general, the 'death' that must be 'introduced' (*pheresthai*) is the *symbolic* death of the covenant maker; the corpses (*nekrois*) over which the covenant is ratified are the sacrificed animals, because a covenant is never in force while the covenant maker is still *ritually* alive. While this interpretation preserves the logical flow of the author's argument and fits much better into the literary and theological context, Hahn (2004: 431) notes two major objections: (a) while a self-maledictory oath may always have been implicit in the making of a covenant, not all covenants were ratified by ritual slaughter; (b) while not impossible, the figurative understanding of 'the *death* of the covenant maker' (v. 16 my trans.) and 'while the covenant maker is *alive*' (v. 17 my trans.) is not the most plausible; the actual death of the covenant maker seems to be implied.[71] In view of such difficulties, therefore, Hahn (2004: 431–436) argues for a more nuanced understanding of *diathēkē* as 'covenant' in these verses.

The key to Hahn's interpretation is the immediate context of these verses: 'It is not covenants in general, but the broken Sinai covenant that forms the context within which the statements of vv. 16–17

---

[68] While recognizing some of the problems, several advocates of the testamentary interpretation suggest that the author is simply engaging in some playful rhetoric, using a clever wordplay to amuse his audience. However, with Hahn one might reasonably challenge the wisdom of doing so in the midst of a serious argument.

[69] Advocates of this position include Westcott (1892), Hughes (1976–7), Lane (1991) and Hahn (2004). Unlike the others, however, Hahn argues that the allusion is to a particular OT covenant; viz. the covenant ratified in Exod. 24.

[70] For more on this practice, see pp. 99–100 above. Hahn (2004: 427ff.) makes the following salient points: (a) the swearing of an oath is closely associated with the making of a covenant in both biblical and ancient Near Eastern covenant-making – cf. their deployment as interchangeable terms, Ezek. 17:13–19; (b) the oath by which a covenant was ratified was almost invariably a conditional self-malediction; (c) the curse for breaking the covenant oath was typically death; (d) in many instances the self-maledictory oath of death (*Drohritus*) was ritually enacted during the making of the covenant – probably giving rise to the typical covenant-*cutting* idiom; e.g. Gen. 15:9–10; Gen. 17; Gen. 22:13; Exod. 24:3–8; Jer. 34:18–20; cf. also the treaty between Ashurnirari V and Mati'ilu (see McCarthy 1963: 195). With the possible exception of Gen. 17 (see my earlier discussion), Hahn's observations are convincing.

[71] Likewise, Gordon 2000: 103–104.

should be understood' (2004: 431). Accordingly, these verses serve to explain why a death for the remission of sins under the first covenant (Heb. 9:15) was necessary. The explanation lies in the fact that these transgressions were committed in a covenantal context – the covenant makers had ritually invoked upon themselves the covenant curse of death.[72] Therefore, under these circumstances (where the covenant in question had been ratified by a bloody oath ritual; cf. Heb. 9:18–22) 'it is necessary for the death of the covenant maker to be borne' (Heb. 9:16 my trans.). As well as giving the verb (*pherō*) its normal rather than some unattested meaning, this interpretation makes sense of the otherwise strange circumlocution:[73] the use of the passive form of 'to carry' leaves open the possibility that the necessary death could be endured by another (i.e. Jesus, their high priest). This is in keeping with the author's insistence that Christ, fulfilling the role of the Suffering Servant,[74] has endured the penalty of death on behalf of those who transgressed under the first covenant (Heb. 9:15).

According to Hahn (2004: 433–435), the author reinforces his main point (i.e. the necessity of death in view of the broken Sinaitic covenant) in the following verse (Heb. 9:17) by pointing out that for such a covenant to be upheld and enforced, the curses of the covenant (i.e. the death of the covenant-makers-turned-covenant-breakers) must be actualized. Thus understood, both 'the covenant maker' (*diathemenos*) and the corpses (*nekrois*) refer to the people of Israel who, having broken the covenant, must experience the curse of death if the covenant is to have any teeth.

While Hahn's interpretation has much to commend it, at some points – particularly his interpretation of verse 17 – it seems somewhat strained. Rather than identifying the 'corpses' with Israel, it seems better to understand them to refer to the slain animals with which self-maledictory covenant oaths were ritually enacted. Such ritual slaughter was certainly part of the covenant-making at Sinai (cf. Exod. 24:5–8), but the author may be making a more general point here.[75]

---

[72] For the covenant curse of death as the necessary consequence of the first covenant, see Heb. 2:15; 3:17; 10:28.

[73] As Hahn (2004: 432) suggests, one might have expected a simple 'it is necessary for the covenant maker to die'.

[74] Cf. the allusions to Isa. 53 in Heb. 9:28. For the linguistic and theological parallels between Heb. 9 and Isa. 53, see Hahn 2004: 433.

[75] While, as noted above, not all covenant-making occasions involved such blood ritual, the immediate context (dealing with the Sinai covenant) may suggest that this type of covenant is particularly in view. This would make better sense in the light of the following verse (Heb. 9:18), which seems to reintroduce and address the Sinai covenant

That is, having established the fact that someone had to carry the necessary death penalty for covenant transgressors, verse 17 explains that this was reflected in the death of the sacrificial animals by which such covenants (i.e. covenants involving self-maledictory oaths) were ratified.[76] So, having made the point about such covenants in general, the writer illustrates it with the Sinai covenant in particular (Heb. 9:18–22).[77] Thus the sequence of thought seems to be as follows: Jesus mediates a new covenant on account of his death, which redeems people from the penalty (the curse of death) warranted by covenant-transgressors; bearing such a penalty is necessary in the context of a covenant involving a self-maledictory oath; this fact is reflected clearly in the normal ritual involved in the making of such a covenant: it is ratified upon corpses, while the covenant maker remains alive. This threat of covenant curse explains the necessity of the bloody ritual involved in the making and maintaining of the first covenant: 'without the shedding of blood there is no forgiveness of sins' (Heb. 9:22 ESV). But all this merely foreshadowed the heavenly reality – when Christ, the one perfect High Priest – would appear 'once for all at the end of the ages to put away sin by the sacrifice of himself' (Heb. 9:26 ESV).

The main thought in the closing verses of this chapter (Heb. 9:23–28) and the first part of the next (Heb. 10:1–18) is the perpetual efficacy of Christ's once-for-all sacrifice. Unlike other priests, there was no need for Jesus to repeat the sacrifice he had made (Heb. 9:25–28),[78] because it accomplished that which the blood of bulls and goats never could – the complete forgiveness of sins (Heb. 10:1–14).[79] The writer emphasizes these facts in order to illustrate his overarching point: the superiority of the new covenant over the old. The latter had been a 'shadow of the good things which were to come',[80] but not

---

more specifically. This seems especially problematic for Hahn's interpretation, since he maintains that the Sinai covenant – and no other – is in focus throughout.

[76] I.e. the verses could be translated as follows: 'For where there is a covenant, the death of the covenant maker must be borne. For a covenant is ratified upon corpses [i.e. the animals sacrificed], since it is not otherwise enforced while the covenant maker lives' (my trans.).

[77] As Hahn (2004: 434) observes, the conjunction with which v. 18 begins (*hothen*) signifies a strong inferential relationship between vv. 16–17 and vv. 18–22.

[78] For the allusion in Heb. 9:28 to the High Priest's anticipated reappearance from the Most Holy Place, thus signifying God's acceptance of the sacrifice offered on the Day of Atonement, see Bruce 1990: 232–233.

[79] Having offered his sacrifice, Jesus 'took his seat at God's right hand' (Heb. 10:12 my trans.), in contrast to the Aaronic priests who remained standing throughout the performance of their duties (Heb. 10:11).

[80] It is important to note that these good things now have come, according to Heb. 9:11 (the majority reading, 'that are to come', should be rejected).

the 'image of these realities' (Heb. 10:1 my trans.).[81] The 'perfection' of which the author speaks (Heb. 10:1, 14) is attainable only under the new covenant, as evidenced by its better promise of permanent forgiveness (Heb. 10:16–18; cf. Heb. 8:6).

Having established the superiority of the new covenant, the writer exhorts his readers to draw near to God with full assurance of faith (Heb. 10:19–22), hold fast to the truths they confess (Heb. 10:23), and spur one another on to love and good deeds in the light of the Lord's return (Heb. 10:25). It is at this point that the writer includes another stern warning passage (Heb. 10:26–39; cf. Heb. 5:11–6:12), in which he refers to the punishment that will be inflicted on those who, among other things, 'profane the blood of the covenant by which he was sanctified' (Heb. 10:29 ESV). What is perhaps surprising here is that the writer again contrasts the old and new covenants, but here seems to envisage a scenario in which the prospect of complete forgiveness held out in the latter does not seem to apply. A rather similar comparison between old and new covenants is found in chapter 12 (Heb. 12:18–29), where again the mention of the 'new covenant' (Heb. 12:24) is set in the context of sombre warning (cf. Heb. 12:14–17, 25–29). Presumably, both these texts (Heb. 10:29; 12:24) serve to remind the readers of this epistle not to take their status under the new covenant for granted, but through perseverance in Christian faith and obedience to 'make [their] calling and election sure' (2 Pet. 1:10 NIV). However, it is clear from the author's final reference to the new covenant (Heb. 13:20) that to do so they were entirely dependent on their covenant Lord (Heb. 13:20–21).

The writer of Hebrews thus contrasts the old and new covenants by emphasizing the superiority of the promises, sacrifice, mediator, blessing and inheritance involved in the latter. While the necessity of this new covenant demonstrates that the old was in some sense deficient, the fault was not in the covenant itself but in those who failed to keep it.[82] Not surprisingly, therefore, it is this intrinsic inadequacy that is taken care of by the spirituality of the new covenant, a fact that the writer is keen to underline (Heb. 8:10–12; 10:16–17). Thus the contrast in Hebrews is similar to that of Paul's (cf. 2 Cor. 3): it is not between something evil and something good, but between something good and something better.

---

[81] The equating of 'image' with 'shadow' suggested in the Chester Beatty papyrus (p[46]) should be rejected.

[82] See p. 201 n.60 above.

Chapter Nine

God's new covenant consummated in the eschatological kingdom

As illustrated in the previous chapter, the climactic covenant anticipated by Jeremiah and other Old Testament prophets has now been
ratified through the death of the Lord Jesus Christ. This new and
everlasting covenant serves as the ultimate divine seal, the blood-oath
which solemnly guarantees the final realization of God's creative
purpose in the kingdom of God.

However, while even now Jesus' death and resurrection have inaugurated this kingdom, we still await the ultimate eschatological
reality, when the hopes held out in the new covenant will come to full
and everlasting expression. This has already been hinted at in the
pages above, but it is important to flesh this out a little lest we fall into
the trap of an overly realized eschatology. The ideal divine–human
relationship – depicted in various Old Testament texts that anticipate
the new covenant era – has found fulfilment in the person and work
of Jesus Christ. Through the blood of the eternal covenant, God's
people have obtained complete forgiveness of sins. Through the
regenerating work of God's Spirit, God's requirements have been
written on the hearts of all his people. Through God's saving initiative in Christ, God's people have been brought into a divine human
relationship that is absolutely and eternally secure. Through Jesus,
the royal seed of Abraham, divine blessing has now been extended to
all the families of the earth. Nevertheless, while these blessings are
already experienced by Christians now, the full realization of the
hopes held out to us in the new covenant will take place only in the
eschaton, when that great petition of the Lord's Prayer will finally be
answered, and God's kingdom will come on earth just as it is in
heaven. Ultimately, the prospect held out by Jeremiah and the other
Old Testament prophets is eschatological in nature. True, we see it
already fulfilled now in part, but only in part. Simply put, the best is
yet to come. These prophetic hopes still await a more comprehensive

and glorious fulfilment when Jesus returns. The restoration hope held out in Jeremiah and the prophets was not exhausted by the repatriation of Jews after the Babylonian exile, but neither is it exhausted in the first coming of Christ and the outpouring of the Holy Spirit. As Dearman (2002: 289) puts it:

> the complete transformation of God's people is still in the future . . . the future redemption promised by God through Jeremiah (or any of the prophets) has dawned in the ministry of Jesus Christ and will be brought to an ultimate fulfilment in his second coming at the end of the age . . . the church has tasted an 'already' of the future Jeremiah foresaw. Nevertheless, there is a 'not yet' as the current age runs its course.

Dumbrell (1984: 181–183) likewise concludes:

> The immediacy of the new situation to which v.34 [Jer. 31] refers us seem [sic.] to take us beyond all biblical personal experience; the limitations of the purely human situation have been transcended. The era to which Jeremiah points here and its characterization by the absence of the need of any human instruction, brings with it the concept of changed natures, indeed perfected human natures . . . in the new age sin will not be required to be dealt with at all. This is a supposition of unfettered mutual fellowship between God and men, the creation of a community in which not only is there no need for instruction but no breach of fellowship occurs, no divisions within the new community are expected . . . Jeremiah is not simply looking forward to the Cross and Resurrection as ushering in the new age, though of course they do that . . . In Jeremiah, we are looking beyond the New Testament age to the community of the end-time, to a situation when the kingdom of God has finally come and God is all in all. In such a situation the blessings of Jeremiah's New Covenant will be achieved. Not only will sin not be imputed, in the new age it will not be a factor.[1]

---

[1] Admittedly, Dumbrell may not give sufficient weight to the 'realized' dimension of Jeremiah's new covenant community, but he is undoubtedly correct in projecting the ultimate fulfilment of this hope into the eschaton.

Thus, while the new covenant is fulfilled in the person and work of Jesus Christ, the ultimate eschatological reality awaits the 'new heavens and new earth, where righteousness is at home' (2 Pet. 3:13 NRSV). It is only after Jesus has put 'all his enemies under his feet' (1 Cor. 15:25 TNIV) and 'the kingdom of the world has become the kingdom of our Lord and of his Messiah' (Rev. 11:15 TNIV), that the blessings of the new covenant – and thus, the eternal blessings foreshadowed in all previous covenants – will come to ultimate fulfilment, and God's universal purpose will at last be realized. Then and only then – in that eschatological reality, the New Jerusalem – will the hope expressed in the age-old covenant formula be most fully experienced: 'God's dwelling place is now among the people, and he will dwell with them. They will be his people, and God himself will be with them and be their God' (Rev. 21:3 TNIV). However long it may be before this eschatological goal is finally realized, the absolute certainty of this great Christian hope can never be in doubt. Our assurance stems from the fact that God has not only spoken his word of promise, but has also sealed it with an oath.

Bibliography

Achtemeier, E. (1996), *Minor Prophets I*, NIBC, Peabody: Hendricksen; Carlisle: Paternoster.

Alexander, T. D. (1995), 'Messianic Ideology in Genesis', in P. E. Satterthwaite, R. S. Hess and G. J. Wenham (eds.), *The Lord's Anointed: Interpretation of Old Testament Messianic Texts*, Grand Rapids: Baker; Carlisle: Paternoster, 19–39.

—— (1997), 'Further Observations on the Term "Seed" in Genesis', *TynB* 48, 363–367.

—— (1998), 'Royal Expectations in Genesis to Kings: Their Importance for Biblical Theology', *TynB* 49.2, 191–212.

—— (2002), *From Paradise to the Promised Land: An Introduction to the Pentateuch*, Grand Rapids: Baker; Carlisle: Paternoster.

Allen, L. C. (1990), *Ezekiel 20–48*, WBC, Dallas: Word.

—— (1994), *Ezekiel 1–19*, WBC, Dallas: Word.

—— (2002), *Psalms 101–150*, WBC; Waco: Word.

Alt, A. (1934), *Die Ursprünge der Israelitischen Rechts*, Leipzig: S. Hirzel (ET 'The Origins of Israelite Law', in *Essays on Old Testament History and Religion*, Oxford: Blackwell, 1966, 79–132).

Andersen, A. A. (1989), *2 Samuel*, WBC, Waco: Word.

Andersen, F. I. and N. Freedman (1980), *Hosea*, AB, New York: Doubleday.

Anderson, B. W. (1994), *From Creation to New Creation: Old Testament Perspectives*, Minneapolis: Fortress.

—— (1999), *Contours of Old Testament Theology*, Minneapolis: Fortress.

Armerding, C. E. (2004), '"Did I Ever Ask For a House of Cedar?" The Contribution of 2 Samuel 7 and 1 Chronicles 17 to the Theology of the Temple', in T. D. Alexander and S. Gathercole (eds.), *Heaven on Earth: The Temple in Biblical Theology*, Carlisle: Paternoster, 35–47.

Arnold, B. T. (2003), *1 & 2 Samuel*, NIVAC, Grand Rapids: Zondervan.

Arnold, B. T. and J. H. Choi (2003), *A Guide to Biblical Hebrew Syntax*, Cambridge: CUP.

Attridge, H. W. (1989), *The Epistle to the Hebrews: A Commentary on the Epistle to the Hebrews*, Hermeneia, Philadelphia: Fortress.

Badcock, G. D. (2001), 'The God of the Covenant', in M. J. Cartledge and D. Mills (eds.), *Covenant Theology: Contemporary Approaches*, Carlisle: Paternoster, 67–83.

Baker, D. L. (2005), 'Covenant: An Old Testament Study', in J. A. Grant and A. I. Wilson (eds.), *The God of the Covenant: Biblical, Theological and Contemporary Perspectives*, Leicester: Apollos, 21–53.

Balla, P. (1997), *Challenges to New Testament Theology: An Attempt to Justify the Enterprise*, Tübingen: Mohr Siebeck, 1997.

—— (2000), 'Challenges to Biblical Theology', in T. D. Alexander and B. S. Rosner (eds.), *New Dictionary of Biblical Theology*, Leicester: IVP, 20–27.

Baltzer, K. (1964), *Das Bundesformular*, WMANT 4; Neukirchen-Vluyn: Neukirchener Verlag (ET *The Covenant Formulary in Old Testament, Jewish and Christian Writings*, Oxford: Basil Blackwell, 1971).

Barnett, P. (1997), *The Second Epistle to the Corinthians*, NICNT, Grand Rapids: Eerdmans.

Barr, J. (1977), 'Some Semantic Notes on the Covenant', in H. Donner, R. Hanhart and R. Smend (eds.), *Beiträge zur Alttestamentlichen Theologie* (Festschrift W. Zimmerli); Göttingen: Vandenhoeck & Ruprecht, 23–38.

—— (1999), *The Concept of Biblical Theology*, Minneapolis: Fortress.

—— (2003), 'Reflections on the Covenant with Noah', in A. D. H. Mayes and R. B. Salters (eds.), *Covenant as Context: Essays in Honour of E. W. Nicholson*, Oxford: OUP, 11–38.

Bartholomew, C. G. (1995), 'Covenant and Creation; Covenant Overload or Covenant Deconstruction,' *CTJ* 30, 11–33.

Barton, J. (2003), 'Covenant in Old Testament Theology', in A. D. H. Mayes and R. B. Salters (eds.), *Covenant as Context: Essays in Honour of E. W. Nicholson*, Oxford: OUP, 23–38.

Batto, B. F. (1987), 'The Covenant of Peace: A Neglected Ancient Near Eastern Motif', *CBQ* 49, 187–211.

Beckwith, R. T. (1987), 'The Unity and Diversity of God's Covenants,' *TynB* 38, 92–118.

Beckwith, R. T. (2000), 'Sacrifice', in T. D. Alexander and B. S. Rosner (eds.), *New Dictionary of Biblical Theology*, Leicester: IVP, 754–762.

Blaising, C. A. (2001), 'The Future of Israel as a Theological Question', *JETS* 44.3, 435–450.

Block, D. I. (1995), 'Bringing back David: Ezekiel's Messianic Hope', in P. E. Satterthwaite, R. S. Hess and G. J. Wenham (eds.), *The Lord's Anointed: Interpretation of Old Testament Messianic Texts*, Grand Rapids: Baker; Carlisle: Paternoster, 167–188.

—— (1997), *The Book of Ezekiel Chapters 1–24*, NICOT, Grand Rapids: Eerdmans.

—— (1998), *The Book of Ezekiel Chapters 25–48*, NICOT, Grand Rapids: Eerdmans.

Boecker, H. J. (1980), *Law and the Administration of Justice in the Old Testament and Ancient East*, London: SPCK (German original, 1976).

Britt, B. (2003), 'Unexpected Attachments: A Literary Approach to the Term *dsh* in the Hebrew Bible', *JSOT* 27, 289–307.

Bruce, F. F. (1990), *The Epistle to the Hebrews*, rev. ed., NICNT, Grand Rapids: Eerdmans.

Brueggemann, W. (1998), *A Commentary on Jeremiah: Exile and Homecoming*, Grand Rapids: Eerdmans.

Bush, F. W. (1992), 'Images of Israel: The People of God in the Torah', in R. L. Hubbard, R. K. Johnston and R. P. Meye (eds.), *Studies in Old Testament Theology: Historical and Contemporary Images of God and God's People*, Dallas: Word, 99–115.

Carpenter, E. (1997), 'Exodus: Theology of', in *NIDOTTE* 4, 605–615.

Carroll, R. P. (1986), *Jeremiah*, OTL, London: SCM.

Carson, D. A. (2004), ' "You Have No Need That Anyone Should Teach You" (1 John 2:27): An Old Testament Allusion That Determines the Interpretation', in P. J. Williams, A. D. Clarke, P. M. Head and D. Instone-Brewer (eds.), *The New Testament in its First Century Setting: Essays on Context and Background in Honour of B. W. Winter on his 65th Birthday* (Grand Rapids: Eerdmans), 269–280.

Carson, D. A., P. T. O'Brien and M. Seifrid (eds.) (2001), *Justification and Variegated Nomism*, vol. 1, *The Complexities of Second Temple Judaism*, Grand Rapids: Baker; Tübingen: Mohr Siebeck.

—— (2004), *Justification and Variegated Nomism*, vol. 2, *The Paradoxes of Paul*, Grand Rapids: Baker; Tübingen: Mohr Siebeck.

Cassuto, U. (1983), *Commentary on the Book of Exodus*, trans. I. Abraham, Jerusalem: Magnes (Hebrew original, 1953).

Chennattu, R. M. (2006), *Johannine Discipleship as a Covenant Relationship*, Peabody: Hendrickson.

Childs, B. A. (1974), *The Book of Exodus: A Critical, Theological Commentary*, OTL, Louisville: Westminster.

—— (1993), *Biblical Theology of the Old and New Testaments*, Minneapolis: Fortress.

Clements, R. E. (1977), '*gôy*', *TDOT* 2, 426–433.

—— (2003), 'The Davidic Covenant in the Isaiah Tradition', in A. D. H. Mayes and R. B. Salters (eds.), *Covenant as Context: Essays in Honour of E. W. Nicholson*, Oxford: OUP, 39–69.

Clines, D. J. A. (1997), *The Theme of the Pentateuch*, 2nd ed., Sheffield: SAP.

Conrad, E. W. (1988), 'The Royal Narratives and the Structure of the Book of Isaiah', *JSOT* 41, 67–81

Craigie, P. C. (1976), *The Book of Deuteronomy*, NICOT, Grand Rapids: Eerdmans.

Cross, F. M. (1998), 'Kinship and Covenant in Ancient Israel', in idem, *From Epic to Canon: History and Literature in Ancient Israel*, Baltimore: Johns Hopkins University Press, 3–21.

Dahood, M. (1963), 'Zacharia 9,1, '*en 'ādām*', *CBQ* 25, 123–124.

Davies, G. (2003), 'Covenant, Oath, and the Composition of the Pentateuch', in A. D. H. Mayes and R. B. Salters (eds.), *Covenant as Context: Essays in Honour of E. W. Nicholson*, Oxford: OUP, 71–89.

Davis, D. R. (1999), *2 Samuel: Out of Every Adversity*, Fearn: Christian Focus.

Davis, J. P. (2005), 'Who are the Heirs of the Abrahamic Covenant?' *Evangelical Review of Theology* 29:2, 149–163.

Day, J. (1986), 'Pre-Deuteronomic Allusions to the Covenant in Hosea and Psalm LXXVIII', *VT* 36, 1–12.

—— (2003), 'Why Does God "Establish" Rather Than "Cut" Covenants in the Priestly Source?', in A. D. H. Mayes and R. B. Salters (eds.), *Covenant as Context: Essays in Honour of E. W. Nicholson*, Oxford: OUP, 91–109.

Dearman, J. A. (2002), *Jeremiah and Lamentations*, NIVAC, Grand Rapids: Zondervan.

Dell, K. J. (2003), 'Covenant and Creation in Relationship', in A. D. H. Mayes and R. B. Salters (eds.), *Covenant as Context: Essays in Honour of E. W. Nicholson*, Oxford: OUP, 111–133.

Dempster, S. G. (2003), *Dominion and Dynasty: A Theology of the Hebrew Bible*, NSBT; Leicester: Apollos; Downers Grove: IVP.

Dillard, R. B. and T. Longman III (1995), *An Introduction to the Old Testament*, Grand Rapids: Zondervan; Leicester: Apollos.

Duguid, I. M. (1999), *Ezekiel*, NIVAC, Grand Rapids: Zondervan.

Dumbrell, W. J. (1984), *Covenant and Creation: A Theology of the Old Testament Covenants*, Exeter: Paternoster.

—— (1988), 'The Prospect of Unconditionality in the Sinaitic Covenant,' in A. Gileadi (ed.), *Israel's Apostasy and Restoration: Essays in Honor of R. K. Harrison*, Grand Rapids: Baker, 141–155.

—— (1989), 'Covenant, Creation and Work', *Evangelical Review of Theology* 13.2, 137–156.

—— (2002a), *The Faith of Israel: A Theological Survey of the Old Testament*, 2nd edn, Grand Rapids: Baker.

—— (2002b), 'Genesis 2:1–17 A Foreshadowing of the New Creation', in S. J. Hafemann (ed.), *Biblical Theology: Retrospect and Prospect*, Downers Grove: IVP; Leicester: Apollos, 52–65.

—— (2004), 'Paul and Salvation History in Romans 9:30–10:4', in C. Bartholomew, M. Healy, K. Möller and R. Parry (eds.), *Out of Egypt: Biblical Theology and Biblical Interpretation*, Scripture and Hermeneutics Series Volume 5, Grand Rapids: Zondervan; Carlisle: Paternoster, 286–312.

Dunn, J. D. G. (1983), 'The New Perspective on Paul', *BJRL* 65, 95–122.

Durham, J. I. (1987), *Exodus*, WBC, Waco: Word.

Eichrodt, W. (1961, 1967), *Theology of the Old Testament*, 2 vols, OTL; London: SCM.

Ellingworth, P. (1993), *The Epistle to the Hebrews: A Commentary on the Greek Text*, NIGTC, Grand Rapids: Eerdmans.

Enns, P. (2000a), 'Exodus', in T. D. Alexander and B. S. Rosner (eds.), *New Dictionary of Biblical Theology*, Leicester: IVP, 146–152.

—— (2000b), *Exodus*, NIVAC, Grand Rapids: Zondervan.

Eslinger, L. (1994), *House of God or House of David: The Rhetoric of 2 Samuel 7*, Sheffield: SAP.

Firth, D. G. (2005), 'Speech Acts and Covenant in 2 Samuel 7:1–17', in J. A. Grant and A. I. Wilson (eds.), *The God of Covenant: Biblical, Theological and Contemporary Perspectives*, Leicester: Apollos, 79–99.

Fox, M. V. (1974), 'The Sign of the Covenant: Circumcision in the Light of the Priestly *'ôt* Etiologies', *RB* 81, 557–596.

Futato, M. D. (1998), 'Because It Had Not Rained: A Study of Genesis 2:5–7 with Implications for Genesis 2:4–25 and Genesis 1:1–2:3', *WTJ* 60, 1–21.

Gerstenberger, E. S. (2002), *Theologies of the Old Testament*, Minneapolis: Fortress (German original, 2001).

Gileadi, A. (1988), 'The David Covenant: A Theological Basis for Corporate Protection', in A. Gileadi (ed.), *Israel's Apostasy and Restoration: Essays in Honor of R. K. Harrison*, Grand Rapids: Baker, 157–163.

Golding, P. (2004), *Covenant Theology: The Key of Theology in Reformed Thought and Tradition*, Geanies House: Mentor (Christian Focus).

Goldingay, J. (2001), 'A Response to Stephen Clark', in M. J. Cartledge and D. Mills (eds.), *Covenant Theology: Contemporary Approaches*, Carlisle: Paternoster, 21–32.

—— (2003), *Old Testament Theology*, vol. 1, *Israel's Gospel*, Downers Grove: IVP.

Gooder, P. (2000), *The Pentateuch: A Story of Beginnings*, Continuum Biblical Studies Series, London: Continuum.

Gordon, R. P. (1986), *I and II Samuel: A Commentary*, Library of Biblical Interpretation, Grand Rapids: Zondervan.

—— (2000), *Hebrews*, Readings: A New Biblical Commentary, Sheffield: SAP.

Gowan, D. E. (1994), *Theology in Exodus: Biblical Theology in the Form of a Commentary*, Louisville: WJK.

Gräbe, P. J. (2006), *New Covenant, New Community: The Significance of Biblical and Patristic Covenant Theology for Contemporary Understanding*, Carlisle: Paternoster (German original, 2001).

Greenberg, M. (1983), *Ezekiel 1–20*, AB, New York: Doubleday.

Grisanti, M. A. (1999), 'The Davidic Covenant', *MSJ* 10:2, 233–250.

Grüneberg, K. N. (2003), *Abraham, Blessing and the Nations: A Philological and Exegetical Study of Genesis 12:3 in its Narrative Context*, BZAW 332, Berlin: de Gruyter.

Gundry, R. H. (1985), 'Grace, Works, and Staying Saved in Paul', *Bib* 66, 1–38.

Hahn, S. W. (2004), 'A Broken Covenant and the Curse of Death: A Study of Hebrews 9:15–22', *CBQ* 66, 416–436.

—— (2005a), 'Covenant, Oath, and the Aqedah: Διαθήκη in Galatians 3:15–18', *CBQ* 67, 79–100.

—— (2005b), 'Covenant in the Old and New Testaments: Some Current Research (1994–2004)', *CRBS* 3.2, 263–292.

Hamilton, V. P. (1990), *The Book of Genesis Chapters 1–17*, NICOT, Grand Rapids: Eerdmans.

—— (1995), *The Book of Genesis Chapters 18–50*, NICOT, Grand Rapids: Eerdmans.

Haran, M. (1997), 'The *Běrît* "Covenant": Its Nature and Ceremonial Background,' in M. Cogan, B. L. Eichler and J. H. Tigay (eds.), *Tehillah le-Moshe: Biblical and Judaic Studies in Honor of Moshe Greenberg*, Winona Lake: Eisenbrauns, 203–219.

Hartley, J. (2000), *Genesis*, NIBCOT, Peabody: Hendricksen; Carlisle: Paternoster.

Hasel, G. (1991), *Old Testament Theology: Basic Issues in the Current Debate*, 4th ed., Grand Rapids: Eerdmans.

Heim, K. (1995), 'The Perfect King of Psalm 72: An Intertextual Inquiry', in P. E. Satterthwaite, R. S. Hess and G. J. Wenham (eds.), *The Lord's Anointed: Interpretation of Old Testament Messianic Texts*, Grand Rapids: Baker; Carlisle: Paternoster, 223–248.

—— (1998), 'The (God-)Forsaken King of Psalm 89: A Historical and Intertextual Enquiry', in J. Day (ed.), *King and Messiah in Israel and the Ancient Near East*, JSOTS 270, Sheffield: SAP, 296–322.

Hess, R. S. (1996), *Joshua: An Introduction and Commentary*, TOTC, Leicester: IVP.

Hill, A. E. (1998), *Malachi: A New Translation with Introduction and Commentary*, AB, New York: Doubleday.

Hillers, D. R. (1969), *Covenant: The History of a Biblical Idea*, Baltimore: Johns Hopkins Press.

Hoeksema, H. (1970), *The Triple Knowledge: An Exposition of the Heidelberg Catechism*, Grand Rapids: Reformed Free Publishing Association.

Holmgren, F. C. (1999), *The Old Testament and the Significance of Jesus: Embracing Change – Maintaining Christian Identity*, Grand Rapids: Eerdmans.

Holwerda, D. E. (1995), *Jesus and Israel: One Covenant or Two?* Grand Rapids: Eerdmans; Leicester: Apollos.

Horton, M. (2006), *God of Promise: Introducing Covenant Theology*, Grand Rapids: Baker.

Hubbard, D. A. (1989), *Hosea*, TOTC, Leicester: IVP.

Huey, F. B., Jr. (1993), *Jeremiah, Lamentations*, Broadman Commentary, Nashville: Broadman.

Hugenberger, G. P. (1994), *Marriage as a Covenant: Biblical Law and Ethics as Developed from Malachi*, Leiden: Brill; republished Grand Rapids: Baker, 1998.

—— (1995), 'The Servant of the Lord in the "Servant Songs" of Isaiah: A Second Moses Figure', in P. E. Satterthwaite, R. S. Hess and G. J. Wenham (eds.), *The Lord's Anointed: Interpretation of Old Testament Messianic Texts*, Grand Rapids: Baker; Carlisle: Paternoster, 105–140.

Hughes, J. J. (1976–7), 'Hebrews IX 15ff. and Galatians III 15ff.: A Study in Covenant Practice and Procedure', *NovT* 21, 27–96.

Hvalvik, R. (1990), 'A "Sonderweg" for Israel: A Critical Examination of a Current Interpretation of Romans 11.25–27', *JSNT* 38, 87–107.

Hyatt, J. P. (1971), *Exodus*, NCBC, Grand Rapids: Eerdmans; London: Marshall, Morgan & Scott.

Jones, D. R. (1992), *Jeremiah*, NCBC, Grand Rapids: Eerdmans; London: Marshall, Morgan & Scott.

Kaiser, W. C., Jr (1972), 'The Old Promise and the New Covenant: Jeremiah 31:31–34', *JETS* 15, 11–23.

—— (1974), 'The Blessing of David: The Charter for Humanity', in J. H. Skilton (ed.) *The Law and the Prophets: Old Testament Studies in Honor of Oswalt T. Allis*, Nutley: Presbyterian & Reformed, 298–318.

—— (1977), 'Davidic Promise and the Inclusion of the Gentiles (Amos 9:9–15 and Acts 15:13–18): A Test Passage for Theological Systems', *JETS* 20, 97–111.

—— (1978), *Toward an Old Testament Theology*, Grand Rapids: Zondervan.

—— (1992), 'Images for Today: The Torah Speaks Today', in R. L. Hubbard, R. K. Johnston and R. P. Meye (eds.), *Studies in Old Testament Theology: Historical and Contemporary Images of God and God's People*, Dallas: Word, 117–132.

—— (1995), *The Messiah in the Old Testament*, SOTBT; Grand Rapids: Zondervan; Carlisle: Paternoster.

—— (2000), *Mission in the Old Testament: Israel as a Light to the Nations*, Grand Rapids: Baker.

Kidner, D. (1973), *Psalms 1–72: A Commentary on Books I and II of the Psalms*, TOTC; Leicester: IVP.

—— (1975), *Psalms 73–150: A Commentary on Books III, IV, and V of the Psalms*, TOTC; Leicester: IVP.

Kitchen, K. A. (1989), 'The Fall and Rise of Covenant, Law and Treaty', *TynB* 40, 118–135.

—— (2003), *On the Reliability of the Old Testament*, Grand Rapids: Eerdmans.

Kittel, R. (1895), *A History of the Hebrews*; London: Williams & Norgate (German original, 1888).

Kline, M. G. (1975), *The Structure of Biblical Authority*, rev. ed., Grand Rapids: Eerdmans.

—— (1986), *Kingdom Prologue*, 3 vols, S. Hamilton, Mass.: M. G. Kline (self-published).

Knoppers, G. N. (1996), 'Ancient Near Eastern Royal Grants and the Davidic Covenant: A Parallel?', *JAOS* 116, 670–697.

——(1998), 'David's Relation to Moses: The Contexts, Content and Conditions of the Davidic Promises', in J. Day (ed.), *King and Messiah in Israel and the Ancient Near East*, JSOTS 270, Sheffield: SAP, 91–118.

Koester, C. R. (2001), *Hebrews: A New Translation with Introduction and Commentary*, AB, New York: Doubleday.

Krasovec, J. (1996), 'Two Types of Unconditional Covenant', *HBT* 18, 55–77.

Kraus, H.-J. (1988), *Psalms 1–59*, CC, Minneapolis: Augsburg (German original, 1978).

Kruse, H. (1985), 'David's Covenant', *VT* 35, 139–164.

Lane, W. L. (1991), *Hebrews 9–13*, WBC, Dallas: Word.

Lehne, S. (1990), *The New Covenant in Hebrews*, JSNTS 44; Sheffield: JSOT Press.

Levenson, J. D. (1979), 'The Davidic Covenant and Its Modern Interpreters', *CBQ* 41, 205–219.

Light, G. W. (1993), 'The New Covenant in the Book of Hosea', *RevExp* 90, 219–238.

Lohfink, N. (1967), *Die Landverheissung als Eid: Eine Studie zu Gn 15*, SBS 28; Stuttgart: Katholisches Bibelwerk.

—— (1991), *The Covenant Never Revoked: Biblical Reflections on Christian– Jewish Dialogue*, New York: Paulist (German original, 1989).

Longenecker, R. N. (1990), *Galatians*, WBC, Dallas: Word.

Loretz, O. (1961), 'The *Perfectum Copulativum* in 2 Sm 7, 9–11', *CBQ* 23, 294–296.

Lucas, E. C. (2002), *Daniel*, AOTC, Leicester: Apollos.

—— (2003), 'Cosmology', in T. D. Alexander and D. W. Baker (eds.), *Dictionary of the Old Testament: Pentateuch* Downers Grove: IVP, 130–139.

Marshall, I. H. (2004), *New Testament Theology: Many Witnesses, One Gospel*, Leicester: Apollos; Downers Grove: IVP.

Mayes, A. D. H. (1979), *Deuteronomy*, NCBC; London: Marshall, Morgan & Scott; Grand Rapids: Eerdmans.

Mays, J. L. (1969), *Hosea*, OTL, London: SCM.

McCarthy, D. J. (1963), *Treaty and Covenant: A Study in the Ancient Oriental Documents and in the Old Testament*, AnBib, Rome: Pontifical Biblical Institute.

—— (1972), '*bᵉrît* in Old Testament History and Theology', *Bib* 53, 110–121.

—— (1973), *Old Testament Covenant: A Survey of Current Opinions*, Oxford: Blackwell.

McComiskey, T. E. (1985), *The Covenants of Promise: A Theology of the Old Testament Covenants*, Leicester: IVP.

McConville, G. J. (1993a), *Grace in the End: A Study in Deuteronomic Theology*, SOTBT, Carlisle: Paternoster; Grand Rapids: Zondervan.

—— (1993b), *Judgment and Promise: An Interpretation of the Book of Jeremiah*, Leicester: Apollos; Winona Lake: Eisenbrauns.

—— (1997), '*bᵉrît*', *NIDOTTE* 1, 747–755.

McGowan, A. T. B. (2005), 'In Defence of "Headship Theology"', in J. A. Grant and A. I. Wilson (eds.), *The God of Covenant: Biblical, Theological and Contemporary Perspectives*, Leicester: Apollos, 178–199.

McKenzie, S. L. (2000), *Covenant*, Understanding Biblical Themes, St Louis: Chalice.

Mendenhall, G. E. (1955), *Law and Covenant in Israel and the Ancient Near East*, Pittsburg: Bible Colloquium.

Mendenhall, G. E. and G. A. Herion (1992), 'Covenant', in *ABD* 1, 1179–1202.

Merrill, E. H. (1991), 'A Theology of the Pentateuch', in R. B. Zuck (ed.), *A Biblical Theology of the Old Testament*, Chicago: Moody, 7–87.

Millar, J. G. (1998), *Now Choose Life: Theology and Ethics in Deuteronomy*, NSBT; Leicester: Apollos; Grand Rapids: Eerdmans.

Miller, P. D. (2000), 'Creation and Covenant', in P. D. Miller, *Israelite Religion and Biblical Theology: Collected Essays*, JSOTS 267; Sheffield: SAP, 470–491.

Mitchell, C. W. (1987), *The Meaning of BRK "To Bless" in the Old Testament*, SBLDS 95; Atlanta: Scholars Press.

Moberly, R. W. L. (1983), *At the Mountain of God: Story and Theology in Exodus 32–34*, JSOTS 22; Sheffield: JSOT Press.

Moo, D. (1996), *The Epistle to the Romans*, NICNT, Grand Rapids: Eerdmans.

Moo, D. (2004), 'Israel and the Law in Romans 5–11: Interaction with the New Perspective', in D. A. Carson, P. T. O'Brien and M. Seifrid (eds.), *Justification and Variegated Nomism*, vol. 2, *The Paradoxes of Paul*, Grand Rapids: Baker, 185–216.

Motyer, J. A. (1993), *The Prophecy of Isaiah*, Leicester: IVP.

—— (1999), *Isaiah: An Introduction and Commentary*, TOTC, Leicester: IVP.

Motyer, S. (1989), *Israel in the Plan of God: Light on Today's Debate*, Leicester: IVP.

Mowinckel, S. (1921–4), *Psalmenstudien I–IV*, Kristiania: Videnskapsselskapts Skrifter.

Mullen, E. T., Jr (1983), 'The Divine Witness and the Davidic Royal Grant: Ps 89:37–38', *JBL* 102, 207–218.

Murray, D. F. (1990), 'MQWM and the Future of Israel in 2 Samuel VII 10', *VT* 40, 298–320.

Murray, J. (1953), *The Covenant of Grace: A Biblico-Theological Study*, reissued 1988, Phillipsburg: Presbyterian & Reformed.

Nicholson, E. W. (1986), *God and His People: Covenant and Theology in the Old Testament*, Oxford: Clarendon.

Niehaus, J. J. (1995), *God at Sinai: Covenant and Theophany in the Bible and Ancient Near East*, SOTBT; Grand Rapids Zondervan; Carlisle: Paternoster.

Noth, M. (1930), *Das System der zwölf Stämme Israels*, BWANT IV/1, Stuttgart: Kohlhammer.

—— (1962), *Exodus: A Commentary*, OTL, Philadelphia: Westminster (German original, 1959).

O'Brien, P. T. (1999), *The Letter to the Ephesians*, PNTC, Grand Rapids: Eerdmans; Leicester: Apollos.

—— (2004), 'Was Paul a Covenantal Nomist?', in D. A. Carson et al. (eds.), *Justification and Variegated Nomism*, vol. 2, 249–296.

Oswalt, J. N. (1986), *The Book of Isaiah Chapters 1–39*, NICOT, Grand Rapids: Eerdmans.

—— (1998), *The Book of Isaiah Chapters 40–66*, NICOT, Grand Rapids: Eerdmans.

Perlitt, L. (1969), *Bundestheologie im Alten Testament*, WMANT, Neukirchen-Vluyn: Neukirchener Verlag.

Polak, F. H. (2004), 'The Covenant at Mount Sinai in the Light of Texts from Mari', in C. Cohen, A. Hurvitz and S. M. Paul (eds.), *Sefer Moshe: The Moshe Weinfeld Jubilee Volume*, Winona Lake: Eisenbrauns, 119–134.

Porter, S. E. (2003), 'The Concept of Covenant in Paul', in S. E. Porter and J. C. R. de Roo (eds.), *The Concept of the Covenant in the Second Temple Period*, JSJSup 71, Leiden: Brill, 269–286.

Pritchard, J. B. (1978), *Ancient Near Eastern Texts Relating to the Old Testament*, 3rd ed., ed. J. B. Pritchard, Princeton: Princeton University Press.

Provan, I. (1995), 'The Messiah in the Book of Kings', in P. E. Satterthwaite, R. S. Hess and G. J. Wenham (eds.), *The Lord's Anointed: Interpretation of Old Testament Messianic Texts*, Grand Rapids: Baker; Carlisle: Paternoster, 67–85.

Provan, I., V. P. Long and T. Longman III (2003), *A Biblical History of Israel*, Louisville: WJK.

Pryor, J. W. (1992), *John: Evangelist of the Covenant People: The Narrative and Themes of the Fourth Gospel*, London: Darton, Longman & Todd.

Rad, G. von (1972), *Genesis*, rev. ed., OTL, London: SCM.

Rendtorff, R. (1993), *Canon and Theology: Overtures to an Old Testament Theology*, Edinburgh: T. & T. Clark (German original, 1991).

—— (1998), *The Covenant Formula*, Edinburgh: T. & T. Clark (German original, 1995).

—— (2005), *The Canonical Hebrew Bible: A Theology of the Old Testament*, Leiderdorp: Deo (German original, 2001).

Riddlebarger, K. (2003), *A Case for Amillennialism: Understanding the End Times*, Grand Rapids: Baker; Leicester: IVP.

Robertson, O. P. (1980), *The Christ of the Covenants*, Phillipsburg: Presbyterian & Reformed.

Robinson, B. P. (2001), 'Jeremiah's New Covenant: Jer 31, 31–34', *SJOT* 15, 181–204.

Roehrs, W. R. (1988), 'Divine Covenants: Their Structure and Function', *Concordia Journal* 14, 7–27.

Rosner, B. S. (2000), 'Biblical Theology', in T. D. Alexander and B. S. Rosner (eds.), *New Dictionary of Biblical Theology*, Leicester: IVP, 3–11.

Rost, L. (1926), *Die Überlieferung von der Thronnachfolge Davids*, BWANT, Stuttgart: Kohlhammer (ET *The Succession to the Throne of David*, Sheffield: Almond, 1982).

Sanders, E. P. (1977), *Paul and Palestinian Judaism: A Comparison of Patterns of Religion*, London: SCM.

Sarna, N. M. (1989), *Genesis*, JPS Torah Commentary, Philadelphia: Jewish Publication Society.

Satterthwaite, P. E. (1995), 'David in the Books of Samuel: A Messianic Expectation?', in P. E. Satterthwaite, R. S. Hess and G. J. Wenham (eds.), *The Lord's Anointed: Interpretation of Old Testament Messianic Texts*, Grand Rapids: Baker; Carlisle: Paternoster, 41–65.

Schibler, D. (1995), 'Messianism and Messianic Prophecy in Isaiah 1–12 and 28–33', in P. E. Satterthwaite, R. S. Hess and G. J. Wenham (eds.), *The Lord's Anointed: Interpretation of Old Testament Messianic Texts*, Grand Rapids: Baker; Carlisle: Paternoster, 87–104.

Schultz, R. (1995), 'The King in the Book of Isaiah', in P. E. Satterthwaite, R. S. Hess and G. J. Wenham (eds.), *The Lord's Anointed: Interpretation of Old Testament Messianic Texts*, Grand Rapids: Baker; Carlisle: Paternoster, 141–165.

Scobie, C. H. H. (2003), *The Ways of Our God: An Approach to Biblical Theology*, Grand Rapids: Eerdmans.

Seitz, C. R. (1992), 'Isaiah, Book of', in *ABD* 3, 472–488.

Seifrid, M. A. (2001), 'Righteousness Language in the Hebrew Scriptures and Early Judaism', in D. A. Carson et al. (eds.), *Justification and Variegated Nomism*, vol. 1, 415–442.

Shead, A. G. (2000a), 'The New Covenant and Pauline Hermeneutics', in P. Bolt and M. Thompson (eds.), *The Gospel to the Nations: Perspectives on Paul's Mission*, Leicester: Apollos, 33–49.

—— (2000b), 'Sabbath', in T. D. Alexander and B. S. Rosner (eds.), *New Dictionary of Biblical Theology*, Leicester: IVP, 745–750.

Sheriffs, D. (1996), *The Friendship of the Lord*, Carlisle: Paternoster.

Smith, B. D. (1996), 'New Covenant', in W. A. Elwell (ed.), *Evangelical Dictionary of Biblical Theology*, Grand Rapids: Baker, 560–561.

Smith, G. V. (1977), 'Structure and Purpose in Genesis 1–11', *JETS* 20, 307–319.

Sohn, S.-T. (1999), '"I Will Be Your God and You Will Be My People": The Origin and Background of the Covenant Formula', in R. Chazan, W. W. Hallo and L. H. Schiffman (eds.), *Ki Baruch Hu: Ancient Near Eastern, Biblical, and Judaic Studies in Honor of Baruch A. Levine*, Winona Lake: Eisenbrauns, 355–372.

Soulen, R. K. (1996), *The God of Israel and Christian Theology*, Minneapolis: Fortress.

Speiser, E. A. (1960), '"People" and "Nation" of Israel', *JBL* 79, 157–163.

Stek, J. H. (1994), '"Covenant" Overload in Reformed Theology', *CTJ* 29, 12–41.

Stuart, D. (1987), *Hosea–Jonah*, WBC 31, Waco: Word.

Suh, M. S. (2003), *The Tabernacle in the Narrative of Israel from the Exodus to the Conquest*, SBL 50, New York: Peter Lang.

Tan, K. H. (2005), 'Community, Kingdom and Cross: Jesus' View of Covenant', in J. A. Grant and A. I. Wilson (eds.), *The God of Covenant: Biblical, Theological and Contemporary Perspectives*, Leicester: Apollos, 122–155.

Taylor, J. B. (1969), *Ezekiel: An Introduction and Commentary*, TOTC, Leicester: IVP.

Thompson, J. A. (1980), *The Book of Jeremiah*, NICOT, Grand Rapids: Eerdmans.

Toews, B. G. (2002), 'Genesis 1–4 The Genesis of Old Testament Instruction', in S. J. Hafemann (ed.), *Biblical Theology: Retrospect and Prospect*, Downers Grove: IVP; Leicester: Apollos, 38–51.

Turner, L. A. (1993), 'The Rainbow as the Sign of the Covenant in Genesis ix 11–13', *VT* 43, 119–124.

—— (2000), *Genesis*, Readings: A New Biblical Commentary, Sheffield: SAP.

Van Groningen, G. (1996), 'Covenant', in W. A. Elwell (ed.), *Evangelical Dictionary of Biblical Theology*, Grand Rapids: Baker, 124–132.

VanGemeren, W. (1988), *The Progress of Redemption: From Creation to the New Jerusalem*, Grand Rapids: Baker.

Vaughn, A. G. (2004), '"And Lot Went with Him": Abraham's Disobedience in Genesis 12:1–4a', in B. F. Batto and K. L. Roberts (eds.), *David and Zion: Biblical Studies in Honour of J. J. M. Roberts*, Winona Lake: Eisenbrauns, 111–123.

Vogels, W. F. (1979), *God's Universal Covenant: A Biblical Study*, Ottawa: University of Ottawa Press.

Wallis, W. (1969), 'Irony in Jeremiah's Prophecy of a New Covenant', *Bulletin of the Evangelical Theological Society* 12, 107–110.

Waltke, B. K. with C. J. Fredericks (2001), *Genesis: A Commentary*, Grand Rapids: Zondervan.

Walton, J. H. (1994), *Covenant: God's Purpose, God's Plan*, Grand Rapids: Zondervan.

—— (2001), *Genesis*, NIVAC, Grand Rapids: Zondervan.

Ward, R. S. (2003), *God and Adam: Reformed Theology and the Creation Covenant*, Melbourne: New Melbourne Press.

Waters, G. P. (2004), *Justification and the New Perspectives on Paul: A Review and Response*, Phillipsburg: Presbyterian & Reformed.

Webb, B. G. (1996), *The Message of Isaiah: On Eagles' Wings*, BST, Leicester: IVP.

Weinfeld, M. (1965), 'Traces of Treaty Formulae in Deuteronomy', *Bib* 41, 417–427.

—— (1970), 'The Covenant of Grant in the Old Testament and in the Ancient Near East', *JAOS* 90, 184–203.

—— (1972), *Deuteronomy and the Deuteronomic School*, Oxford: Clarendon.

—— (1975), '*Běrît*. Covenant vs. Obligation', *Bib* 56, 120–128.

—— (1976), 'The Loyalty Oath in the Ancient Near East', *UF* 8, 379–414.

—— (1977), '*běrît*', TDOT 2, 253–279.

Weiser, A. (1925), *Die Bedeutung des Alten Testaments für den Religionsunterricht*, Giessen: Töpelmann.

Wellhausen, J. (1885), *Prolegomena to the History of Israel*, Edinburgh: A. & C. Black.

Wells, P. (1986), 'Covenant, Humanity, and Scripture: Some Theological Reflections', *WTJ* 48, 17–45.

Wenham, G. J. (1982), 'The Symbolism of the Animal Rite in Genesis 15: A Response to G. F. Hasel', *JSOT* 22, 134–137.

—— (1987), *Genesis 1–15*, WBC, Waco: Word.

—— (1994), *Genesis 16–50*, WBC, Dallas: Word.

—— (2003), *Exploring the Old Testament: A Guide to the Pentateuch*, Downers Grove: IVP; London: SPCK.

Westcott, B. F. (1892), *The Epistle to the Hebrews: The Greek Text with Notes and Essays*, 2nd ed., London: Macmillan.

Westermann, C. (1969), *Isaiah 40–66*, OTL, London: SCM.

—— (1984), *Genesis 1–11*, London: SPCK; Philadelphia: Fortress (German original, 1974).

Whybray, R. N. (1995), *Introduction to the Pentateuch*, Grand Rapids: Eerdmans.

Williamson, H. G. M. (1985), *Ezra, Nehemiah*, WBC, Waco: Word.

Williamson, P. R. (2000a), *Abraham, Israel and the Nations: The Patriarchal Promise and its Covenantal Development in Genesis*, JSOTS 315; Sheffield: SAP.

—— (2000b), 'Covenant', in T. D. Alexander and B. S. Rosner (eds.), *New Dictionary of Biblical Theology*, Leicester: IVP, 419–429.

—— (2003), 'Covenant', in T. D. Alexander and D. W. Baker (eds.), *Dictionary of the Old Testament: Pentateuch*, Downers Grove: IVP, 139–155.

—— (2005), 'Land', in B. T. Arnold and H. G. M. Williamson (eds.), *Dictionary of the Old Testament: Historical Books*, Downers Grove: IVP, 638–643.

Wilson, A. I. (2005), 'Luke and the New Covenant: Zechariah's Prophecy as a Test Case', in J. A. Grant and A. I. Wilson (eds.), *The God of Covenant: Biblical, Theological and Contemporary Perspectives*, Leicester: Apollos, 156–177.

Witsius, H. (1990), *The Economy of the Covenants between God and Man: Comprehending a Complete Body of Divinity*, trans. from original Dutch and rev. W. Crookshank, 2 vols., reprinted Escondido, Calif.: den Dulk Christian Foundation.

Wolff, H. W. (1974), *Hosea*, Hermeneia, Philadelphia: Fortress (German original, 1961).

Woudstra, M. H. (1971), 'The Everlasting Covenant in Ezekiel 16:59–63', *CTJ* 6, 22–48.

—— (1981), *The Book of Joshua*, NICOT, Grand Rapids: Eerdmans.

Wright, C. J. H. (2001), *The Message of Ezekiel: A New Heart and a New Spirit*, BST, Leicester: IVP.

—— (2005), 'Covenant: God's Mission through God's People,' in J. A. Grant and A. I. Wilson (eds.), *The God of Covenant: Biblical, Theological and Contemporary Perspectives*, Leicester: Apollos, 54–78.

Wright, N. T. (1991), *The Climax of the Covenant: Christ and the Law in Pauline Theology*, Edinburgh: T. & T. Clark (1991); Minneapolis: Fortress (1992).

Zimmerli, W. (1978), *Old Testament Theology in Outline*, Edinburgh: T. & T. Clark (German original, 1975).

Index of modern authors

227

Index of Scripture references

230

236

Adopted into God's Family
Exploring a Pauline metaphor
Trevor J. Burke

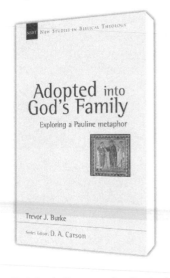

' ... you received the Spirit of adoption'
(Romans 8:15).

The relationship between God and his people is understood in various ways by the biblical writers, and it is arguably the apostle Paul who uses the richest vocabulary.

Unique to Paul's writings is the term *huiothesia*, the process or act of being 'adopted as son(s)'. It occurs five times in three of his letters, where it functions as a key theological metaphor.

Trevor Burke argues that *huiothesia* has been misunderstood, misrepresented, or neglected through scholarly preoccupation with its cultural background. He redresses the balance in this comprehensive study, which discusses metaphor theory; explores the background to *huiothesia*; considers the roles of the Father, Son and Holy Spirit; examines the moral implications of adoption, and its relationship with honour; and concludes with the consequences for Christian believers as they live in the tension between the 'now' and the 'not yet' of their adoption into God's new family.

'Not only the importance of God's family, but also the enormous privilege of belonging to it, are powerfully underscored by Paul's understanding of what it means to be the adopted sons of God. With such themes in view, a wide array of pastoral implications soon springs to light. In other words, this volume not only probes a neglected theme — it also edifies' (D. A. Carson).

Available from your local Christian bookshop or via our websites at
www.ivpbooks.com or **www.ivpress.com** in North America
Paperback 233 pages, ISBN: 978-1-84474-146-5 or 978-0-8308-2623-0 in North America

Shepherds after My own Heart

Pastoral traditions and leadership in the Bible

Timothy S. Laniak

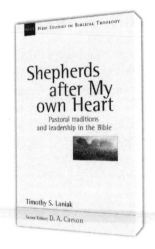

'I will give you shepherds after my own heart, who will lead you with knowledge and understanding' (Jeremiah 3:15).

Most of the Bible's pastoral imagery is grounded in two traditions: Israel's 'wilderness drama', in which Moses functioned as God's under-shepherd; and the shepherd-king David and his dynasty, with its messianic promises. Old Testament prophets like Jeremiah made sustained use of pastoral imagery, seeing the LORD revealing himself as the ultimate Shepherd of his flock, and creating expectation of a new exodus, a renewed community, and a unique shepherd king.

These traditions provided proto-types for leaders that followed, and formed the background for the ministry of Jesus – the 'good shep-herd'. His disciples were sent as shepherds to feed his sheep – and as sheep among wolves. The pastoral role was central to the ongoing life of local churches in the Christian movement, and today's pastors are still called to be shepherds after God's own heart, to lead his people, living on the margins of settled society, to their eternal home.

In this excellent study, Timothy Laniak draws on a wide range of Old and New Testament texts to develop a biblical theology of 'shepherd' imagery, and concludes with some principles and implications for contemporary 'pastoral' ministry.

Dominion and dynasty

A theology of the Hebrew Bible

Stephen G. Dempster

Christian theologians rarely study the Old Testament in its final Hebrew canonical form, even though this was very likely the Bible used by Jesus and the early church. However, once read as a whole, the larger structure of the Hebrew Bible *(Tanakh)* provides a 'wide-angle lens' through which its contents can be viewed.

In this stimulating exposition, Stephen Dempster argues that, despite its undoubted literary diversity, the Hebrew Bible possesses a remarkable structural and conceptual unity. The various genres and books are placed within a comprehensive narrative framework which provides an overarching literary and historical context. The many texts contribute to this larger text, and find their meaning and significance within its story of 'dominion and dynasty', which ranges from Adam to the Son of Man to David, and to a coming Davidic king.

'Dr Dempster's reading of the storyline of the Old Testament is fresh, provocative, helpful — and doubtless will prove to be the stuff of many sermons and lectures. His closing chapter points to some of the links that bind the Old and New Testaments together, an obviously urgent goal for the Christian preacher and teacher' (D. A. Carson).